TEXT BOOK OF

# PHARMACEUTICS - II

FOR

SECOND YEAR DIPLOMA IN PHARMACY
(As per E. R. 1991)

**Dr. P. V. KASTURE**
M. Pharm. Ph. D.
Ex. Professor of Pharmacy,
D.Y. Patil College of Pharmacy,
Pimpri,
**Pune** 411 018.

**Prof. S. B. GOKHALE**
M. Pharm. A.I.C.
Ex. Coordinator
R.C. Patel Institute of Pharmaceutical
Education and Research, Shirpur,
Dist. **Dhule** 425 405

**Dr. S. R. PARAKH**
M. Pharm. Ph. D. (Tech.)
Ex. Principal & Professor of Pharmaceutics,
Maharashtra Institute of Pharmacy,
M.I.T Campus, **Pune** - 411 038.

**Dr. A. R. PARADKAR**
M. Pharm. Ph. D.
Ex. Professor of Pharmacy,
Poona College of Pharmacy,
**Pune** - 411 038.

N1249

**PHARMACEUTICS – II**
**Fourteenth Edition** : **July, 2015**
© : **Authors**

The text of this publication, or any part thereof, should not be reproduced or transmitted in any form or stored in any computer storage system or device for distribution including photocopy, recording, taping or information retrieval system or reproduced on any disc, tape, perforated media or other information storage device etc., without the written permission of Authors with whom the rights are reserved. Breach of this condition is liable for legal action.

Every effort has been made to avoid errors or omissions in this publication. In spite of this, errors may have crept in. Any mistake, error or discrepancy so noted and shall be brought to our notice shall be taken care of in the next edition. It is notified that neither the publisher nor the authors or seller shall be responsible for any damage or loss of action to any one, of any kind, in any manner, therefrom.

**ISBN : 978-81-85790-22-0**

**Published By :**
**NIRALI PRAKASHAN**
Abhyudaya Pragati, 1312, Shivaji Nagar,
Off J.M. Road, PUNE – 411005
Tel - (020) 25512336/37/39, Fax - (020) 25511379
Email : niralipune@pragationline.com

**Printed By :**
**Repro Knowledgecast Limited,**
Thane

### ☞ DISTRIBUTION CENTRES
**PUNE**
Nirali Prakashan : 119, Budhwar Peth, Jogeshwari Mandir Lane, Pune 411002, Maharashtra
Tel : (020) 2445 2044, 66022708, Fax : (020) 2445 1538
Email : bookorder@pragationline.com, niralilocal@pragationline.com
Nirali Prakashan : S. No. 28/27, Dhyari, Near Pari Company, Pune 411041
Tel : (020) 24690204 Fax : (020) 24690316
Email : dhyari@pragationline.com, bookorder@pragationline.com
**MUMBAI**
Nirali Prakashan : 385, S.V.P. Road, Rasdhara Co-op. Hsg. Society Ltd.,
Girgaum, Mumbai 400004, Maharashtra
Tel : (022) 2385 6339 / 2386 9976, Fax : (022) 2386 9976
Email : niralimumbai@pragationline.com

### ☞ DISTRIBUTION BRANCHES
**JALGAON**
Nirali Prakashan : 34, V. V. Golani Market, Navi Peth, Jalgaon 425001,
Maharashtra, Tel : (0257) 222 0395, Mob : 94234 91860
**KOLHAPUR**
Nirali Prakashan : New Mahadvar Road, Kedar Plaza, 1st Floor Opp. IDBI Bank
Kolhapur 416 012, Maharashtra. Mob : 9850046155
**NAGPUR**
Pratibha Book Distributors : Above Maratha Mandir, Shop No. 3, First Floor,
Rani Jhanshi Square, Sitabuldi, Nagpur 440012, Maharashtra
Tel : (0712) 254 7129
**DELHI**
Nirali Prakashan : 4593/21, Basement, Aggarwal Lane 15, Ansari Road, Daryaganj
Near Times of India Building, New Delhi 110002
Mob : 08505972553
**BENGALURU**
Pragati Book House : House No. 1, Sanjeevappa Lane, Avenue Road Cross,
Opp. Rice Church, Bengaluru – 560002.
Tel : (080) 64513344, 64513355,Mob : 9880582331, 9845021552
Email:bharatsavla@yahoo.com
**CHENNAI**
Pragati Books : 9/1, Montieth Road, Behind Taas Mahal, Egmore,
Chennai 600008 Tamil Nadu, Tel : (044) 6518 3535,
Mob : 94440 01782 / 98450 21552 / 98805 82331,
Email : bharatsavla@yahoo.com

niralipune@pragationline.com | www.pragationline.com
Also find us on www.facebook.com/niralibooks

# PREFACE TO THE FOURTEENTH EDITION

We are pleased to release the revised Thirteenth edition of Pharmaceutics - II.

It is needless to say that, overwhelming response from the students and colleagues has made this possible.

Suggestions, criticism and comments are most welcome to make the future editions of this book more valuable.

We hope we shall keep receiving the same co-operation in future as received in the past.

June 2015                                                                                                              Authors

# PREFACE TO THE FIRST EDITION

It is an exclusive pleasure to introduce the first edition of **Pharmaceutics – II** book for Second Year Diploma in Pharmacy according to Education Regulation 1991.

When the Pharmacy profession is passing through a critical modification it is paramount to go for a substantial change in the type and variety of educational needs of the future pharmacist, and it becomes critically necessary to validate the pharmaceutical academics in the light of new drug laws, policies and ever-changing technology.

This book encompasses the different sections of the curriculum of Pharmaceutics designed for Second Year Diploma in Pharmacy.

The pharmacist generates a link between the physician and patient. The knowledge of the current aspects of the pharmacy profession and pharmaceutical technology becomes an indispensable parameter in developing the "would be pharmacist".

The book covers different basics of pharmaceutics and dispensing of medications. It combines the dispensing Pharmacy aspects such as prescription, incompatibilities and posology with dosage form technology including solid, liquid and semi-solid formulations. Certain dosage forms such as pastes, jellies, poultices and suppositories have also been discussed. The book also touches the delicate areas such as *"Cosmeticology"* and *"Parenteral Dosage Forms"*.

Parenteral Dosage Forms, today have changed their faces and it is the need of the hour to brush the technicalities in this important and vital dosage form.

This is our sincere attempt to infuse the knowledge of Pharmaceutical technology and professional pharmacy to the students of Diploma in Pharmacy in a simple language.

This book would not see completion without the suggestions and criticisms from our colleagues, teachers and educational authorities.

We shall ever welcome suggestions and criticism from all the strata of profession to make improvements in the next edition of the book.

We thank our Publisher **Shri Dineshbhai Furia** and Staff members of **Nirali Prakashan, Pune**, for their kind co-operation.

07/7/1994                                                                  **Authors**

# SYLLABUS

## PHARMACEUTICS – II

**Lectures : 75**  **Marks : 100**

### I. Dispensing Pharmacy

(i) **Prescriptions :** Reading and understanding of prescriptions; Latin terms commonly used (Detailed study is not necessary), Modern methods of prescribing, adoption of metrics system. Calculations involved in dispensing.

(ii) **Incompatibilities in Prescriptions :** Study of various types of incompatibilities-physical, chemical and therapeutic.

(iii) **Posology :** Dose and dosage of drugs. Factors influencing dose. Calculations of doses on the basis of age, sex and surface area. Veterinary doses.

### II. Dispensed Medications :

(**Note :** A detailed study of the following dispensed medication is necessary. Methods of preparation with theoretical and practical aspects, use of appropriate containers and closures. Special labeling requirements and storage conditions should be high-lighted.

(i) **Powders :** Types of powders – Advantages and disadvantages of Powders, Granules, Cachets and Tablet triturates. Preparation of different types of powders encountered in prescriptions. Weighing methods, possible errors in weighing, minimum weighable amounts and weighing of a material below the minimum weighable amount, geometric dilution and proper usage and care of dispensing balance.

(ii) **Liquid Dosage Forms :**

(a) **Monophasic Liquid Dosage Forms :** Theoretical aspects including commonly used vehicles, essential adjuvants like stabilizers, *colourants* and *flavours,* with examples.

Review on the following monophasic liquids with details of formulation and practical methods.

| Liquids for Internal Administration | Liquids for External administration or used on Mucous Membranes |
|---|---|
| Mixtures and Concentrates, Syrups, Elixirs. | Gargles, Mouth washes, Throat-paints, Douches, Ear drops, Nasal drops and Sprays, Lotions. |

**(b) Biphasic Liquid Dosage Forms :**

**(i) Suspension** (elementary study) : Suspensions containing diffusible solids and liquids and their preparations. Study of the adjuvants used like thickening agents, *wetting agents*, their necessity and quantity to be incorporated. Suspensions of precipitate forming liquids like tinctures, their preparations and stability. Suspensions produced by chemical reaction. An introduction to flocculated/non-flocculated suspension system.

**(ii) Emulsions** : Types of emulsions, identification of emulsion systems, formulation of emulsions, selection of emulsifying agents. Instabilities in emulsions. Preservation of emulsions.

**(c) Semi-Solid Dosage Forms :**

**(1) Ointments** : Types of ointments, Classification and selection of dermatological vehicles. Preparation and stability of ointments by the following processes : (i) Trituration, (ii) Fusion, (iii) Chemical reaction, (iv) Emulsification.

**(2) Pastes** : Differences between ointments and pastes. Bases of pastes. Preparation of pastes and their preservation.

**(3) Jellies** : An introduction to the different types of jellies and their preparation.

**(4)** An elementary study of poultice.

**(5) Suppositories and pessaries** : Their relative merits and demerits, types of suppositories, suppository bases, classification, properties, preparations and packing of suppositories. Use of suppositories for drug absorption.

**(6) Dental and Cosmetic Preparations** : Introduction to Dentrifices, Facial cosmetics, Deodorants, Antiperspirants, Shampoos, Hair dressings and Hair removers.

**III. Sterile Dosage Forms :**

**(a) Parenteral dosage forms** : Definition, general requirements for parenteral dosage forms. Types of parenteral formulations, vehicles, adjuants, processing, personnel facilities and quality control. Preparation of intravenous fluids and admixtures – Total parenteral nutrition, dialysis fluids.

**(b) Sterility testing** : Methods of testing, Particulate matter monitoring – Faulty seal-packaging.

**(c) Ophthalmic products** : Study of essential characteristics of different ophthalmic preparations. Formulation additives, special precautions in handling and storage of ophthalmic products.

## PRACTICAL PHARMACEUTICS – II

**Practical Hours : 100**                                                                 **Marks : 100**

Dispensing of at least 100 products covering a wide range of preparations such as Mixtures, emulsions, lotions, liniments, E.N.T. preparations, ointments, suppositories, powders, incompatible prescriptions etc.

# CONTENTS

## I. DISPENSING PHARMACY

1. Prescriptions — 1.1 – 1.22
2. Incompatibilities in Prescriptions — 2.1 – 2.10
3. Posology — 3.1 – 3.14

## II. DISPENSED MEDICATIONS

4. Powders — 4.1 – 4.12

### (a) Monophasic Liquid Dosage Forms

**Liquids for Internal Use**

5. Mixtures and Concentrates — 5.1 – 5.14
6. Elixirs and Syrups — 6.1 – 6.4

**Liquids for External Use**

7. Mouth washes, Gargles and Throat Paints — 7.1 – 7.14
8. Ear drops, Nasal drops, Douches and Sprays — 8.1 – 8.6
9. Liniments and Lotions — 9.1 – 9.10

### (b) Biphasic Liquid Dosage Forms

10. Suspensions — 10.1 – 10.10
11. Emulsions — 11.1 – 11.20

### (c) Semi-solid Dosage Forms

12. Ointments and Pastes — 12.1 – 12.14
13. Jellies and Poultices — 13.1 – 13.6
14. Suppositories and Pessaries — 14.1 – 14.10
15. Dental and Cosmetic Preparations — 15.1 – 15.20

## III. STERILE DOSAGE FORMS

16. Parenteral Dosage Forms — 16.1 – 16.12
17. Sterility Testing — 17.1 – 17.6
18. Ophthalmic Products — 18.1 – 18.6
- Bibliography — B.1 – B.2
- Index — I.1 – I.5

# SECTION - I
# DISPENSING PHARMACY

# CHAPTER 1

# PRESCRIPTIONS

## (A) READING AND UNDERSTANDING OF PRESCRIPTIONS

**Definition :** *A prescription is a written order from a registered physician, a dentist, or a veterinarian or a surgeon or any other person licensed by law to prescribe drugs, containing instructions for preparation and dispensing to the pharmacist along with the mode of administration for the patient. Pharmacist may accept a prescription on telephone in an emergency and it needs to be followed by a regular written prescription.*

**Importance :** In the modern era of potent drugs, if a wrong prescription is delivered, a patient is likely to suffer from serious consequences.

While considering the safety of the patient, a prescription

1. Should be written in ink.
2. Should not have over-writing.
3. Should be legible.
4. Should have only official abbreviations of weights and measures.
5. As far as possible only generic names of the drugs be used in the prescription.
6. Full names of medicaments be used and no abbreviations.

**Parts of a Prescription :**

An ideal prescription consists of the following parts :

(a) Superscription, (b) Inscription, (c) Subscription, (d) Signature.

**(a) Superscription :** It consists of the name, qualification and address of the physician, date, name, age and address of the patient. The physician's name, qualification and address are essential for the identity of the prescriber, particularly for a narcotic prescription.

Date helps in judging the interval between the issue of prescription and that of dispensing it. It is important to know the date of prescription particularly when the drugs like narcotics and cumulative drugs like digitalis, santonin, arsenic etc. are prescribed.

The name, sex and address of the patient are important to facilitate proper handling. It helps to avoid confusion among prescriptions meant for some other patient. These are especially required for prescriptions of drugs like narcotics. The age of the patient is important particularly in case of children. From the age, the pharmacist can recheck the correctness of the dose.

It consists of the symbol $R_x$. R stands for the Latin word Recipe meaning, *'take thou of,* the oblique dash after R is considered as an ancient invocation of the physician to Jupiter.

**(b) Inscription :** It is the body of the prescription and contains the official English name and the amount of each ingredient. Abbreviations should be avoided since they are likely to result in errors. The name of each drug is placed on a separate line directly under the preceding one. First letter of the name of the drug should be in capital. If there are more than one ingredient, their ideal order should be as follows :

**(i) Basis :** It is the principal active drug and gives the prescription its chief action.

**(ii) Adjuvant :** It aids or increases the action of the base.

**(iii) Corrective :** It modifies or corrects any undesirable effect of the basis of adjuvant. It may be a flavouring, colouring or a sweetening agent.

**(iv) Vehicle :** It is an inert agent used to distribute the above ingredients. It may serve either as a solvent or to increase the bulk or both. In the case of a liquid, if it is intended merely to dilute the active drug, it is called a *diluent*. In powders, an inert powder may serve as a diluent. The inert substance added to medicine to give it a proper consistency, as in pills, is known as an *excipient*. In ointments, the soft or greasy substance in which a more active drug is incorporated is usually called the *ointment base*.

The inscription also consists of doses of drugs in metric system.

**(c) Subscription :** It contains directions to the pharmacist, which is usually only *'Mix'* or *'Send such ... tablets or capsules, etc"*.

**(d) Signature :** The word signature is derived from the Latin *'signature'* meaning 'write', 'make' or 'label'. It consists of directions to the patient regarding the use of medicine. The directions should be simple, complete, and clear to the patient. It also contains the signature of the physician with his registration number, which is especially necessary when any narcotic drug is prescribed. Occasionally this part of prescription is called *transcription* and the term signature is then reserved for the *physician's name*.

**Refill information :** The prescription is never to be repeated unless the physician so desires, particularly in case of dangerous drugs and narcotics.

**The Prescriber's signature :** A prescription is never complete without the signature of the prescriber. In case, the prescription is through a phone message, pharmacist must obtain the signature later on.

After dispensing, the pharmacist should prepare a label to be attached to the container. This label includes :

(a) Type of preparation e.g. mixture, lotion, ointment etc.
(b) Special directions e.g. *'Shake well before use'* or *'For external use only', 'Poison';* to be *diluted before use* etc.

```
┌─────────────────────────────────────────────────────────────┐
│            Ghanshyam Kochure Accident Hospital              │
│              Visanjinagar, JALGAON 425 001.                 │
│  Phone : (0257) 222 54 50                                   │
├─────────────────────────────────────────────────────────────┤
```

                                            Dr. Ghanshyam Kochure
                                                    M. S. (Ortho).
                                                   Reg. No. 64829
                                              Date : 3/12/2011

Shri. Prakash Supe,
    14/4 Pratap Nagar,
    Jalgaon.
Male - 35 years

    Δ    Compound fracture tibiafibula R

        R̥
            Tab. Ciprofloxacin 500 mg   1 BD
            Tab. Paracetamol 500 mg    1 t ds.
            Tab. B-plex c̄  Vit C 1 BD
            For 7 days

            —  Elevation on pillow
            —  Not to walk
            —  Care of plasters
            —  Dressing.

(c) Name of the patient in full.
(d) Directions to the patient, signature of pharmacist, date, and place of dispensing.
(e) Quantity of the medicament.

If the directions are lengthy they should be written on a separate sheet of paper and handed over to the patient. When the directions are embarassing for the patient they should not be written on the label but given to the patient in private.

**Nature of bottles used for liquid preparations :**

White, round and small bottle should be used for draughts, gargles mouthwashes, etc. Fig. 1.1.

Round, blue or amber coloured and ribbed bottles should be used for preparations for external use such as lotions and liniments, in order to prevent the reaction of light and to make it identifiable from a distance.

Vertically fluted bottles with bakelite caps and attachments should be used for eye drops, ear drops and nasal preparations.

Fig. 1.1 : Containers for Mixtures

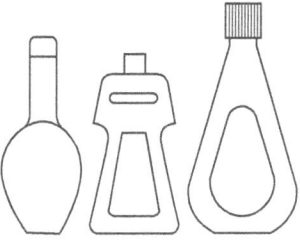

Fig. 1.2 (a) : Containers for liniments and lotions

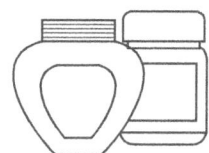

Fig. 1.2 (b) : Wide mouth containers for creams and ointments

Graduated, flat blue or amber coloured bottles with uniform internal diameter should be used for mixtures. It is not ideal, if graduation marks are incorrect, hence a dose marking slip is necessary.

**Example of a prescription :**

| | | For<br>Mr. XYZ<br>Age : 27 Years<br>Address : | | Dr. A. B. C.<br>Address :<br>Date : |
|---|---|---|---|---|
| **Superscription** | | | | |
| | I<br>n<br>s | $R_x$ | | |
| (Basis) | c | Liquor ammonium acetate fortis | 9 | g |
| (Adjuvant) | r<br>i | Potassium acetate | 3 | g |
| (Adjuvant) | p<br>t | Spiritus aetheris nitrosi | 3 | g |
| (Corrective) | i<br>o | Orange syrup | 6 | g |
| (Vehicle) | n | Water upto | 90 | ml |
| **Subscription :** Mix and prepare a mixture. Divide into 3 doses.<br>**Signature :** *Direction :* One dose to be taken 3 times a day.<br>ABC<br>Regd. No. xxxx | | | | |

### Handling of Prescription :

Receiving, checking the prescription, finishing and delivering of medicaments to the patient is part and parcel of the duty of a pharmacist. While receiving a prescription, never show carelessness. In an hospital, it is wise to have a method at hand to see that the prescription goes to the right person. A suitable method would be to give prescription number on three slips. One slip is given to the patient, the second slip is attached to the prescription and the third slip is fixed to the final container. This will ensure identification.

### Checking the Prescription :

Never depend on guess work. When in doubt about the ingredients on their quantities, always fall back and contact the prescriber and confirm the authenticity of your own interpretation.

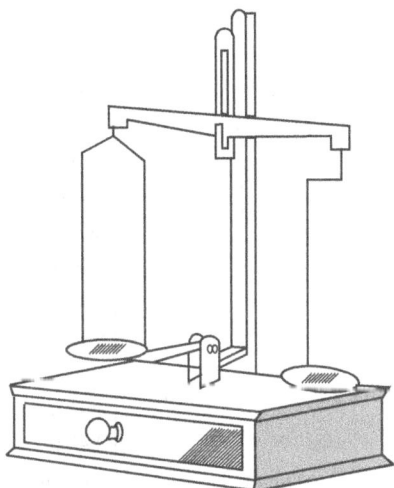

Fig. 1.3 : Dispensing balance

### Compounding the Prescription :

When handling the prescription for compounding, always check for the picking up of correct drug from the shelf and again recheck from the label when returning the container of medicine to the shelf.

### Compounding Accuracy :

Choose a balance which gives a good accuracy. A balance, shown in Fig. 1.3 is a typical Dispensing balance used for the purpose. When the product is finished, choose a suitable container, label it, see that it is presentable and then deliver it to the patient.

### (B) LATIN TERMS USED IN PRESCRIPTIONS

Physicians still use abbreviations, which on writing at length are latin terms. A short but useful English translation appears as mentioned below :

Table 1.1 : Abbreviations and Translation of Latin terms

| Abbreviation | Latin | English |
|---|---|---|
| a | Ante | Before |
| aa | Ana | Of each |
| a.c | Cibos | Before meals |
| ad | – | Sufficient to produce |
| add | Addature | Let it be added |
| aq | Aqua | Water |
| b.i.d. | Bis in die | Twice a day |
| sig | Signetur | Let it be labelled |
| coach | Cochleare | Spoonful |
|  | Amplum | Following the word |
|  | Magnum | Cochleare means |
|  | Maximum | One tablespoonful |
|  | Plenum |  |
|  |  | Following the word |
|  | Medium | Cochleare means one |
|  | Modicium | desert spoonful. |
|  | Minimum | Following the word |
|  | Parvum | Cochleare means one teaspoonful |
| t.i.d. | Ter in die | Thrice a day |
|  | Post cibos | after meals |
|  | Ante cibos | before meals |
|  | Sumendum | To be taken |
|  | Capiendum |  |
| mitt | Mitte | Send |
|  | Semi hora | Half an hour |
|  | Ante Jentaculum | Before breakfast |
|  | Secundis horis | Every two hours |
|  | Ex Lacte | With milk |
|  | Dolore urgente | When the pain is severe |
|  | Fiat Mistura | Let a mixture be made. |
|  | Fiat haustus | Let a draught be made |
|  | Statim | At once |
|  | More dicto danda | Let it be given |
|  | Utenda | To be used |
|  | Quotidie | Daily |

| Abbreviation | Latin | English |
|---|---|---|
| | Secundum artem | in pharmaceutical manner. |
| | Hora sommi | At bed time. |
| | Collunarium | A nasal douche |
| | Guttae | Drops |
| | Haustus | A draught |
| | Insufflation | An insufflation |
| | Nebula | A spray solution |
| past | Pasta | A paste |
| ung | Unguentum | An ointment |
| pil | Pilula | A pill |
| pulv | Pulvis | A powder |
| | Pulvis conspersus | A dusting powder |
| troch | Trochiscus | A lozenge |
| n.p. | Nomen Proprium | Label with name of article |
| chart | Charta | A powder |
| | In phiala | In a bottle |
| p.p.a | Phiala pirus agitata | The bottle being Shaken first |
| tal | Talis, Tales Talia | Such |
| dimid | Dimidium | The half |
| reliq | Reliquum | The remainder |
| infricand | Infricandus | To be rubbed in |
| sugatur | Sugatur | Let it be sucked |
| | Sumat | Let him take |
| d | Da | Give |
| | ut antea | As before |
| ad lib | Ad libtum | As much as you please |
| dos | Dosis | A dose |
| – | Pro | For |
| | Prodosi | As a dose |
| Terquot | Terqotidie | Three times daily |

| Abbreviation | Latin | English |
|---|---|---|
| prim luc. | Prima luce / Primo mane | Early in the morning. |
|  | Mane | In the morning |
|  | Nocte | At night |
|  | Nocte et mane | Night and morning |
|  | Hac nocte | Tonight |
|  | Cras vespere | Tomorrow evening |
| q.i.d. | Quarter in die | Four times a day |
| m. d. | More dicto | As directed |
|  | Lente | Slowly |
| p. r. n. | Pro re nata | Occasionally |
| quot. o. s. | Quoties opus sit | As often as necessary |
| s. o. s. | Si opus sit | When necessary |
| tuss urg | Tussi urgente | When the cough is troublesome. |
| cyath | Cyathyus | A glass |
|  | Ex | With |
| ligament | Ligamentum | Bandage |
| gutt | Guturi | To the throat |
| ocul | Oculis | For the eyes |
|  | Prococulo lacvo | For the left eye |
|  | Inoculum dextrum | Into the right eye |

### Numerals

| | | | |
|---|---|---|---|
| unus | 1 | undecim | 11 |
| duo | 2 | duodecim | 12 |
| tria | 3 | tredicim | 13 |
| quartor | 4 | quatturodecium | 14 |
| quinque | 5 | quindecium | 15 |
| six | 6 | sedecim | 16 |
| septum | 7 | septemdecim | 17 |
| octo | 8 | duodeviginti | 18 |
| novem | 9 | undeviginti | 19 |
| decem | 10 | viginti | 20 |

## (C) MODERN METHODS OF PRESCRIBING

Apart from the general prescription which we have discussed, there are prescriptions which are commonly encountered. In general, the prescriptions are classified as follows :

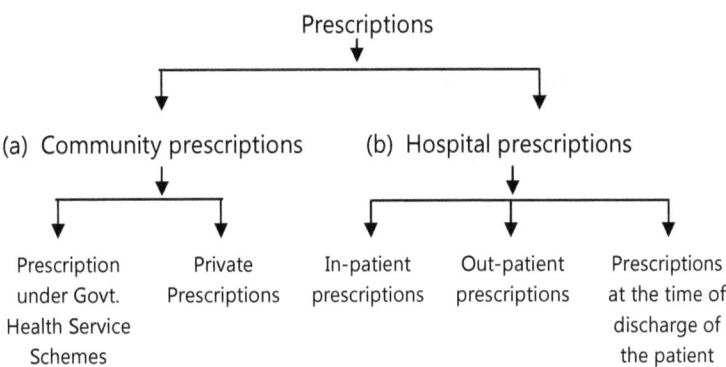

**(a) Community Prescriptions :** The doctors and dentists who are approved by the Government (may be State or Central under Health service schemes may prescribe the drugs, medicines or other appliances in a special prescription form.

In this form, along with the general parts of the prescription, there is an endorsement section for completion by the pharmacist. The pharmacist should enter the details of the medicaments supplied and date in the endorsement section. At one corner there will be the stamp of the name and address of the pharmacy with date of dispensing.

For such prescriptions, remuneration will be paid only if the prescription is in the specific format. The remuneration will be paid to the pharmacist every month after endorsement and submitted to the pricing authority. Thus, such prescriptions are to be retained for a month then they are sent for pricing.

In private prescriptions, now-a-days the physicians prescribe the ready-made dosage forms which do not need any compounding instructions for the pharmacist.

In private prescription apart from general prescription, **veterinary prescriptions** are increasing in number in recent time.

A typical veterinary prescription is given below :

> **Thakur S. M.**
> B. V. Sc.
> Petcare Clinic
> Paud Road, Pune 38.
>
> This prescription is for an animal under my care.
>
> **Mr. S. S. Joshi (for Tommy)**
> 3/4 Kailash Apts; Paud Road.
> Pune 38.
> Age : 2 Years
>
> $R_x$
>
> 30 Tabs. Oxytetracycline 50 mg
> 1 Tablet three times daily
>
> 10 ml. Gentamicin eye drops
> Use four times daily
>
> Signature    11/7/94

Of the private prescriptions received, prescriptions containing only medicine or controlled drug are to be retained for two years. After dispensing the medicines, the prescription is stamped, dated and given the reference number.

### (b) Hospital Prescriptions :

**1. In-patient Prescription :** In most of the hospitals, the physician writes the prescription on a patient's record sheet. This prescription contains the patient identification, name of the drug, route of administration, dose, time of the administration and the prescriber's signature.

In these prescriptions, for drugs which are taken only on one occasion are written as 'once only', for drugs which are to be taken prior to surgery 'pre-medication drugs'. Some drugs are prescribed which are to be taken after regular intervals or on requests. Such drugs include laxatives, post-operative analgesics, sedatives etc.

In hospitals pharmacist may receive a parenteral prescription or intravenous admixture prescription. The prescription may be as follows :

```
┌─────────────────────────────────────────────────────────┐
│          MAHATMA GANDHI HOSPITAL, MUMBAI                │
│  For                                    Date : 12/10/93 │
│     Mr. Jain S. V.                                      │
│     Age : 16 yrs.                                       │
│     Ward No. 10                                         │
│  Rx                                                     │
│                    NSS 1000 ml                          │
│                    125 ml/hr.                           │
│                                                         │
│                         Physician's Signature  11/7/94  │
└─────────────────────────────────────────────────────────┘
```

In the above prescription of the patient's record will be sent to the pharmacist. The above prescription means sodium chloride injection (normal saline solution) 1000 ml, is to be administered at the flow rate of 125 ml per hr.

There may be *prescriptions for total parenteral nutrition (TPN) mixture* as :

```
┌─────────────────────────────────────────────────────────┐
│            MUNICIPAL HOSPITAL, LONAWALA                 │
│  For                                    Date : 26/12/93 │
│  Roy P. N.                                              │
│  Age : 38 years                                         │
│  Male ward                                              │
│     Rx                                                  │
│        1000 Hyperal + 10 NaCl                           │
│        + 10 KCl + 5 MgSO$_4$ + 10 Insulin               │
│                                                         │
│                              Physician's Signature      │
└─────────────────────────────────────────────────────────┘
```

This is a prescription for the preparation of one litre of the hospital's basic TPN solution which is to be provided with the addition of 10 m Eq. sodium chloride, 10 m Eq. potassium chloride, 5 m Eq. magnesium sulphate and 10 units of insulin.

These prescriptions should be checked for proper dose, compatibility, drug allergies, drug interaction and stability. Expiration period for such preparations is usually 24 hours from the time of preparation.

**2. Out-patient Prescriptions :** The out-patient dispensing prescriptions are given in the form where identification of patient, name, address, age and hospital registration number are mentioned. Generally, the medicines prescribed are sufficient to last until the next out-patient appointment.

**3. Prescriptions for patients at the time of discharge :** These are similar to out-patient prescription or may be written on the patient's chart. Depending on the hospital's policies, the quantity prescribed may be for one or two weeks period.

There can be the following types of prescription depending upon the conditions under which they have been prescribed.

(1) Preventive prescriptions

(2) Pathological prescriptions

(3) Drug-induced prescriptions

(4) Etiological prescriptions

(5) Miasmatic prescriptions

(6) Constitutional prescriptions

(7) Prescriptions on totality of symptoms

(8) Prescriptions on key-note symptoms

## (D) ADOPTION OF METRIC SYSTEM

In pharmacy, two unit systems viz. the Metric and the Imperial system are in use. The leaning is more towards the metric system. Yet, it is felt that a working pharmacist must be familiar with both. With this view in mind, the imperial system is included in this chapter.

### THE IMPERIAL SYSTEM

**Measures of Weight (Mass) :**

The standard is the Imperial Standard Pound. This is defined as a cylindrical block made up of platinum and having a diameter 1.15 inch and 1.35 inch in thickness, with an encircling groove into which fits an ivory fork to lift the cylinder. The weight of this cylinder in vacuum is the Imperial Standard Pound.

**1. Avoirdupoise System :**

(Avoirdupoise : Fr *Avoir* : to have + *du* : of the + *pois* : weight)

All other measures of mass are derived from the Imperial Standard Pound.

1 ounce (oz) Avoirdupoise = $16^{th}$ part of 1 pound = 537.5 grains

1 grain (gr) = $7000^{th}$ part of 1 pound

**2. Apothecaries System :**

Apothecary (G. *Apotheke* : Storing place)

It includes a set of special weights, known as Apothecaries or Troy weights.

The details together with their symbols are given below :

| Troy-weight | Symbol |
|---|---|
| 20 grains = 1 scruple | ∋ |
| 60 grains = 1 drachm | ʒ |
| 480 grains = 1 Apothecaries or Troy ounce | ℥ |

12 Apothecaries OR Troy ounces = 1 Troy Pound or 5760 grains. *lb*

Arabic numbers are used in conjunction with the English words.

Examples are :

2 grains, 4 drachms, 3 oz (Troy) etc. Hence 2, 4, 3 are Arabic numbers which precede the English words grain, scruple, etc.

The Avoirdupoise ounce is indicated by the abbreviation 'oz'.

The Apothecaries ounce is indicated either by the symbol, '℥' or is written out as ounce (Troy or Apothecaries).

If symbols are used (which is generally the case when a prescription is given), the Roman numerals follow the symbol.

For example :

One scruple is written as        ∋ i

Two drachms are written as      ʒ ii

Six ounces Troy are written as   ℥ vi

i, ii, iii, iv, v etc. are roman numerals.

The letters, 'SS' or 'fs' following a symbol means 'half'.

For example :

ʒ SS means half a drachm

∋ fs means half a scruple

The symbol for Imperial Standard Pound is 'lb'

## Measures of Capacity (Volume) :

The standard in the Imperial System is the Imperial Standard Gallon and this is a secondary standard related to the Imperial Standard Pound. Therefore, it is called a *derived* standard.

The Gallon is defined as the volume occupied by ten Imperial Standard pounds weight of distilled water weighed in air at 62°F at 30 inches pressure. All other weights are called derived weights.

**Derived Weights :**

| | |
|---|---|
| 1 pint (o) | = 8th part of a gallon |
| 1 fluid ounce (fl. oz) | = 20th part of a pint |
| 1 fluid drachm (fl. dr) | = 8th part of 1 fluid ounce |
| 1 fluid drachm | = 60 minims |
| | = 60th part of a fluid drachm |
| 1 Gallon (c) | = 160 fluid ounces |
| 1 fluid ounce | = 8 fluid drachms or 480 minims |
| 1 fluid drachm | = 60 minims |

| Units | Symbols |
|---|---|
| Minim | m |
| Gutta (drop) | gtt |
| Fluid drachm | ʒ |
| Fluid ounce | fl ʒ |
| Pint | O |
| Gallon | C |

1. Solids are weighed and liquids measured. Hence, confusion cannot occur even if the symbol viz ... 'ʒ' is the same in measures for mass as well as capacity.

2. Similarly as before, Arabic numerals are placed before the English words, and roman numerals follow the symbols.

## THE METRIC SYSTEM

The Metric Units system was legalised in India from 1st April, 1957.

In order to establish standards of weights and measures and to regulate trade or commerce in weights and measures, the Standards of Weights and Measures Act 1976 have been passed by the Government of India.

**Measures of Weight (Mass) :**

The standard for weight is a *Kilogramme*. A kilogram is defined as *the weight of a piece of platinum-iridium whose weight is equal to 1000.027 c.c. of pure water at 4°C and 760 mm Hg pressure.*

All other measures of mass are derived from kilogramme.

| | | |
|---|---|---|
| 1 kilogram | = | 1000 grams |
| 1 Gram | = | 1000 milligrams i.e. $10^{-3}$ kg |
| 1 milligram | = | 1000 micrograms i.e. $10^{-6}$ kg |
| 1 microgram | = | $10^{-9}$ kg |

## Measures of Capacity (Volume):

The litre is a secondary standard measurement of volume. The standard is a litre. The litre is defined as the *volume of 1 kg of pure water at 4°C and 760 mm Hg pressure.*

| Symbols of weight | | Symbols for capacity |
|---|---|---|
| Kilogram | (kg) | Litre $l$ |
| Gram | (g) | |
| Milligram | (mg) | Millilitre $ml$ i.e. $10^{-3}\ l$ |
| Microgram | (µg) | Micro litre $\mu l\ 10^{-6}\ l$ |

The cubic centimetre (c.c.) is less than one ml.

$$1\ ml = 1.000027\ c.c.$$

## Relations of capacity to weight:

| | |
|---|---|
| 1 minim | = 0.9114 grain of water at 62°F |
| 1 fluid drachm | = 54.688 grains of water at 62°F |
| 1 fluid ounce | = 437.5 grains of water at 62°F |
| | = 1 ounce (avoirdupoise) |
| 110 minims | = 100 grains of water |

## Imperial equivalents of Metric weights and measures:

| | |
|---|---|
| 1 microgram (µg) | = $15.432 \times 10^{-6}$ grain |
| 1 milligram (mg) | = 0.015432 grain |
| 1 gram (g) | = 15.432 grains |
| | = 0.03215 ounce (apothecaries) |
| | = 0.03527 ounce (avoirdupoise) |
| 1 kilogram | = 2.2046 pounds |
| 1 millilitre (m$l$) | = 16.894 minims |
| 1 litre ($l$) | = 0.21997 gallon |
| | = 1.7598 gallon |
| | = 35.196 fluid ounces |

**Metric equivalents of Imperial weights and measures :**

| | |
|---|---|
| 1 grain (gr) | = 0.064799 g |
| 1 ounce (avoirdupoise) (oz) i.e. 437.5 grains | = 28.350 g |
| 1 ounce (apothecaries) (480 grains) | = 31.104 g |
| 1 pound (lb) | = 453.59 g |
| 1 minim (min) | = 0.05919 g |
| 1 fluid drachm (fl. dr) | = 3.3515 ml |
| 1 fluid ounce (fl. ox) | = 28.412 ml |
| 1 pint (pt) | = 568.25 ml |
| 1 gallon (gal) | = 4.546 litres |

**Approximate Equivalents :**

| | |
|---|---|
| 30 ml | = 1 fluid ounce |
| 30 g | = 1 oz Avoir |
| 0.1 g | = 15 grains |
| 1 ml | = 15 minims |
| 1 Teaspoonful | = 4 ml |
| 1 Desert spoonful | = 8 ml |
| 1 Table spoonful | = 15 ml |

Recently, SI units (System International) have been adopted everywhere. However, it will have very little effect on dispensing of medication.

As compared to metric system which has many units including Calorie, horse power etc. the S.I. system has only seven primary units.

Kilogramme primary unit of mass in metric system is available in S.I. system, while the unit of capacity (volume) litre is a secondary unit.

### (E) CALCULATIONS INVOLVED IN DISPENSING

#### (I) Alligation :

It is a method used in Pharmacy to bind quantities together through lines drawn and in order to arrive at solutions to simple problems.

**Example 1 :**

In what proportion should 10 per cent salicylic acid ointment be mixed with white soft paraffin in order to obtain a mixture of 2 per cent salicylic acid ointment ?

**Solution :**

1. Put the known strengths on left corner of a rectangle.
2. Place the required strength at a point where the diagonals meet.

3. Subtract the smaller figure from the bigger one on the same diagonal and place the figure on the other end of a diagonal.

4. The figures so obtained represent the number of parts of strength of the solution to be mixed.

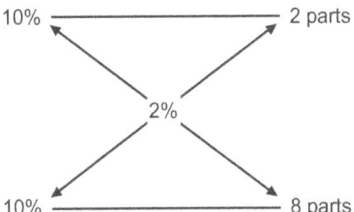

Take 8 parts of soft paraffin and mix with 2 parts of ten per cent of salicylic acid ointment. The 10 parts of mixture will contain 2 per cent salicylic acid.

**Example 2 :**

In what proportion should 10 per cent, 8 per cent and 2 per cent sulphur ointments be mixed in order to obtain a mixture of 4 per cent sulphur ointment ?

**Solution :**

```
        10%              ┐            – 2 parts
                         │
        8%               │            – 2 parts
                         │
                        4%
                         │
        2%               ┘            – 6 parts + 4 parts
```

2 parts of 10%
2 parts of 8%
$\frac{10}{14}$ parts of 2%

1. Link the 10, 8 and 2 per cent ointments as shown. Put the required percentage in the centre of two vertical lines.

2. Subtract the lowest from the required and put the result across the two higher values.

3. Subtract the required percentage from the highest and second highest and put the results against the lowest.

Thus, 14 parts of the above mixture will contain 4 per cent of sulphur.

**Example 3 :**

A pharmacist has three lots of ichthammol ointments containing 40 per cent, 20 per cent and 10 per cent of ichthammol respectively. In what proportions should these be mixed in order to obtain an ointment containing 15 per cent of ichthammol ?

## Solution :

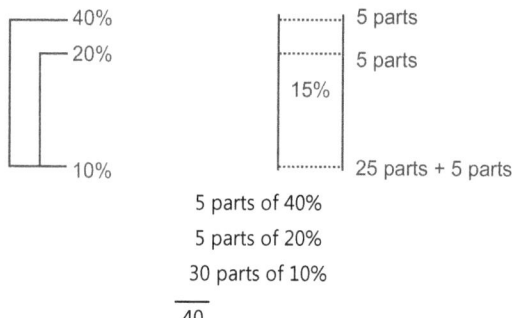

5 parts of 40%
5 parts of 20%
30 parts of 10%
―――
40

Thus, 40 parts of the above mixture will contain 15 per cent of ichthammol in the ointment.

### Example 4 :

How many parts of 90 per cent, 80 per cent, 60 per cent and 40 per cent alcohols be mixed so as to obtain alcohol of 70 per cent strength ?

### Solution :

1. Pair of a higher strength and lower strength alcohol. Make such two pairs and link them together as shown below.
2. Place the required strength in between two vertically drawn lines.
3. Subtract the required strength from the higher values. Place the result against the lower strengths horizontally.
4. Subtract the lower percentage from the required percentage and place the result across and horizontal to the higher strengths.

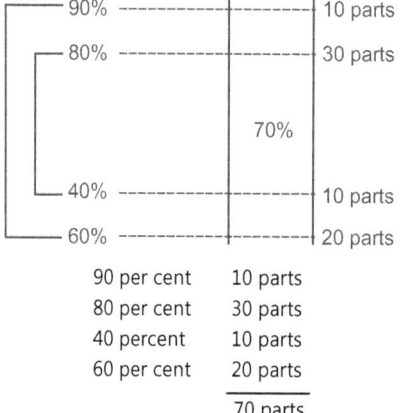

| | |
|---|---|
| 90 per cent | 10 parts |
| 80 per cent | 30 parts |
| 40 percent | 10 parts |
| 60 per cent | 20 parts |
| | 70 parts |

The mixture of 70 parts will contain 70 per cent of alcohol.

### (II) To find out the percentage strength of a mixture :

**Example 5 :**

20 gallons of 40 per cent, 30 gallons of 60 per cent and 40 gallons of 80 per cent alcohols are mixed. What is the percentage strength of the mixture ?

**Solution :**

1. Multiply the volume by percentage
2. Divide the product by total volume

$20 \times 90 = 800$
$30 \times 60 = 1800$
$40 \times 80 = 3200$
$\overline{\phantom{00}90\phantom{00}}\quad\overline{5800}$

$\therefore \quad \dfrac{5800}{90} = 64.44$ per cent

### (III) To find out the specific gravity of a mixture of liquids with different dilutions :

Observe the following rules :

1. Multiply the volume with corresponding specific gravity of individual solution.
2. Add the volume of all liquids.
3. Add all the products of multiplication.
4. Then use the following formula.

$$\text{Specific gravity} = \dfrac{\text{Sum of the product of multiplication}}{\text{Sum of the volumes}}$$

**Example 6 :**

What is the resultant specific gravity if the following solutions are mixed ?

100 ml solution of 0.9 specific gravity
200 ml of distilled water of 1 specific gravity
300 ml of solution with 1.1 specific gravity

**Solution :**

$100 \times 0.9 = 90.0$
$200 \times 1.0 = 200.0$
$300 \times 1.1 = 330.0$

Total volume = 600 ml    620 Sum of products

$\text{Specific gravity} = \dfrac{620}{600}$

Specific gravity = 1.03 of resultant mixture

### (IV) Percentage calculations :

Before a student proceeds to undertake percentage calculations, he is advised to become familiar with weights and measures.

**Per cent solutions are of the following types :**

1. Per cent weight by volume (w/v) means 1 gram of solute in 100 ml of the product. In terms of grain and minims, it is 1 grain of solute in 110 minims of product.
2. Per cent weight by weight (w/w) means 1 gram of solute in 100 grams of product.
3. Per cent volume by volume (v/v) means number of millilitres of solute (liquid) in 100 ml of product.
4. Per cent volume by weight (v/w) means number of millilitres in 100 grams of product.

Generally, solutions are ordered in w/v or v/v, while w/w is used only when the prescriber so desires.

## WEIGHT BY VOLUME SOLUTIONS IN IMPERIAL SYSTEM

Solute 1 oz Avoir, and solvent to produce 100 fluid ounces

$$= 1\% \text{ w/v solutions}$$

437.5 grains in 100 fluid ounces is 1% solution.

Therefore, to produce 1% w/v 1 fluid ounce quantity of solute necessary will be,

$$= \frac{437.5}{100}$$

= 4.375 grains dissolved to produce 1 fluid ounce of 1% w/v solution.

Or

4.375 × 4 = 17.5 grains in 4 ounces is 1% w/v.

Or

35 grains in 8 ounces is 1% w/v solution.

**Example 1 :**

Prepare Xylometazoline hydrochloride 1/2 per cent w/v

Water     ad ℥ ij

Label - The Nasal drops

1 grain in 110 minims is 1 per cent w/v

Therefore, 1 grain in 220 minims is 1/2 per cent

Dissolve 1 grain in 220 minims

Dispense 120 minims, reject the rest.

At times a solution may contain more than one medicament. If there are two medicaments separately, prepare the solution of individual medicament at double the strength and mix. If there are three medicaments prepare the individual solutions with triple strength and then mix. Wastage is prevented by using such methods.

## Example 2 :

℞

    Physostigmine salicylate    0.01%
    Hyoscine hydrobromide    0.01%
    Send 200 ml

Prepare the individual solutions at double strength.
Physostigmine salicylate solution is to be prepared at double strength.
    10 mg in 100 ml will be 0.01%
    20 mg in 100 ml will be 0.02% i.e. double strength.
Prepare the solution in water.
    Hyoscine hydrobromide 10 mg in 100 ml will be 0.01%
    20 mg in 100 ml will be 0.02% i.e. double strength.
Prepare this solution to produce 100 ml.
Mix the two solutions and dispense 200 ml of solution.

## Solution of High Dilutions :

## Example 3 :

Send 2 ounces of 1 in 10,000 solution of potassium permanganate.

It is always convenient to prepare a solution of higher concentration and then dilute to the required strength.

    $10,000 = 100 \times 100$

Therefore, prepare 1 in 100 solution and dilute it 100 times.

    1 grain in 110 minims is 1 in 100 solution.

Prepare this and dilute 10 minims of this solution to 1000 minims and dispense 960 minims i.e. 2 ounces.

## Example 4 :

Send one quart of 1 in 5000 of copper sulphate solution.

    1 quart = 40 ounces
    35 grains in 8 ounces is 1 in 100 solution

Therefore, for 1 in 5000 solution = $\frac{35 \times 100}{5000} = \frac{35}{50}$ grains of copper sulphate in 8 ounces will be 1 in 5000 solution.

But 40 ounces are required.

∴    $\frac{35}{50} \times \frac{40}{8}$ = 3.5 grains in 40 ounces will be 1 in 5000 solution

Solutions are sometimes issued in the concentrated form and the patient is directed to dilute the solution before use.

**Example 5 :**

Required 8 ounces of a solution so that 2 teaspoonful diluted to a pint will give 1 in 2000 solution.

35 grains in 8 ounces will give 1 in 100 solution.

$$\therefore \frac{35 \times 100}{2000}$$

i.e. $\frac{35}{20}$ grains in 8 ounces will give 1 in 2000 solution.

$$\frac{35}{20} \times \frac{20}{8} = \frac{35}{8}$$ grains must be contained in each teaspoonful

In 8 ounces, there are 64 teaspoonful.

Therefore, the quantity required will be

$$\frac{35}{8} \times \frac{64}{2} = 140 \text{ grains will be required}$$

**Example 6 :**

Required 4 ounces of solution so that when a table spoonful is diluted to quart will give 1 in 1000 solution.

35 grains in 8 ounces is 1 in 100 solution

$$\frac{35 \times 100}{1000} = \frac{35}{10}$$ grains in 8 ounces will make 1 in 1000 solution,

1 quart = 40 ounces

2 table spoonful = 1 ounce

$$\therefore \frac{35}{10} \times 40 = 140 \text{ grains will be required to give 1 in 1000 solution}$$

In 4 ounces, there are 8 table spoonfuls

$$\therefore \quad 140 \times 8 = 1120 \text{ grains will be required}$$

## QUESTIONS

1. What is prescription ? Comment on various parts of prescription.
2. What is alligation ? How does it helps in solving the simple mathematical problems, explain with suitable example ?
3. What is metric system ? Name the units of weight of capacity in Imperial and Metric system.

# CHAPTER 2

# INCOMPATIBILITIES IN PRESCRIPTIONS

## DEFINITIONS

*The undesired change, taking place in the physical, chemical or therapeutic properties of the medicament, when two or more ingredients of a prescription are mixed together is termed as incompa-tibility.*

While handling a prescription containing combinations, many a times, problems associated with therapeutic, physical and chemical properties of the drugs, arise.

Incompatibilities are, therefore, grouped into three classes :

1. Therapeutic Incompatibility.
2. Physical Incompatibility.
3. Chemical Incompatibility.

### 1. Therapeutic Incompatibility :

In this type, problems arise in combining drugs or dosages prescribed. It is the responsibility of a physician. However, it forms a part of the duty of the pharmacist to bring this problem to the notice of the *prescriber*.

### 2. Physical Incompatibility :

In this type, mixing or combination of drugs produce a preparation unacceptable in appearance or inaccuracy in dosage or immiscibility problems. For example, combination of oil and water presents a problem of immiscibility and this defect is corrected by emulsification. Eutectic mixture of powders is another example of physical incompatibility.

### 3. Chemical Incompatibility :

In this type, two or more drugs react to give new compound which may be toxic or inactive. Remedy lies in replacing one or more ingredients of the same medical usefulness, yet inert.

There are mainly two types of incompatibilities viz. *Intentional* where the prescriber wants that the prescription, be dispensed as it is and the *Unintentional* where the prescriber has inadvertently combined such drugs as to give unexpected results e.g. precipitation of drug, which is not what the prescriber wanted.

## I. THERAPEUTIC INCOMPATIBILITY

**Exercise 1 :**

R$_x$

Codeine Phosphate           0.5 g

Prepare 10 powders.

**Label :** One dose to be taken at bed time.

This is an example of over-dosage. Probably, the physician intended to write 5 milligrams and yet prescribed 500 mg of codeine phosphate. This prescription must be referred back to the prescriber.

**Exercise 2 :**

R$_x$

Tetracycline hydrochloride    250 mg

Send ten capsules.

**Label :** Take one capsule every six hours with milk.

In this prescription, the dose is alright but the direction is wrong. Tetracycline is inactivated by calcium which is present in milk. Water replaces the milk.

**Exercise 3 :**

R$_x$

Amphetamine sulphate     20 mg

Ephedrine sulphate        100 mg

Syrup                       ad 100 ml

Let a mixture be made.

**Label :** Take 25 ml every four hours.

In this prescription, there is a combination of two sympathomimetic drugs with additive effect and there is a need to reduce the dose of each. Refer the prescription back to the prescriber.

**Exercise 4 :**

R$_x$

Acetyl salicylic acid        1.5 g

Probenecid               1.0 g

This is an example of antagonism between the two drugs. Both help in the treatment of gout being unicosuric agents. However, the combination leads to neutralization. Refer back the prescription.

### Exercise 5 :

R$_x$

| | |
|---|---|
| Acetophenetidin | 150 mg |
| Acetyl salicylic acid | 200 mg |
| Caffeine | 30 mg |

**Label :** Take as directed.

Acetophenetidin is an analgesic and so is aspirin. Acetophenetidin depresses the C.N.S. This side effect is undesirable. Caffeine, a central stimulant is included to overcome the side effect of acetophenetidin. Incompatibility is intentional. Dispense as it is.

## II. PHYSICAL INCOMPATIBILITY

### Exercise 6 :

R$_x$

| | |
|---|---|
| Castor oil | 15 ml |

Make an emulsion

**Label :** Take at once.

This is a case of physical incompatibility. Oil and water do not mix. Emulsification corrects the incompatibility. Dispense as an emulsion.

### Exercise 7 :

R$_x$

| | |
|---|---|
| Thymol | 250 mg |
| Menthol | 2 mg |
| Camphor | 2 mg |

Send five powders.

This is another example of physical incompatibility. The combination forms an eutectic mixture. Refer to the chapter no. 4 'Powders' and dispense accordingly.

## III. CHEMICAL INCOMPATIBILITY

All chemical incompatibilities must be corrected before the prescriptions are dispensed unless the prescriber wants the incompatible combination to be dispensed.

Classification of chemical incompatibilities could be done in three ways :

Classification based on chemical nature of reacting substances.

(a) Inorganic incompatibility

(b) Organic incompatibility

(c) Miscellaneous chemical incompatibility.

Chemical interactions between the drugs of prescription lead to chemical incompatibility. These incompatibilities include effervescence, precipitation, colour changes and at times formation of toxic substances. It is the duty of the pharmacist to correct the incompatibilities with, ofcourse, the consent of the prescriber. At times, the incompatibility is immediately apparent and at other times, the changes occur at a slower rate and the incompatibility is not detectable immediately. It is a practice that such a delayed incompatibility be dispensed in such a way that the prescription is used up before ten per cent of therapeutic activity is lost.

**1. Incompatibility of metals :**

Many metallic salts are used to fill in prescription. Sodium and potassium salts are commonly used. Generally, precipitation occurs by way of incompatibility. Following example will illustrate it.

**Exercise 8 :**

$R_x$

| Sodium salicylate | 10 g |
|---|---|
| Potassium iodide | 2 g |
| Potassium bicarbonate | 4 g |
| Water | 100 ml |

**Label :** Take 25 ml every four hours.

**Type :** Incompatibility of metals.

Sodium salicylate and potassium bicarbonate react and sodium bicarbonate is formed which is in excess of its solubility (1 in 10) and hence precipitated. Solution also darkens due to the presence of salicylate in alkaline solution.

**Correction :** Refer the prescription back to the prescriber for his consent to dispense Potassium bicarbonate separately.

Generally, where a precipitate is expected to be formed, it is convenient to allow it to be formed in as dilute solution as possible. In order to do this, dissolve the reactant in one portion of the vehicle and the second reacting substance in second portion of the vehicle and then mix the two portions.

When it is expected that an indiffusible precipitate is going to be formed, mix compound powder of tragacanth to one of the reacting substances to one portion of the vehicle and the second reacting substance to the second portion of the vehicle and then mix the two portions.

**Exercise 9 :**

$R_x$

| Morphine hydrochloride solution I.P. | 0.5 ml |
|---|---|
| Aromatic spirit of ammonia | ad 30 ml |

**Label :** Take 15 ml. before bedtime.

**Type :** Incompatibility of alkaloidal salt with alkaline substances.

In the present prescription there are 20 mg of morphine hydrochloride present in 2 ml of solution. It has been found that as long as the morphine hydrochloride concentration is 8 mg per 30 ml there will be no precipitation of morphine hydrochloride by alkaline substance such as aromatic spirit of ammonia. Hence, the incompatibility is apparent and not real.

Follow the procedure of a simple mixture.

**Exercise 10 :**

R$_x$

| | |
|---|---|
| Tincture opium | 10 ml |
| Aromatic spirit of ammonia | ad 30 ml |

**Label :** Take 15 ml at bedtime.

**Type :** Incompatibility of alkaloidal salts with alkaline sub-stances.

Tincture opium contains an equivalent of 20 mg of anhydrous morphine per 2 ml. The solubility of anhydrous morphine is 1 in 18 and therefore, the morphine will be precipitated. Secondly, the maximum dose of tincture opium is 2 ml. While each dose contains 5 ml of tincture in the above prescription. The prescription is to be referred back to the prescriber.

However, the student should prepare the mixture as it is, observe the precipitation and then discard it.

**Exercise 11 :**

R$_x$

| | |
|---|---|
| Quinine hydrochloride | 1.2 g |
| Sodium salicylate | 2.4 g |
| Water | ad 100 ml |

**Label :** Take 25 ml every four hours.

**Type :** Incompatibility of alkaloidal salt with salicylate and benzoates.

A precipitate of quinine salicylate is formed. Use method for precipitate yielding combinations.

**Exercise 12 :**

R$_x$

| | |
|---|---|
| Quinine bisulphate | 10 g |
| Dilute sulphuric acid | 20 ml |
| Potassium iodide | 3.0 g |
| Water | ad 200 ml |

**Label :** Take 20 ml every four hours.

**Type :** Incompatibility of Quinine acid sulphate with soluble iodides.

The quinine bisulphate is dissolved in dilute (with equal volume of water) sulphuric acid. The potassium iodide is dissolved in the remaining quantity of vehicle and the two portions mixed and the mixture dispensed.

The mixture is quite clear at first and remains so for three days after which it begins to deposit olive green scales which is the outcome of *Herapath reaction for Quinine.*

The sequence of events are as follows :

Dilute sulphuric acid liberates hydroiodic acid (HI) from potassium-iodide, hydroiodic acid is partly oxidised to give iodine. The free Iodine + HI and quinine sulphate then combine to form a compound called *Herapathite*. There is no problem if the mixture is given for a period of less than three days. Over three days it is better to send potassium iodide in one bottle and other ingredients in another bottle.

## 2. Incompatibility of Soluble Iodides :

### Exercise 13 :

R$_x$

| | |
|---|---|
| Solution of ferric chloride | 2 ml |
| Potassium iodide | 3 g |
| Water | to 120 ml |

**Label :** Take as directed by the physician.

**Type :** Incompatibility of Iodide with ferric salt.

Ferric chloride solution reacts with potassium iodide to liberate free iodine which is undesirable. The remedy lies in replacing ferric chloride with ferrous ammonium citrate. Refer back to prescriber.

### Exercise 14 :

R$_x$

| | |
|---|---|
| Solution of ferric chloride | 2 ml |
| Potassium iodide | 3 g |
| Potassium citrate | 6 g |
| Water | ad 120 ml |

**Label :** Take as directed.

Incompatibility as in Exercise 13 is avoided by the inclusion of alkali citrate which helps in converting ferric chloride to an organic compound before addition of potassium iodide. The organic iron compound does not liberate iodine from potassium iodide.

**Method :**

Dissolve potassium citrate in a part of the vehicle then add solution of ferric chloride and then potassium iodide. Make up the volume and dispense.

## Exercise 15 :

R<sub>x</sub>

| Solution of ferric chloride | 2 ml |
|---|---|
| Sodium salicylate | 3 g |
| Water | ad 150 ml |

**Label :** Take one tablespoon full of solution every four hours.

**Type :** Incompatibility of soluble salicylate with ferric salt.

Ferric salicylate is formed which is insoluble and indiffusible hence use the method for indiffusible precipitate.

### 3. Incompatbility of Soluble Salicylates and Benzoates with Acids :

## Exercise 16 :

R<sub>x</sub>

| Sodium salicylate | 3.0 g |
|---|---|
| Quinine sulphate | 600 mg |
| Dilute sulphuric acid | 2.0 ml |
| Water | ad 150 ml |

**Label :** Take as directed.

Incompatibility (Example of tolerated incompatibility)

The sulphuric acid will precipitate salicylic acid from sodium salicylate.

**Remedy :** Sulphuric acid is included to dissolve quinine sulphate, omit sulphuric acid and a clear mixture will be formed.

## Exercise 17 :

R<sub>x</sub>

| Sodium salicylate | 3 g |
|---|---|
| Syrup of lemon | 15 ml |
| Water | ad 60 ml |

**Label :** Take 15 ml every four hours.

Syrup of lemon contains citric acid which will precipitate salicylic acid from sodium salicylate.

**Remedy :**

Replace syrup of lemon with simple syrup and 1 ml of Tincture lemon. This is an example of adjusted incompatibility.

## 4. Incompatibility Concerned with Liberation of Carbon-dioxide Gas :

Some combinations yield carbon dioxide gas immediately and others very slowly. When the combination yield gas slowly, can break the bottle containing the mixture through explosion due to slowly built up pressure.

General remedy is to prepare the mixture in an open vessel, allow the gas to escape and then bottle the mixture. Where the reaction proceeds very slowly and gas is evolved slowly, methods such as using hot water or heating may be employed to hasten the formation and escape of gas in an open vessel.

### Exercise 18 :

$R_x$

| | | |
|---|---|---|
| Sodium bicarbonate | | 2 g |
| Borax | | 1 g |
| Glycerin | | 10 ml |
| Water | ad | 50 ml |

**Type :** Evolution of Carbondi-oxide gas.

**Method :** Mix all the ingredients in an open vessel. Allow carbon dioxide to escape. Make up the volume and dispense.

## 5. Incompatibility of Soluble Barbiturates :

At times sodium salts of barbiturates are used in mixtures. These solutions are alkaline and, therefore, incompatibility occurs with ammonium salts and acids with precipitation of barbiturate.

### Exercise 19 :

$R_x$

| | | |
|---|---|---|
| Sodium phenobarbitone | | 120 mg |
| Ammonium bromide | | 1.2 g |
| Water | ad | 100 ml |

**Label :** Take 25 ml of solution every night.

**Incompatibility :**

Phenobarbitone is precipitated by ammonium bromide. Prepare as it is and observe indiffusible precipitate. Repeat the exercise by using sodium bromide and observe.

Dispense by using compound powder of Tragacanth.

### Exercise 20 :

℞

| | |
|---|---|
| Bismuth sub-nitrate | 4 g |
| Kaolin pectin mixture | ad 50 ml |

This combination forms a cake on standing. Refer back to the physician.

## 6. Incompability of Emulsifying agents :

### Exercise 21 :

℞

| | | |
|---|---|---|
| Phenol | | 0.5 g |
| Menthol | | 0.1 g |
| Tragacanth | | 0.5 g |
| Olive oil | | 50 ml |
| Lime water | ad | 100 ml |

**Label :** Take as directed by the physician.

The free acids in olive oil form a divalent soap with lime water. The divalent soap promotes w/o emulsion. While tragacanth favours o/w emulsion. Consult the physician and replace lime water with purified water, or omit tragacanth.

### Exercise 22 :

℞

| | |
|---|---|
| Chloral hydrate | 250 mg |
| Send ten capsules | |

**Label :** Take one capsule at night.

### Incompatibility :

Capsules may collapse as the chloral hydrate softens gelatin capsules.

### Remedy :

Send chloral hydrate in solution form. Alternatively use magnesium carbonate as a diluent and store in a refrigerator.

## Exercise 23 :

℞

Acriflavine 0.1%         15 ml

Dakin's Solution     ad  100 ml

**Label :** Use as directed by the physician.

The Dakin's solution is a source of chlorine. The chlorine reacts with acriflavine and changes the colour of the solution. Consult the prescriber and omit Dakin's solution.

### QUESTIONS

1. Define incompatibility. How incompatibilities are classified ? Describe one example of each.

2. What you know about therapeutic incompatibility ? How will you overcome Herapath reaction of Quinine in a mixture.

# CHAPTER 3

# POSOLOGY

Posology deals with doses of drug. The Greek term *posos* means how much; and *logos* means science. So it is a science of how much (dose) drug is to be given for its expected effect. Doses of different medicines are different. They are dependent on the state of patient, sex, age and severity of the disorder. It is also dependent on the factors such as :

1. **Route of Administration :** Effectiveness of drug formulation is controlled by the route of administration. Injection gives a quick effect in a small dose whereas comparatively large doses are required when administered orally.

2. **Rate of Elimination :** If the rate of drug elimination from the body is increased due to some reason or the other, the same drug shows a prolonged effect.

3. **Formulation :** Type of formulation also affects the dose size. Same drug in repeated single dosage form requires more quantity than does the prolonged drug formulation.

4. **Drug Interaction :** Simultaneous administration of the drug may give synergistic effect reducing the dose of one or both of the drugs.

5. **Idiosyncrasy :** Sometimes one comes across a patient or person, who, on administration of a minimum dose of certain drug, suffers unpleasant symptoms of a temporary nature, or individual intolerance. Such a person is said to be suffering from idiosyncrasy arising from that particular drug. e.g. quinine, aspirin, etc. Remedy is to discontinue the drug.

## NATURAL AND ACQUIRED TOLERANCE

Some individuals tolerate comparatively large doses, while others may get an adverse effect. Similarly, repeated doses of a drug for a prolonged period affect the individual in such a way that the dose is required to be increased in order to produce therapeutic effect. Normally, the quantity of drug or dose decreases in the following order.

$$\text{Oral} \rightarrow \text{Subcutaneous} \rightarrow \text{Intramuscular} \rightarrow \text{Intravenous}$$

**Frequency :**

Generally, a dose is repeated three or four times a day. The frequency depends on the effective blood concentration of the drug, rate of metabolism and excretion.

## PAEDIATRIC DOSE

Pharmacopoeia gives the range of quantities for adult dose for 24 hours by oral route and by any other specified route. Adult dose and paediatric doses are different. In order to calculate paediatric dose, the following formulae are used:

1. **Young's Rule**

    $$\frac{\text{Age in Years}}{\text{Age in Years} + 12} = \text{Proportion of adult dose}$$

    Example: For a child of 6 years.

    $$\frac{6}{6 + 12} = \frac{6}{18} = \frac{1}{3} \text{ of adult dose.}$$

    If adult dose is 150 mg then child dose is 50 mg.

2. **Dilling's Rule**

    $$\frac{\text{Age in Years}}{20} = \text{Part of adult dose}$$

    Example: For a child of 6 years

    $$\frac{6}{20} = \frac{3}{10} \text{ parts of adult dose}$$

    If adult dose is 150 mg then child dose is 45 mg.

3. **Fried's Rule for Infants**

    [Below the age of 2 years]

    $$\frac{\text{Age in months} \times \text{Adult dose}}{150}$$

    If the age is 6 months and adult dose is 600 mg

    then $\frac{6 \times 600}{150} = 24$ mg dose of a child.

4. **Clark's Rule for Infants**

    $$\frac{\text{Weight in pounds} \times \text{Adult dose}}{150}$$

    If adult dose is 300 mg and weight is 20 pounds

    then $\frac{20 \times 300}{150} = 40$ mg dose of a child

5. **Cowling's Rule**

    $$\frac{\text{Age at next Birthday (in years)} \times \text{Adult dose}}{24}$$

    If the adult dose is 240 mg and age is 6 years

    then $\frac{6 \times 240}{24} = 60$ mg

Sometimes, dose is calculated on the basis of body weight. This is essential because quantity of drug at site is dependent on the size of the patient and hence heavily built person should receive more drug than does a normal person. Therefore, for some drugs, doses are prescribed on the basis of body weight. For example, propanidid dose is 10 mg per kg of body weight. For a person weighing 60 kg, the dose becomes :

$$60 \times 10 = 600 \text{ mg by intravenous route.}$$

**Surface Area :**

In 1966, Catzel devised a method for calculating doses based on surface area of a body. Some of the formulae are given below. Tables according to weight and age are also available to find out surface area of the body. Although this method is good for calculation of dose, it is tedious for calculating the surface area.

1. $\dfrac{\text{Surface area of patient in m}^2}{\text{Average adult surface area}} \times \text{Adult dose} = \text{Dose for patient}$

2. Surface area of patient in m² × Dose of drug per m² = Dose of patient

**Dose Table :**

The following is a dose table for commonly used drugs. Maximum dose and route of administration is also specified :

Unless and otherwise mentioned, doses are suitable for adults.

In the range of doses, lower dose applies at the lower age and higher dose applies at the higher age limit. Although the doses are based on the opinions of medical experts and are for general guidance they are not binding on the prescriber. A pharmacist must ensure the intention of the prescriber before he advises. Unless specifically mentioned dose is to be administered by oral route.

I.M. : Intra-muscular, I.V. : Intra-venous

| Name of the Drug | Maximum dose and route |
|---|---|
| Acetazolamide | 500 mg initial dose, 250 mg subsequently every six hours. |
| Acetyl salicylic acid | 1 g for headache, 8 g daily in divided doses in rheumatism. |
| Acetomenaphthone | 5-10 mg daily, one week before delivery. |
| Adrenaline acid tartarate | 1 mg by subcutaneous injection as single dose. |
| Adrenaline injection | 0.5 ml by subcutaneous injection. |
| Allopurinol | 200 - 400 mg daily, 1.8 g daily in divided doses, 8 mg as emetic, 100 mg by intravenous, 200 mg daily maintenance dose. |

| | |
|---|---|
| Aloes | 300 mg. |
| Alpha amylase | 0.2 to 5 g |
| Aluminium hydroxide gel | 7.5 -15 ml |
| Amantadine HCl | 200 mg daily |
| Amino caproic acid | 5 g followed by 1 - 1.25 g every hour. |
| Aminophylline | 250 - 500 mg by slow I.M. injection, 300 mg oral. |
| Amitriptyline HCl | 75 - 150 mg daily. |
| Ammonium chloride | 3 - 6 g daily in divided doses before the administration of mersalyl injection. |
| Amodiaquine | 400 mg suppressive dose. |
| Amoxycillin trihydrate | 0.75 to 4.5 g daily |
| Amphetamine sulphate | 10 mg morning and mid day. |
| Ampicillin trihydrate | 2 to 6 g daily |
| Amylobarbitone | 100 - 200 mg oral sedative |
| Amylobarbitone sodium | 100 - 200 mg sedative |
| Analgin | 0.5 to 3.0 g daily |
| Aneurine hydrochloride | 50 mg oral. Prophylactic dose, 100 mg daily, therapeutic oral dose. |
| Antazoline hydrochloride | 100 mg oral antihistaminic |
| Anise oil | 0.2 ml oral |
| Ascorbic acid injection | 1 g intramuscular |
| Ascorbic acid | Oral 75 mg daily prophylactic, 500 mg therapeutic |
| Atropine sulphate | 2 mg orally, 0.2 mg by intramuscular injection. |
| B. C. G. vaccine | 0.1 ml by intra-cutaneous injection as prophylactic. |
| Bacitracin | For amoebasis 80000 to 120000 IU. orally. |
| Barbitone sodium | 600 mg orally, sedative |
| Bel liquid extract | 8 ml orally as digestive and astringent |
| Belladonna dry extract | 60 mg orally |
| Belladonna tincture | 2 ml orally |
| Bemegride | 1 g total. 50 mg at intervals of ten minutes by intravenous injection in the treatment of barbiturate poisoning. |
| Bendrofluazide | 5 - 20 mg daily |

| | |
|---|---|
| Benzathine penicillin | 0.9 g prophylactic by intramuscular injection every two or three weeks. |
| Benzyl penicillin | 500 mg every four hours orally. 600 mg by I.M. injection, 2 to 4 times daily. |
| Bephenium hydroxyna - Phlthoate | 5.0 g single dose |
| Betamethazone | 0.5 - 5 mg daily |
| Bethanidine sulphate | 10 - 20 mg daily |
| Bisacodyl | 5 to 10 mg daily |
| Bismuth sodium – subcarbonate | 200 mg by I.M. injection antisyphilic Antacid 2 g daily. |
| Busulphan | 2 - 4 mg daily |
| Caffeine | 600 mg daily, C.N.S stimulant |
| Caffeine citrate | 600 mg daily. |
| Calciferol | Prophylactic (antiricketic) 400 to 1000 units, 5 mg or 200,000 units in the treatment of hypothyroidism |
| Calcium levulinate | 1.0 g daily |
| Calcium aminosalicylate | 10 - 20 g daily |
| Calcium gluconate | 1 to 5 g daily |
| Calcium lactate | 5 g orally |
| Calcium pentothenate | 10 - 100 mg |
| Carbamazepine | 0.2 to 1.2 g daily |
| Carbenicillin disodium | 10 to 30 g daily |
| Carbimazole | 30 - 60 mg daily |
| Castor oil | 20 ml single dose as purgative |
| Cephalexin | 1 - 4 g daily |
| Cephaloridine | 1 - 4 g daily |
| Chloral hydrate | 0.5-2 g |
| Chloramphenical | 1.5 - 3 g daily, children dose 500 mg per kg of body weight |
| Chlorcyclizine HCl | 50 - 200 mg daily |
| Chloroquine phosphate | Antimalarial suppressive 0.5 g weekly, therapeutic initial 1 g – 0.5 g daily |
| Chloroquine sulphate | 400 mg - 1.2 g |
| Chlorpheniramine maleate | 4 - 16 mg daily |
| Chlorpropamide | 100 - 500 mg daily |

| | |
|---|---|
| Chlorpromazine HCl | 75 - 800 mg daily |
| Chlortetracycline | 3 g in divided doses daily, children 30 mg per kg body weight |
| Chlorthalidone | 100 - 200 mg daily |
| Cholera vaccine | 0.5 ml |
| Chordiazepoxide | 10 - 100 mg daily |
| Cloxacillin sodium | 1.5 - 3.0 g |
| Cimetidine | 200 - 400 mg |
| Clofazimine | 100 mg six times weekly |
| Clofibrate | 2 g daily |
| Clonidine HCl | 100 - 300 mg daily |
| Cod liver oil | 10 ml daily |
| Codeine phosphate | 60 mg |
| Corticotrophin | 40 - 80 mg daily |
| Cortisone acetate | 50 - 400 mg daily |
| Cyanocobalamine | 1 - 2 mg by I.M. injection in divided doses |
| Cyclizine HCl | 25 - 50 mg daily |
| Cyclophosphamide | 100 - 200 mg daily |
| Cycloserine | 250 - 750 mg daily |
| Cypraheptadine HCl | 4 - 20 mg daily |
| D-panthenol | 0.25 - 0.5 g |
| Dapsone | 25 - 50 mg twice weekly |
| Dehydro-emetine HCl | 60 - 90 mg by I.M. injection |
| Deslanoside | 0.8 - 1.2 mg by I.M. injection |
| Dexamethazone | 0.5 - 10 mg |
| Di-iodohydroxy quinoline | 2 g daily for 20 days in amoebasis |
| Diazepam | 5 mg for inducing sleep |
| Diethylcarbamazine | 100 - 500 mg daily |
| Digitalis prepared | 1.5 g initial dose in divided doses for rapid digitilisation |
| Digitoxin | 0.05 - 0.2 mg daily |
| Digoxin | 1 - 1.5 mg daily |
| Dilute hydrochloric acid | 10 ml |
| Diloxamide furoate | 1.5 g daily |
| Dimenhydrinate | 25 - 100 mg |

| Drug | Dose |
|---|---|
| Dimercaprol | 2 - 3 mg daily |
| Diphenhydramine HCl | 50 - 200 mg daily |
| Diphenoxylate HCl | 5 - 30 mg daily |
| Diphtheria antitoxin | 50 - 2000 IU |
| Doxycyclin | 100 mg daily, antibiotic |
| Emetine HCl | 30 - 60 mg daily |
| Ephedrine HCl | 15 - 60 mg daily |
| Ergometrin maleate | 1 mg |
| Ergotamine tartarate | 1 - 2 mg daily |
| Erythromycin | 1 - 2 g daily |
| Ethambutol | 15 - 25 mg/kg |
| Ethionamide | 0.5 - 1 g daily |
| Ethopropazine HCl | 50 - 100 mg daily |
| Ferric ammonium citrate | 3 g daily |
| Ferrous fumarate | 0.2 - 0.6 g daily |
| Ferrous gluconate | 1.2 - 1.8 g daily |
| Ferrous gluconate | Prophylactic 300 mg daily |
| Ferrous sulphate | Prophylactic 300 mg daily |
| Fludrocortisone acetate | 1 - 2 mg daily |
| Fluorouracil | 3 mg/kg of body weight |
| Fluphenazine HCl | 1 - 2 mg daily |
| Folic acid | 5 - 20 mg daily |
| Frusemide | 40 - 120 mg daily |
| Furazolidone | 400 mg daily |
| Gentamycin sulphate | 80 - 120 mg by I.M. injection |
| Glibenclamide | 2.5 - 20 mg daily |
| Griseofulvin | 0.5-1 g daily |
| Guanethidine sulphate | 10 - 20 mg daily |
| Heparin sodium | 20000 - 50000 units |
| Hyaluronidase | 500 - 1000 units by I.V. injection. |
| Hydrochlorthiazide | 25-100 mg |
| Hydrochloride | Weekly or once every two weeks in malaria. |
| Hydrocortisone | 50 mg by intravenous route |
| Hyoscine hydrobromide | 600 microgram sub-cutaneous injection |

| | |
|---|---|
| Hyoscyamus dry extract | 60 mg |
| Hyoscyamus liquid extract | 0.5 ml |
| Hyoscyamus tincture | 5 ml |
| Ibuprofen | 0.6 - 1.2 g daily |
| Imipramine | 50 - 150 mg daily |
| Indomethacin | 75 - 100 mg daily |
| Insulin | According to requirement of patient |
| Ipecac liquid extract | 0.1 ml |
| Ipecac tincture | 1 ml |
| Isocarboxazid | 10 - 20 mg daily. |
| Isoniazid | 600 mg in divided doses |
| Isoprenaline sulphate | 5 - 20 mg daily |
| Kanamycin sulphate | 0.5 - 1 g by I.M. injection |
| Lanatoside C | 1 - 1.5 mg |
| Leptazol | 50 - 100 mg |
| Levodopa | 250 mg daily |
| Light kaolin | 75 g |
| Light magnesium carbonate | 0.3 - 0.6 antacid |
| Lincomycin | 1.5 g daily |
| Liquid paraffin | 30 ml oral |
| Liquorice liquid extract | 5 ml |
| Magnesium hydroxide | 10 ml as antacid |
| mixture | 50 ml as laxative |
| Magnesium trisilicate | 0.5 - 2 g |
| Mebendazole | 100 mg single dose |
| Meclizine HCl | 25 - 50 mg |
| Mephenesin | 0.1 - 1 mg |
| Meprobamate | 0.4 - 1.2 g daily |
| Metformin HCl | 0.5 - 2 g daily |
| Methodilazine HCl | 8 mg daily |
| Methotrexate | 50 - 100 mg |
| Methyldopa | 0.5 - 3.0 g |
| Metronidazole | 200 mg 3 times daily for seven days |
| Morphine hydrochloride | 5 - 10 mg |

| | |
|---|---|
| Morphine sulphate | 10 - 20 mg |
| Neomycin sulphate | 0.7 - 2 g |
| Nikethamide | 2 g by I/V injection |
| Noscapine | 15 - 30 mg |
| Nuxvomica tincture | 2 ml |
| Nystatin | 1 - 2 million units daily |
| Opium tincture | 2 ml |
| Oxprenolol HCl | 40 mg - 2 g daily |
| Oxyphenbutazone | 200 - 400 mg daily |
| Oxytetracycline | 1 - 2 g |
| Oxytocin | 1.5 unit by I/V injection |
| Paracetamol | 0.5 - 1 g every four hours |
| Paraldehyde | 8 ml orally or rectal injection |
| Pentazocine HCl | 25 - 100 mg after food |
| Pethidine hydrochloride | 100 mg, 25 - 100 mg by I/M or I/V injection. |
| Phenobarbitone | 120 mg |
| Phalcodeine | 60 mg daily |
| Phenobarbitone sodium | 120 mg |
| Phenyl butazone | 400 mg daily |
| Piperazine citrate | 2 g daily |
| Phenytoin sodium | 50 mg daily |
| Potassium citrate | 2g |
| Potassium iodide | 500 mg as expectorant |
| Prednisolone | 5 - 60 mg daily |
| Prednisone | 5 - 60 mg |
| Prepared belladonna herb | 200 mg orally |
| Primaquine phosphate | 15 mg daily |
| Probenecid | 2 g daily |
| Procaine penicillin | As penicillin 900 mg by I/M daily |
| Proguanil HCl | 0.1 to 0.3 g daily |
| Promethazine HCl | 20 - 50 mg daily |
| Propranolol HCl | 3 - 10 mg I/V injection. |
| Pyridoxin HCl | 10 - 150 mg daily |
| Quinidine | 200 mg three to four times a day in the prophylaxis of cardiac arrhythmia. |
| Quinine hydrochloride | 300 - 600 mg in malaria |

| | |
|---|---|
| Quinine sulphate | 300 - 600 mg in malaria |
| Reserpine | 5 mg daily in divided doses in psychiatric state |
| Rhubarb powder | 1 g |
| Rifampicin | 450 - 600 mg |
| Senna leaf powder | 2 g |
| Small pox vaccine | 0.02 ml prophylactic |
| Sodium bicarbonate | 5 g as an antacid |
| Sodium citrate | 4 g |
| Sodium iodide | 500 mg as an expectorant |
| Sodium salicylate | 10 gm daily in divided doses for acute rheumatism |
| Streptomycin sulphate | 1 g daily |
| Sulpha methoxazole | 2 g daily |
| Sulphadiazine | 3 g initial dose. Subsequently 4 gm daily in divided doses. |
| Sulphafurazole | 3 g daily |
| Sulphadimidine | 3 g initial dose. Afterwards 6 gm daily in divided doses |
| Streptomycin sulphate | 1 g daily |
| Tolbutamide | 0.5 - 1.5 g daily |
| Trimethoprim | 100 - 200 mg |
| Thyroid | 250 mg daily |
| Testosterone | 60 mg |
| Tolu syrup | 10 ml |

## VETERINARY DOSES

It was mentioned earlier that doses depend upon the type of formulation, age of the patient, sex of the patient, idiosyncracy, drug interaction, body weight, surface area and the severity of the disorder. Thus, as compared to human beings, the doses required for animals are more or on the higher side, obviously because the weight and surface area of animals in normally more than in the case of human beings, except very few small animals.

Doses for animals are normally mentioned on body weights. Morever unless otherwise mentioned specifically, doses are applicable to 'all-species'.

The term *'all species'* as referred in British Pharmacopoeia Veterinary 1977 First Edition is restricted to

| | |
|---|---|
| Horse and cattle | 500 kg |
| Pigs | 150 kg |
| Sheeps, goats, calves, and foals | 50 kg |
| Dogs | 10 kg |
| Cats | 5 kg |

For heavier animals, the daily doses may vary. The word daily means once in twenty four hours.

Doses mentioned are per kg of body weight of animals.

Veterinary doses of some important medicaments are as below :

| Name of the Medicament | Maximum dose and route |
|---|---|
| Adrenaline acid tartarate | 10 microgram/kg |
| Ampicillin | 4 - 12 mg/kg |
| Apomorphine hydrochloride | 0.3 to 0.6 mg/kg |
| Arsanillic acid | 100 - 250 g /tonne of feed |
| Ascorbic acid | 50 - 300 mg/kg |
| Acetyl salicylic acid | 30 - 100 mg/kg |
| Atropine sulphate | 20 - 60 microgram/kg subcutaneously |
| Azaperone | 0.5 - 2 mg/kg |
| Benzyl penicillin | 3 - 6 mg by I.M. injection |
| Betamethazone | 20 microgram/kg |
| Calciferol | 12 - 100 microgram/25 - 50 mg/tonne of feed |
| Calcium gluconate | 100 - 300 mg/kg I.M. or I.V. injection |
| Calcium lactate | 50 - 100 mg/kg of body weight |
| Carbon tetrachloride | 1 to 3 ml |
| Castor oil | 1 to 2 ml/kg |
| Catechu | 10 - 20 mg/kg |
| Chalk | 0.3 - 0.5 g/kg |
| Chloral hydrate | 60 - 100 mg/kg |
| Chloramphenicol | 50 mg/kg |
| Chlorpropamide | 5 - 15 mg/kg |
| Chlortetracycline HCl | 130 mg/litre of drinking water |
| Cloxacillin benzathine | 500 mg as a single dose |

| | |
|---|---|
| Cod-liver oil | 0.2 ml/kg |
| Danthrone | 20 - 50 mg/kg |
| Dapsone | 4 g daily by I.M. injection |
| Decoquinate | 40 g/tonne of feed |
| Dexamethasone | 25 - 100 microgram/kg |
| Dextrose | 1 g/kg |
| Diamphenethide | 100 mg/kg |
| Diaveridine | 15 g/tonne of feed |
| Dienostrol | 20 mg/kg |
| Dihydro streptomycin sulphate | 20 mg/kg daily by I.M. injection |
| Dimercaprol | 2.5 - 3 mg/kg by I.M. injection |
| Dinitolmide | 200 g/tonne of feed. |
| Erythromycin | 2 - 20 mg/kg daily |
| Ethopabate | 5 - 8 g/tonne of feed |
| Ferrous sulphate | 10 - 30 mg/kg |
| Fluanisone | 5 mg/kg |
| Framycetine sulphate | 7000 units/kg daily |
| Frusemide | 5 mg/kg daily |
| Furazolidone | 400 g/tonne feed for ten days |
| Griseofulvin | 15 - 20 mg/kg daily |
| Haloxon | 50 mg/kg |
| Hexachlorophene | 10 - 15 mg/kg |
| Hexoestrol | 15 - 45 mg by implantation in non-edible part of the body of animal. |
| Hydrochlorothiazide | 0.2 to 5 mg/kg daily |
| Hydroxycobalmin | 5 - 10 microgram/kg |
| Hyoscine hydrobromide | 30 - 60 microgram/kg |
| Lincomycin HCl | 20 mg/kg daily |
| Magnesium carbonate | 15 - 30 mg/kg |
| Magnesium sulphate | 0.5 - 1 g/kg |
| Mepyramine maleate | 5 -10 mg/kg |
| Methandienone | 500 mg/kg daily |
| Methyl prednisolone acetate | 400-1000 microgram/kg once a week |

| Drug | Dose |
|---|---|
| Methyl testosterone | 0.25 mg/kg daily |
| Metronidazole | 20 mg/kg |
| Neomycin sulphate | 4000 - 8000 units/kg daily |
| Nicotinamide | 3 - 5 mg/kg |
| Nitrofurazone | 500 g/tonne of feed |
| Nitroxynil | 10 mg/kg |
| Nystatin | 1,00,000 units daily |
| Oxyclozanide | 10 - 15 mg/kg |
| Oxytetracycline | 10 - 55 mg/kg |
| Oxytocin | upto 50 milliunits/kg |
| Paracetamol | 20 mg/kg |
| Liquid paraffin | 1 - 2 ml/kg |
| Pentobarbitone sodium | 20 - 35 mg/kg |
| Pethidine HCl | 1 to 5 mg/kg by I.M. injection |
| Phenobarbitone | 6 - 12 mg/kg |
| Phenoxylmethyl penicillin | 16 mg/kg daily |
| Phenyl butazone | 2 - 20 mg/kg |
| Phenytoin sodium | 10 to 20 mg/kg |
| Piperazine adipate | 100 - 300 mg/kg |
| Prednisolone | 0.25 to 0.5 mg/kg |
| Procain penicillin | 20 - 40 mg/kg by I.M. injection |
| Progesterone | 200 - 500 microgram/kg |
| Promethazine HCl | 2.5 - 10 mg/kg |
| Reserpine | 0.1 kg/tonne of feed |
| Serum gonadotrophin | 5 - 15 units/kg by I.M. injection |
| Sodium acid phosphate | 10 - 30 mg/kg daily |
| Sodium bicarbonate | 50 - 100 mg/kg |
| Sodium salicylate | 50 - 200 mg/kg |
| Stilbesterol | 50 mg by implantation in non-edible part of the animal |
| Streptomycin sulphate | 10 mg/kg |
| Sulfamerazine | upto 100 mg/kg |
| Sulfadiazine | 200 mg/kg |
| Sulfadimidine | 100 mg/kg daily |
| Sulphamethoxypyridazine | 22 mg/kg |
| Testosterone | 0.5 - 2 mg/kg |

| Thiabendazole | 50 - 100 mg/kg |
| Thiamine HCl | 5 - 10 mg/kg |
| Thyroxine sodium | 100 microgram/kg daily |
| Tolbutamide | 10 - 30 mg/kg |
| Trimeprazine tartrate | 2 - 4 mg/kg |
| Turpentine oil | 15 - 60 ml as a single dose |

### QUESTIONS

1. What is dose of a drug ? What are the different factors which control the dose of a drug, describe them in short.
2. How is the paediatric dose worked out ? Name and describe at least three formulae for fixing the doses of drugs.
3. What is Posology ? Give the minimum and maximum doses of Reserpine.

❑❑❑

# SECTION - II
# DISPENSED MEDICATIONS

# CHAPTER 4

# POWDERS

## INTRODUCTION

Powders are a useful dosage form and usually consist of mixtures of two or more powdered medicaments meant for internal use. The size of the particles range from 10,000 microns (μ) to 0.1 micron (0.1 μ) depending upon the method employed for grinding. The size of the particle determines the effectiveness of the physiological properties. Powders are economical and easy to manufacture as compared to Tablet triturates, granules and cachets.

**Tablet Triturates or Moulded Tablets :** These are small tablets prepared extemporaneously. The potent medicament is diluted with lactose, moistened with 50-60% alcohol and then the paste is filled in mould and dispensed.

**Granules :** These are the formulation of medicinal substances with small irregular particles of 2 to 4 millimeters. Granules contain pharmaceutical adjuvants. These are provided in sachets each containing 5 gm of granules, Bephenium, Methylcellulose granules are official.

**Cachets :** These are the dosage forms like capsules made of rice flour and water moulding into suitable shape to enclose the medicaments with unpleasant taste. There are two types of cachets, dry closing and flanged type, to hold the drug material from 0.2 to 2.0 gm. Cachets are official products. They are required to be immersed in water for a few seconds placed on tongue and swallowed with water.

**Advantages of Powders :**
1. The dose variation depending on the condition of the patient, is possible.
2. Powders are more stable than liquid dosage forms.
3. Many a times, the desired effect depends on the particle size and where a diffusion is desired powder meets the required need i.e. it diffuses more rapidly than the tablets and pills.
4. Relatively easy to swallow.

**Disadvantages of Powders :**
1. Bitter powders cause discomfort.
2. Powders affected by atmospheric conditions, cannot be safely handled.
3. Time consuming.
4. Quantity less than 60 mg or so cannot be weighed conveniently on dispensing balance.

**Mixing of Powders :** In a small scale work, it is better to use hand mixing methods.

**Spatulation :** Small amounts of powders with the same range of particle size and densities, may be mixed with the help of spatula, the powders being placed on a tile.

**Trituration :** This is carried out in a mortar. In case of combination of a small amount of one drug with a large quantity of a diluent, it is better to triturate first with one volume of drug, with equal volume of the diluent and then adding twice as much diluent and continue the trituration. This procedure i.e. adding twice as much diluent as there is material in the mortar is continued until the total bulk of powder is in the mortar.

By the term trituration, it is meant the pestle be moved (with pressure) in circle, starting from the centre, reaching the periphery and returning to the pestle to the centre. This cycle is repeated several times or until the mixing is satisfactorily completed.

**Sifting :** Brushing of powders through sieves is known as sifting. Sifting is useful where free flowing light powders are desired as in case of snuffs.

**Fig. 4.1 : Sieves**

**Tumbling :** Tumbling is carried out in a wide mouth closed container. It is obvious that this procedure avoids pressure gradient.

**Fig. 4.2 : Powder Mixer**

Powders are required not to occupy more than half or less than half the capacity of the container. The container is rotated in such a manner that during the motion the powder particles float in the air. Tumbling is used for mixing powders with density differences.

On a large scale, powders are mixed in mixers, a typical of which is shown in Fig. 4.2.

## Special Problems

**(a) Hygroscopic Powders :** Powders which absorb moisture from the atmosphere are called hydroscopic powders. Some powders absorb moisture to such a great extent that they go into the solution. Such powders are called *Deliquescent powders*. Remedy lies in dispensing these powders in granular form in order to reduce the surface area of powders and to expose less area to the air. If powdering is necessary, it may be carried out in a dry mortar. Double wrapping of powders as described is to be carried out.

**(b) Efflorescent Powders :** Some substances lose their water of crystallization on exposure, particularly to dry atmospheric conditions. Such substances are said to be efflorescent. Such powders may lose water of crystallization during trituration causing the powder to become pasty. This difficulty can be overcome by using corresponding anhydrous salt or by drying the crystalline form to a constant weight. When such steps are being taken, the dose is required to be adjusted.

**(c) Eutectic Mixtures :** Many substances, when combined with other powders turn into liquid or give rise to a pasty mass. This is undesirable when powders are being dispensed. Such combinations i.e. which liquify are known as Eutectic Mixtures.

**Examples :** Acetanilide, antipyrine, menthol, camphor, chloral-hydrate, phenol, salol, thymol and acetyl salicylic acid.

When two or more of these are combined, liquification occurs. Liquification is avoided in the following ways :

1. If each substance is in sufficient quantity, dispense each separately advising the patient to use one sample powder to each as a dose.
2. Alternatively, use starch, talc or calcium phosphate as an absorbent powder equal in proportion of liquifiable substances. Each liquifiable substance is triturated with equal quantity of absorbent powder. The second liquifiable substance is separately triturated with the absorbent powder and then both the mixtures are lightly mixed.

**(d) Explosive Mixtures :** These are generally a mixture of oxidising and reducing substance. For example, a combination of potassium chlorate and tannic acid is an explosive mixture particularly so when pressure is applied. In trituration, there is a pressure gradient. In order to avoid explosion, the substances should be powdered separately and then combined by mixing lightly.

## Containers and Closures for Powders :

Powders may be wrapped or sent out in bulk. In wrapped powders, each dose is enclosed in a paper. For powders less than six powder packs, a suitable size of box is chosen. The wrapped powders may be placed flat if the number of powders is less and when the number is large, they may be stacked on edges.

Powders are supplied in plain white glass bottles or jars with close fitting lids. Deliquescent or powders containing volatile ingredients are wrapped in waxed paper which further can be enclosed in metal foils. Individually wrapped powders are enclosed in cartons or rigid slide boxes of paper of plastic material. Now-a-days, they are supplied in aluminium sachets.

**Wrapping of Powders :** Take a clean paper of a suitable length, generally 1/8 inch less than twice the inside length of box. The width of paper may be three times the inside width of the box.

Turn up one edge of paper to 1/7$^{th}$ of its width. Weigh out material for each powder and put it in the centre of the paper. The free end of the paper is then folded and placed under the previously folded edge. Fold this through the centre. Turn the ends under symmetrically so that the size is now less than inside length of the box. Pair off the powders and place a rubber band so that the paper does not unfold itself.

**Double Wrapping :** Double wrapping is carried out with the help of two sheets of papers. The inner sheet of paper is a waxed paper. Double wrapping is carried out exactly as the single paper wrapping. It is necessary for powders containing volatile or hygroscopic substances.

**List of Volatile and Hygroscopic Substances :**

Camphor, Chlorbutol, Menthol, Thymol and Volatile oils. Hygroscopic substances include citric acid, iron and ammonium citrate, potassium citrate, pepsin and sodium chloride.

**Bulk Powders :**

Generally, the quantity prescribed is more and is required to be taken in teaspoonfuls or tablespoonfuls and consequently they are sent out in wide mouth screw capped bottles.

A powder is considered to be simple if it has one ingredient. While a compound powder is a mixture of two or three or more ingredients.

**Labelling :** Label on the container must provide the direction for taking the powder, along with all other details, like name, quantity, batch number, date of manufacture and date of expiry and dose.

Number of powders to be dispensed should be stated by the prescribers.

**Storage of powders :** Powders should be stored in air-tight well closed containers in a cool place away from moisture.

**Exercise 1 :**

R$_x$

Acetyl salicylic acid          5 grains

Send 4 powders

**Label :** Take one every 4 hours.

**Type :** Simple powder.

Each powder contains 5 grains. Weigh out excess of the total quantity of acetyl salicylic acid and powder it. Weigh out 5 grains of the powder four times, wrap, label and dispense. Reject the excess.

Before a student begins to study and carry out exercises on compound powders, he should bear the following points in mind :

1. Weigh out material for one powder more than required.
2. If the total quantity arrived at, is a fraction not directly weighable, take sufficiently (nearest) extra number of powders which will give directly weighable quantities.
3. If the total quantity of each powder includes a fraction, calculate the quantity of lactose (diluent) necessary to make it directly weighable.
4. If the prescription contains a liquid, adjusting the mixed material by adding lactose so that each powder is directly weighable.
5. While mixing, mix the powdered ingredients in ascending order of their weight.

Supposing 1 mg of a substance is to be mixed with second substance (say about 12 mg), do it as follows :

1 mg + 1 mg of second substance.

2 mg of mixture + 4 mg of second substance

6 mg of mixture + 6 mg of second substance or the remaining

**Exercise 2 :**

$R_x$

| Aspirin | 0.25 g |
| Paracetamol | 0.25 g |

Let a powder be made.

**Type :** Compound powder

Send such nine.

**Label :** One to be taken when the pain is severe.

Nine powders are to be sent. Calculate for ten powders.

| Aspirin | 2.5 g |
| Paracetamol | 2.5 g |

Each powder must contain 0.5 g of the mixture.

**Method :**

Mix by trituration and dispense in a powder box or in an envelope.

### Exercise 3 :

R_x

| | |
|---|---|
| Tragacanth powder | 15 g |
| Acacia powder | 20 g |
| Starch powder | 20 g |
| Sucrose powder | 45 g |

**Type :** A compound powder.

**Use :** Suspending agent, for use in pharmacy.

### Method :

Finely powder the substances and mix them in a laboratory mixer.

### Exercise 4 :

R_x

| | |
|---|---|
| Mercurous chloride | gr 1/5 |
| Sodium bicarbonate | gr iii |
| Powdered rhubarb | gr ss |

Let the powder be made. Send twelve powders.

**Label :** Take one, three times a day between meals.

**Type :** Compound powder.

Taking one extra powder will give 13/5 grains of mercurous chloride. This is not a directly weighable quantity, hence calculate for 15 powders.

| | |
|---|---|
| Mercurous chloride | 3 gr |
| Sodium bicarbonate | 45 gr |
| Powdered rhubarb | 7.5 gr |
| | 55.5 gr of mixture |

55.5 gr is again a quantity which is not weighable. Therefore, use lactose as diluent, 4.5 grains of lactose may be added. The total would then be 60 grains of mixture and each powder will amount to 60/15 = 4 grains.

### Method :

Mix mercurous chloride with lactose, and rhubarb powder and then sodium bicarbonate. Wrap 15 powders.

### Powder containing small doses :

At times potent medicaments are prescribed in fractions or in too small a bulk. In such cases, the following rules are applicable.

For imperial quantities : Make the weight of the ingredient upto 2 grains for each powder by addition of lactose (diluent).

For metric quantities make the weight for each powder upto 100 mg with lactose. Exercises 5 and 6 illustrate the point.

**Exercise 5 :**

R<sub>x</sub>

    Codeine phosphate     gr 1/6

    Send five powders

**Label :** Take one before going to bed.

Calculate for six powders.

Take Codeine phosphate 1/6 × 6 = 1 grain.

Each powder must weigh two grains. Hence, quantity of lactose would be 6 × 2 = 12 grains. We already have 1 grain of Codeine phosphate. Weigh 11 grains of lactose.

**Method :**

Triturate Codeine phosphate with 11 grains of lactose, mixing being carried out in ascending orders of weight. Dispense five powders.

**Exercise 6 :**

R<sub>x</sub>

    Diazepam              5 mg

    Send nine powders

**Label :** Take one at bed time.

**Type :** Powder containing a small dose.

Calculate for ten powders.

Diazepam 5 × 10 = 50 mg

But each powder must weigh 100 mg.

Therefore, quantity of lactose to be taken is (100 × 10) – 50 = 950 mg.

**Method :**

Weigh out 50 mg of diazepam and triturate with 950 mg of lactose. Weigh out powder (100 mg) and dispense nine.

**Exercise 7 :**

R<sub>x</sub>

    Hyoscine hydrobromide 1/150 grain.

    Send 12 powders.

**Label :** Take twice a day.

**Type :** Powder containing small dose.

Calculate for 15 powders.

Hyoscine hydrobromide 15 × 1/150 = 1/10 gr.

Take one grain of Hyoscine hydrobromide and triturate with nine grains of lactose. One grain of the mixture will contain 1/10 grains of Hyoscine hydrobromide.

**Method :**

1 grain of mixture + 29 grains of lactose (repeated) be triturated and twelve powders dispensed.

**Exercise 8 :**

R$_x$

| | |
|---|---|
| Diazepam | 1/9 grain |
| Aspirin | 3 gr |
| Paracetamol | 3 gr |

Send ten.

**Label :** Use one at bed time

**Type :** Compound powder containing a small dose.

Calculate for 11 powders :

Diazepam 11 × 1/9 – 11/9 = 11/9 gr

Aspirin 33 gr

Paracetamol 33 gr

Diazepam is not directly weighable.

Take 2 grains and triturate with 16 grains of lactose.

Total 18 grains of mixture. One grain of this mixture will contain 1/9$^{th}$ grain of diazepam and 11 grains will contain 1/9 × 11 = 11/9 grains.

**Method :**

Take 11 grains of the mixture and triturate with 33 grains each of Aspirin and Paracetamol respectively.

Total bulk would be 33 + 33 + 11 = 77 grains

Each powder will therefore weigh $\frac{77}{11}$ = 7 grains

Wrap and dispense the powders.

**Exercise 9 :**

℞

| Sodium bicarbonate | gr X |
|---|---|
| Powdered rhubarb | gr iii |
| Oil of peppermint | mss |

Let a powder be made. Send nine.

**Label :** Take one dose after meals.

**Type :** Powder containing a liquid volume.

Calculate for ten powders.

| Sodium bicarbonate | 100 gr |
|---|---|
| Powdered rhubarb | 30 gr |
| Oil of peppermint | 5 minim |
| Lactose | q. s. 140 gr |

**Method :**

Mix the dry ingredients. Then add oil of peppermint. Each powder will weigh between 13 and 14 grains. Weigh the mixture. Then add lactose to weigh 140 grains. Each powder will now be 14 grains. Double wrap the powders as the oil of peppermint is volatile. The inner wrapper must be waxed paper. Wrap and dispense nine powders.

## EFFERVESCENT POWDERS

As the name indicates, a powder of this type effervescences on coming in contact with moisture.

Obviously, it will be a mixture of acid and substance like sodium bicarbonate. Generally, medicaments may also be incorporated. Effervescent granules effectively mask the taste of a nauseous drug.

The commonly used acids for preparation of effervescent granules are citric and tartaric acids together with sodium bicarbonate. The acids are slightly more in quantity than is necessary to neutralise the bicarbonate. This imparts a pleasant sour taste.

If a medicament is being incorporated it is best to heat it at 100°C in order to let it lose its water of crystallization because the effervescent granules are required to be treated at 100°C.

**Laboratory method of Preparation :**

Preheat a porcelain dish over a boiling water bath. Finely powder the acids and bicarbonate of soda in ascending order of weight.

Place the mixture in the preheated porcelain dish. The citric acid loses the molecules of water of crystallization and this is sufficient to make a mixture of powders, moist and coherent. This operation takes about five minutes. As soon as the powder mixture falls into the hand, pass it through a No. 8 sieve superimposed by No. 20 sieve. The finer granules will fall through number 20 sieve. Collect these granules and place them in a warm place for drying.

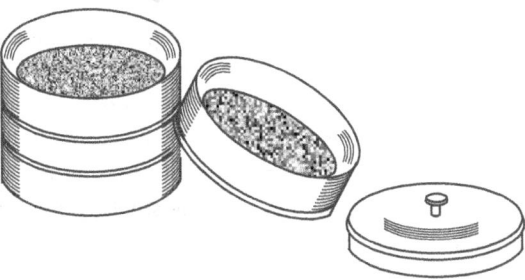

**Fig. 4.3 : Sieves**

Pack the granules in a wide mouth bottle for easy removal and dispense.

**Note :** If there is no effervescence when it comes in contact with water, the preparation is considered to be useless.

**Exercise 10 :**

$R_x$

| | |
|---|---|
| Sodium bicarbonate | 20.4 g |
| Sugar | 60.0 g |
| Tartaric acid | 10.80 g |
| Citric acid | 07.2 g |
| Iron and ammonium citrate | 2.15 g |

Follow the above procedure.

**Exercise 11 :**

$R_x$

| | |
|---|---|
| Menthol | 12 grains |
| Camphor | 12 grains |
| Ammonium chloride | 72 grains |
| Light magnesium carbonate | 144 grains |

Let a insufflation be made.

**Label :** For the nose.

**Type :** Powders containing liquifiable substances.

**Method :**

Separately powder each ingredient and weigh out the required quantities of each. Lightly mix menthol with ammonium chloride and camphor with magnesium carbonate and then mix both. Pass the mixture so obtained through No. 80 sieve and then dispense the sieved mixture of powders.

## POWDERS FOR EXTERNAL USE

There are three types :

**1. Dusting Powders :** The characteristics of these powders are that the powders are in the state of very fine particles capable of passing through and required to pass through a No. 80 sieve. They are mixture of such substances as zinc oxide, starch, boric acid, kaolin and talc. The last two are obtained from mineral sources and generally expected to contain the pathogenetic organism viz. *Clostridium tetani*. Hence, when kaolin or talc, being natural mineral ingredients included in a formula, they must be sterilised by dry heat (160°C) for one hour (from the time that the powder attains 150°C temperature) before use. The dusting powders are not meant to be applied to open wounds.

Unless otherwise directed, 50 g of powder be dispensed for external use.

**2. Insufflations :** These powders are intended for body cavities or areas where direct access to affected part is not possible. They are sent out in wide mouth bottles from which the required quantity is removed and transferred to an insufflator (a device to blow the powder) for use.

**3. Snuffs :** These are sent out in hinged boxes similar to a pill box and meant to be inhaled through nose for local action.

### Exercise 12 :

$R_x$

| Zinc oxide | 20 g |
|---|---|
| Salicylic acid | 0.2 g |
| Starch | 78 g |

Let a powder be made.

**Label :** The dusting powder.

**Method :** Each of the ingredients is finely powdered in a little excess and mixed in ascending order of weight. The mixture is passed through a No. 80 sieve and then dispensed in bottles with a perforated cap.

### Exercise 13 :

$R_x$

| Magnesium oxide | 2.5 g |
|---|---|
| Starch | 5.0 g |
| Purified talc sterilised | 50.0 g |

**Label :** The dusting powder.

## QUESTIONS

1. What are powders ? How powders are prepared ?
2. What are the advantages of powders over other dosage forms of medicaments ? How powders are dispensed ?
3. Describe the various types of powders for internal and external use.
4. What are effervescent powders and how are they prepared ?

# 5
CHAPTER

# MIXTURES AND CONCENTRATES

## INTRODUCTION

A **mixture** is a solution or suspension of soluble, partially soluble or insoluble solids or liquids in a vehicle (solvent) for internal use of which one or several doses are contained in a bottle, where only one dose is prescribed, it is then called a **draught.**

Mixtures are not formulated to keep for long periods and hence should be freshly prepared. They should be used within a month. When the dose of a mixture is less than 5 ml, it should be diluted with vehicle used during preparation to 5 ml or multiple thereof, the diluted product is less stable and should be consumed within 15 days.

**Advantages of Mixtures :**

1. Previous disintegration as in the case of solid dosage forms (e.g. tablets, moulded tablets, pills, cachets) is not required and hence they are more quickly effective.
2. Certain substances can be given in liquid form because they are available in liquid form and giving such liquids in relatively large doses in any other form is not possible e.g. castor oil and liquid paraffin.
3. Some substances are required to be administered in diffuse form so as to adsorb toxic substances in the alimentary canal e.g. light kaolin.
4. It is difficult for small children to swallow capsules or tablets. Mixtures are easy to swallow.
5. Potassium iodide and bromide cause pain if administered in the dry form.
6. Mixtures are economic as compared to other dosage forms.

**Disadvantages of Mixtures :**

1. Some substances are likely to undergo hydrolysis giving rise to toxic substances. For example, acetyl salicylic acid when in contact with water undergoes hydrolysis giving rise to salicylic acid, which is toxic.
2. If proper care is not taken during handling of mixtures, they may be contaminated with bacteria thereby spoiling the mixture, in such a case there is always a danger of infection.

**Containers for Mixtures :**

Plain glass bottles with uniform internal diameters may be used. The capacities should be predetermined depending upon whether the mixture (assuming that there are six doses per 24 hours) is for one day or two days or three days.

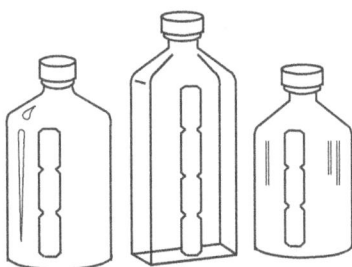

**Fig. 5.1 : Containers for Mixtures**

In other words, the mixture bottles or containers for mixture should be of three different capacities. It is suggested that not more than three days doses be dispensed at one time. The bottle should be fitted with a suitable size of cork which will ensure easy removal and non-spilling of mixture.

Unless otherwise mentioned, 90 ml or 6 doses should be dispensed.

**Label on Mixture :** The following information should be given on the label :

**Label for a Simple Mixture**

| | | |
|---|---|---|
| **THE MIXTURE** | | |
| Quantity | : | 60 ml. |
| Prescription No. | : | 106 |
| For | : | Mr. AVP |
| Direction | : | Take 15 ml after every four hours |
| Date of Dispensing | : | 21 - 7 - 98 |
| Dispensed by | : | Name of the pharmacist. |

| |
|---|
| J and J Hospitals, Chennai |

In case of certain mixtures, the label should include the words. Shake well before use'

**Label for a Mixture containing insoluble substances :**

| | | |
|---|---|---|
| **THE MIXTURE** | | |
| Quantity | : | 60 ml |
| Prescription No. | : | 123 |
| For | : | SBC |
| Direction | : | Take as directed |
| Date of Dispensing | : | 20 - 7 - 98 |
| Dispensed by | : | PVK |
| **SHAKE WELL BEFORE USE** | | |

| |
|---|
| Navbharat Dispensary, Chennai |

Directions for storage should be mentioned on label. Directions for dilutions if any should also be indicated on the label.

If no dose is mentioned, one tablespoonful three times a day, with water should be mentioned on the label.

**Concentrates :** When the mixtures are made stronger they are known as concentrates. Concentrated aromatic waters and concentrated infusions are the suitable examples.

## VEHICLES FOR MIXTURES

**Water :**

Tap water should never be used as a vehicle for mixtures. Trace metallic salts and dissolved gases in tap water give rise to incompatibilities, particularly with sensitive drugs. Distilled water is to be used. Sterility of purified water is to be maintained. Any evidence of contamination calls for rejection of the lot and fresh supply to be used. For this purpose, it is better to purchase a distilled water still. It is better to have as much purified water as is necessary for day's work. Purified water is by far the most cheap and inert vehicle for mixtures.

**Concentrated Aromatic Waters :**

The strength of concentrated aromatic water is 40 times the strength of ordinary aromatic water. One volume diluted with 39 volumes of purified water will produce the ordinary strength. Most of the aromatic waters are carminative in nature and generally improve palatability and impart flavour to the mixtures containing nauseating drugs. Examples of aromatic waters are peppermint water, cinnamon water, etc.

**Concentrated Infusions :**

One volume added to seven volumes of purified water produces the ordinary strength of infusion. The carminative properties as well as the property of being bitter are associated with infusion. They are not frequently used.

**Syrup Vehicles :**

Solution of sugar in water is known as syrup. Naturally, these are sweetening agents. The syrups are good vehicles for salines. A simple syrup is one which has the solution of sugar in purified water. Raspberry and cherry syrups impart their characteristic flavour since they are prepared from the juice of fresh ripe fruits.

**Diabetic Syrup :**

A diabetic patient requires non-glycogenetic vehicle. Only one formula for this type of syrup has been given below :

| | |
|---|---|
| Orange oil | 0.05 |
| Tween 20 | 3.00 |
| Citric acid | 0.35 |
| Carboxy methyl cellulose solution | ad 50.00 |

(The C.M.C. solution contains 1% sodium carboxy methyl callulose and 1% sodium cyclamate, non-carbohydrate sweetening agent).

## ALCOHOLIC VEHICLES

**Elixers :**

Elixers are sweetened and flavoured solutions in alcohols. At times, a hydro-alcoholic vehicle is needed to dissolve drugs.

**Tinctures and Spirits :**

They are not frequently used as they are rather potent preparations and have a high alcoholic content.

**Stabilizers :**

These are the substances, which make the solution, suspension, mixture or state stable and are known as stabilizers.

Even the substances which retard the rate of reaction or preserve a chemical euqilibrium or act as antioxidants keeping pigments and other components in emulsion and prevent the particles in a colloidal suspension from precipitating are also stabilizers.

Thus, sodium citrate an anti-peptizing agent, sodium meta bisulphite as antioxidant and gums as emulsifying or suspending agents are the good examples of stabilizers in Pharmacy.

**Colourants :**

Substances which impart colours to the solutions or mixtures are colourants or colouring agents. They are added for any of the following purposes :

(1) For identifying similar looking products,

(2) To mask the undesired colour.

(3) To improve the aesthetic value or marketing value.

Since, availability of natural and safe colours is limited many synthetic colours are used in the pharmaceutical industry. But these colours must be safe and approved by Food and Drug Administration. They are water soluble or slightly soluble in water or alcohol. Most of them are anthraquinone, azodyes or coal-tar compounds. They are used in very small concentration. Some of the natural safe colours are curcuma (turmeric) carmine, litmus, saffron, indigo, chlorophyll and walnut oil. Animal dye like cochineal may also be used safely.

**Flavours :**

Flavours are added to mixture to mask undesired smell of the substances. Normally, the flavours are volatile oils or synthetic compounds like vanilline.

These are used in very small concentrations upto 1.0% either alone or by dissolving in alcohol as found suitable. Examples : Lemon oil, orange oil, cardamom, peppermint etc.

## OTHER FORMS OF MIXTURES

**Drops :**

Drops are considered to be a form of mixtures. They are generally dispensed without dilution with water as this may lead to decomposition. If at all they are prescribed with other liquids, it is generally alcoholic liquid such as Compound cardamom tincture.

Since, this type of mixture is given in drops, it is necessary to bear in mind that viscid liquids produce large drops and lighter liquids produce small drops. In order to arrive at a correct solution, it is advisable to use a standard dropper with an external diameter of 3 mm.

Drops are sent out in plain bottles or vials accompanied by a standard dropper.

**Linctuses :**

These are viscid solutions of medicines meant to be licked. They have local action on the throat. A viscid vehicle is used to ensure prolonged action. They are generally simple solutions.

Mixtures can be classified as follows :

Class I – Simple mixtures containing soluble substances only, e.g.

   (a) Carminative mixture

   (b) Iron and ammonium citrate mixture.

Class II – Mixtures containing diffusible solids; e.g. Alba mixture.

Class III – Mixtures containing indiffusible solids

     e.g. Antidiarrhoeal mixture with prepared chalk.

Class IV – Mixtures containing precipitate-forming liquids;

     e.g. Ammoniated solution of quinine.

Class V – Mixtures containing slightly-soluble liquids; e.g. creosote.

Class VI – Miscellaneous mixtures; e.g.

     (a) Castor oil or liquid paraffin emulsion

     (b) Effervescent mixture.

**Notes on Mixtures Containing Indiffusible Solids or Liquids :**

At times, it is necessary to prepare mixtures containing insoluble and indiffusible substances. A solid is regarded as indiffusible when it will not remain uniformly distributed through the body of the liquid in which, it is distributed. In pharmacy, when a mixture of this type is dispensed without making an effort to remedy this situation, it leads to inaccuracy in dosage. It has now been accepted that addition of Compound Powder of Tragacanth (suspending agent), serves to keep the particles, uniformly suspended after shaking the mixture and then administering the stated dose.

The Compound Powder of Tragacanth (C.P.T.) is a mixture of the following :

(i) Acacia, (ii) Starch, (iii) Sucrose, (iv) Tragacanth.

The C.P.T. is used in the following proportion :

In imperial system, 10 grains per ounce of mixture.

In metric system, 2 g per 100 ml of mixture.

Mucilage of tragacanth is also used as a suspending agent. The proportion to be used is **one quarter of the volume of mixture.**

*Theory of protective effect of Gums* (used as suspending agents) *on colloidal precipitates.*

Colloids represent a system in which a substance of certain particle size is distributed throughout a liquid medium. Colloidal particles range in size from 1 millimicron to 0.1 micron. Suspending particles may fall within the colloidal range. However, in the mixtures containing indiffusible substances range, the particle size is above 10 microns. Suspending agents function in the colloidal range i.e. in colloidal state the particles remain in suspension. At times, these colloidal solutions assist in holding the particles of other solution in suspension. Gums such as acacia and tragacanth as also the Compound Powder of Tragacanth have protected properties when in solution. These solutions when added to other solutions impart a similar charge and also increase the viscosity of the whole solution and keep the particles in suspension and in addition prevent flocculation if any electrolyte is added to the solution. This can be verified by undertaking the following experiment :

***Expt :***

5 ml of tincture of myrrh

+

10 ml of mucilage of acacia        No precipitation.

+

10 % solution of sodium chloride

Repeat the above experiment without addition of mucilage of acacia. A precipitate of agglomerated resin contained in the tincture of myrrh will be formed. Under such circumstances, it is said that mucilage of acacia has a protective effect by virtue of its property of forming a film around the colloidal particles of Tincture of myrrh affording protection against the electrolyte viz. sodium chloride solution in the above experiment.

Practical exercises on mixtures containing soluble solids and liquids are labelled as "Simple Mixtures".

While preparing a mixture, the instructions given below should be followed.

(i) The volume of vehicle (solvent) taken at the beginning should be half or three fourth of the total volume depending upon the presence of other medicinal liquids i.e. subtract the quantity of liquid medicaments. The final volume should not exceed the stated volume in the prescription.

(ii) Solids occurring in the prescription should be crushed into powder. This helps the solute going into the solution quickly.

(iii) Add the liquid medicaments after the solids are dissolved.

(iv) Transfer to a measure and make up the final volume by addition of more of vehicle.

Before the actual exercises begin, let it be understood, that should a prescription occur in Latin, it must be translated into English, before it is dispensed. A "student pharmacist" should write down the original Latin prescription on the left side of the *Practical Note book* and the translation should appear on the right hand page. The following Exercise (1) will make it clear.

**Exercise 1 :**  Translation

$R_x$   Take

Potassii bromidi ℨiij   Potassium bromide ....... three-drachms

Tincture nucis vomicae ℨii   Tincture of nux-vomica two-drachms

Aquam chloroformi ad ℨ vi   Chloroform water.....quantity

sufficient to produce six ounces

Flat mistura.   Let a mixture be made.

Signa cochleare magnum   Label One tablespoonful to be

ter in die post cibos sumendum   take three times after meals.

**Type :** Simple Mixture

**Method :**

(1) Dissolve Potassium bromide in chloroform water (1/2 to 3/4$^{th}$ of the total volume of vehicle) previously measured and placed in a beaker. Stir with a glass rod. At this stage, see if there are foreign particles present in the solutions, one or two particles may be removed by means of a glass rod, or if there are many particles of foreign matter, take a funnel and plug it with cotton wool, and pour the solution through it. Pour a little of vehicle over the plug to displace the solution trapped in the cotton plug.

(2) Now, measure the tincture in a dry measure and pour it into the solution. Rinse the measure with a little of vehicle and add this to the solution. Transfer the whole of mixture into a measure and make up the volume to six ounces.

(3) Transfer the mixture to a previously cleaned bottle.

(4) Label the mixture and dispense.

**Note :** When actually performing the exercise, see that the method appears in the past tense.

**Exercise 2 :**

Rx

| Glucose | 100 g |
|---|---|
| Lemon flavour | q. s. |
| Distilled water | ad 300 ml |

**Label :** Take at once.
**Note :** Solution for Glucose tolerance test. Solution must be freshly prepared.
**Type :** Simple Mixture.

**Exercise 3 :**

Rx

| Potassium iodide | 0.3 g |
|---|---|
| Ammonium carbonate | 0.15 g |
| Distilled water | to 30 ml |
| Send | 60 ml |

**Label :** Simple Mixture

Follow the method given in Exercise 1.

**Exercise 4 :**

Rx

| Sodium bicarbonate | 04 g |
|---|---|
| Tincture nuxvomica | 02 ml |
| Compound infusion of gentian, | ad 120 ml |

**Label :** Take one table spoonful twice a day, before meals. Follow the method for simple mixture.

Compound Infusion of gentian, if available in concentrated form, is eight times stronger than ordinary strength. Hence, dilute 1 volume with 7 volumes of distilled water.

**Exercise 5 :**

Rx

| Tincture of opium | 1.3 ml |
|---|---|
| Chloroform water | ad 05 ml |
| Send 100 ml | |

**Label :** Take 5 ml thrice daily.
**Type :** Simple Mixture.

## Exercise 6

R<sub>x</sub>

| | |
|---|---|
| Magnesium sulphate | 31 g |
| Magnesium carbonate | 4 g |
| Peppermint water | ad 180 ml |

**Label :** Take two table spoonful, half an hour before breakfast.

**Type :** Mixture containing diffusible solid. **"Shake well before use"** label is necessary.

**Method :**

Magnesium sulphate and magnesium carbonate were powdered in the mortar. Three fourth of the vehicle was slowly added with trituration until a smooth cream was formed. The cream was transferred to measure. The mortar was rinsed with a little of the vehicle and this was added to the measure. The volume was made up by addition of more of vehicle and the mixture was dispensed after proper labelling.

**Note :**

Whenever a mixture containing diffusible or indiffusible solid is present and there is presence of foreign particles, these must be removed by passing the mixture (before addition of liquid medicinal substance) through a muslin cloth and **not cotton plug.**

Magnesium carbonate is a diffusible solid in the above prescription.

## Exercise 7 :

R<sub>x</sub>

| | |
|---|---|
| Bismuth carbonate | 1.0 g |
| Sodium bicarbonate | 0.7 g |
| Tincture of belladonna | 0.4 ml |
| Water | ad 30 ml |

**Label :** Take 15 ml before each meal.

**Type :** Mixture containing diffusible solid.

Follow the method explained in Exercise 6. Add Tincture of belladonna after the foreign particles are removed. Bismuth carbonate is the diffusible solid. In all cases, where there is a diffusible or indiffusible solid present **"Shake well before use"**. Label must appear on the container.

## Exercise 8 :

R<sub>x</sub>

| | |
|---|---|
| Barium sulphate | 100 g |
| Vanillin | q.s. |
| Water | ad 200 ml |

**Label :** The Barium metal. **Shake well before use**. Take at once.

Follow the method as given in Exercise 7.

**Note :** Freshly prepared mixture is to be dispensed.

**Exercise 9 :**

R$_x$

| | |
|---|---|
| Boric acid | 1 g |
| Tincture hyoscyamus | 2 ml |
| Distilled water | ad 15 ml |

Send six doses.

Label : Take twice a day.

The boric acid is partly soluble. The insoluble part is diffusible. "**Shake well before use**" label is necessary. Follow the method as given in Exercise 8.

**Exercise 10 :**

R$_x$

| | |
|---|---|
| Quinine sulphate | 1.6 g |
| Potassium iodide | 08 g |
| Waters | ad 180 ml |

**Label :** Take 15 ml after every four hours.

Quinine sulphate is diffusible. **Shake well before use** label is necessary.

Follow the method used for mixtures containing diffusible solids.

**Exercise 11 :**

R$_x$

| | |
|---|---|
| Sulphadimidine | 12 g |
| Syrup of orange | 15 ml |
| Water | ad 160 ml |

Label : Take twenty ml after every four hours.

Type : Mixture containing indiffusible substances.

Note : Sulphadimidine is indiffusible substance.

"**Shake well before use**" *label* is necessary.

**Method :**

A clean dry mortar was taken. 12 g of sulphadimidine was added to it and was finely powdered. Then 2.6 g of Compound powder of tragacanth was added to it and the powders were properly mixed by trituration. Added the vehicle little by little. The trituration was continued until a smooth cream was formed. The cream was then transferred to a glass measure. The mortar was rinsed with a little of vehicle and this was added to the measure.

The syrup of orange was then added to the mixture and then the volume made upto 160 ml. The mixture was transferred to a clean bottle, labelled and dispensed.

**Method** for **indiffusible solids** using **Tragacanth mucilage.** The proportion of mucilage to be used is one quarter of the volume of mixture.

### Exercise 12 :

Rx

| | |
|---|---|
| Acetyl salicylic acid | 1.5 g |
| Oxyphenbutazone | 0.25 g |
| Simple syrup | 15 ml |
| Water         ad | 80 ml |

**Label :** Take 20 ml after every four hours.

**Type :** Mixture containing indiffusible solids.

**Note :** Both the solids require suspending agents, 'Shake well before use' label is necessary.

**Method :**

Both the solid ingredients were reduced to a fine powder separately then intimately mixed. The mixture was then triturated with twenty ml of mucilage of tragacanth until a smooth cream was formed. Then the cream was diluted with about half the volume of vehicle. Then the syrup was added in the centre of the mixture in all the stream and the trituration was continued. The mixture was transferred to a measure. The mortar was rinsed with a little portion of remaining vehicle and the rinsing added to the mixture. The volume was then made up with addition of more of vehicle and then mixture was dispensed in the usual manner.

### Exercise 13 :

Rx

| | |
|---|---|
| Prepared chalk | 02 g |
| Tincture catechu | 01 ml |
| Cinnamon water    ad | 180 ml |

Label :  Take 30 ml after every two hours.

Type :   Mixture containing indiffusible substance.

**Method :** Follow the method used in Exercise 12.

### Exercise 14 :

Rx

| | |
|---|---|
| Potassium iodide | 02 g |
| Ethereal tincture of lobelia B.P.C. | 08 ml |
| Water | 180 ml |
| Send | 60 ml |

**Label :** Take 15 ml four times a day.

**Type :** Mixture containing precipitate forming liquid.

**Note :** Ethereal tincture of lobelia is precipitate forming liquid.

**Method :**

Took about 45 ml of mucilage of tragacanth and was mixed with equal volume of water. The precipitate forming liquid was measured in a dry measure and poured slowly into the centre of the mucilage with constant stirring. Separately took 45 ml of water and potassium iodide dissolved in it. This was then added to the first portion. The volume was made up with addition of more water and the mixture dispensed. "*Shake well before use*" label is necessary.

**Exercise 15 :**

R$_x$

| | |
|---|---|
| Oxyphenbutazone | 1 g |
| Syrup of orange | 15 ml |
| Water ad | 120 ml |

**Label :** Take one tablespoonful when the pain is severe.

**Type :** Mixture containing indiffusible substance.

Follow the method using 'Mucilage of tragacanth'.

**Exercise 16 :**

R$_x$

| | |
|---|---|
| Phenobarbitone | 60 mg |
| Water | ad 30 ml |

Let a draught be made.

Lable : Take at bed time.

Type : Mixture containing indiffusible substance.

Note : This is a single dose mixture "*Take at once*", label is necessary.

Follow the method used in Exercise No. 11 using Compound powder of tragacanth.

**Exercise 17 :**

R$_x$

| | |
|---|---|
| Paraldehyde | 4 ml |
| Syrup | 8 ml |
| Liquid extract of glycyrrhiza | 2 ml |
| Water | ad 30 ml |

Let a draught be made.

**Lable :** Take as directed.

**Type :** Mixture containing slightly soluble liquid.

The paraldehyde was placed in a bottle together with about 3 ml of water and the mixture was shaken vigorously. The liquid extract was added to it. The mixture was then transferred to a measure and the volume was made up and the mixture rebottled, labelled and dispensed.

**Special Mixtures :**

**Exercise 18 :**

Rx

| Potassium bromide | 1 grain |
| Arsenical solution | 3 minims |
| Water | to one ounce |

**Note :** In this prescription, the main drug is potassium bromide. In some patients, this produces a rash and the arsenical solution is included to prevent this. However, the use of solution affords the required quantity, which would present a problem if the given quantity is in fraction of unit.

**Type :** Mixture containing fraction of a potent medicament.

Follow method for Simple Mixture.

**Exercise 19 :**

Rx

| | Take |
|---|---|
| Strychnine hydrochloridi gr. 1/150 | Strychnine hydrochloride gr. 1/150 |
| Aqua chloroform ad ℥ ii | Chloroform water…ad.. ℥ ii |
| Flat mistura | Let a mixture be made |
| Signa : Ter in die sumenda | Label : Take three times a day |
| Mitte ℥ iii | Send three ounces. |

Type : Mixture containing potent medicament occurring in a fractional non-weighable quantity.

**Calculation :**

Each dose of Strychnine hydrochloride is 1/150 grain given in 2 drachms of mixture. The total volume is three ounces which is equal to $3 \times 8 = 24$ drachms or 12 doses.

$1/150 \times 12$ doses = 2/25 grain of Strychnine hydrochloride total quantity, which is not weighable.

Solution lies in accurately weighing one grain of Strychnine hydrochloride and dissolving it in 250 minims of solvent. 20 minims of this solution will contain the required quantity of Strychnine hydrochloride.

Take 20 minims of the solution and make up the volume to three ounces and dispense it. It is a simple mixture.

**Paediatric Mixture :**

The age and dose must be written on the label.

**Exercise 20 :**

R̥

| | |
|---|---|
| Sulphadimidine, in a fine powder | 500 mg |
| Compound tragacanth powder | 200 mg |
| Raspberry syrup | 0.1 ml |
| Benzoic acid solution | 0.1 ml |
| Amaranth solution | 0.05 ml |
| Chloroform water | ad   5 ml |

**Age :** 6 months.

**Label :** 2.5 ml every six hours. 100 ml to be dispensed unless otherwise directed.

Follow the method for mixture containing indiffusible substance Sulphadimidine, Exercise 11.

### QUESTIONS

1. What are mixtures. How do they differ from draughts ? How mixtures are classified, explain with suitable examples ?
2. What are diffusible and indiffusible mixtures ? How indiffusible mixtures are stabilized ?
3. Comment on the various vehicles used for the preparation of mixtures.
4. What do you know about colours, flavours, suspending agents, and stabilizers ?

# CHAPTER 6

# ELIXIRS AND SYRUPS

## (1) ELIXIRS

Elixirs are usually clear sweet, aromatic preparation, sometimes containing considerable proportion of alcohol and consequently requiring dilution at the time of use. Some elixirs are employed as a flavouring agent. They differ from syrups in containing much less or sometimes no sugar. The preparation may be sweet due to the use of soluble saccharin or glycerine. They are excellent solvents for many drugs and mask the disagreeable odour and taste of many drugs dissolved in them.

**Containers for Elixirs :**

Elixirs are supplied in well filled, well closed, airtight glass containers.

100 ml of elixir to be dispensed unless otherwise instructed.

**Storage of Elixirs :** Elixirs are stored in a cool place, protected from light. Diluted elixirs are used within a week of preparation.

**Labelling :** Label on container must give directions for storage; duration for which potency is retained. Elixirs supplied in the form of powder or granules to which specified amount of water is to be added to prepare elixirs should be mentioned. Diluted elixirs are unstable, their shelf-life is short and detailed information should be given on the label itself.

**Example 1 :**

$R_x$

| Orange tincture | 75 ml |
|---|---|
| Syrup | 400 ml |
| Chloroform water | to 1000 ml |

**Method of Preparation :**

Mix all the ingredients with shaking to form sparkling clear liquid.

**Example 2 :**

$R_x$

| Terpine hydrate | 50 g |
|---|---|
| Orange oil | 0.2 ml |
| Glycerine | 400 ml |
| Alcohol | 425 ml |
| Syrup | 100 ml |
| Purified water | to 1000 ml |

**Label :** Take as directed by the Physician.

**Method of Preparation :**

Dissolve terpine hydrate in alcohol and add successively the orange oil, glycerine, syrup and sufficient purified water to make the product 1000 ml. Mix and filter if necessary.

**Example 3 :**

℞

| | |
|---|---|
| Piperazine citrate | 180 g |
| Chloroform spirit | 0.5 ml |
| Glycerine | 100 ml |
| Orange oil | 0.25 ml |
| Syrup | 500 ml |
| Purified water | to 1000 ml |

**Label :** Take as directed by the physician.

**Method of Preparation :**

Dissolve piperazine citrate in part of water. Then mix with agitation orange oil, glycerine, syrup in chloroform spirit and pour in watery solution of piperazine citrate. Adjust the volume with sufficient purified water.

## (2) SYRUPS

They are concentrated solutions (66.7% W/W) of sucrose or other sugars in water. Such syrups are called simple syrups. When they contain some added medicinal substance, they are called medicated syrups; e.g. chloral hydrate, piperazine citrate, etc. When they contain any flavouring substance, they are called flavoured syrups; e.g. Cherry, orange, etc.

Glycerine, sorbitol and propylene glycol in small quantities are added to syrup to prevent the crystallization of sucrose or even to increase the solubility of medicinal ingredients. Normally, the growth of micro-organisms does not take place in syrups due to higher concentration of sucrose, but the diluted syrups are highly susceptible for growth of yeasts, moulds and other microbes. Therefore in diluted syrups, sodium benzoate, methyl or propyl parabenes are used as preservatives.

**Containers for Syrups :** In well-filled, well-closed, sterile containers.

50 ml of syrup should be dispensed unless otherwise directed.

**Storage :** Freshly prepared syrups should be used, unless special precautions are taken to prevent their contamination.

**Syrups are used as under :**

(i) They act as demulcents in cough. They act by coating the mucous membrane and thus decrease pharyngeal irritation.

(ii) They increase the viscosity of the solution; thereby help in suspension of insoluble substances.

(iii) They act as preservatives, because sugar in strong solution preserves many vegetable substances from decomposition.

**Exercise 1 :**

R$_x$

| Lemon spirit | 0.5 ml |
|---|---|
| Citric acid | 25 g |
| Invert syrup | 10 ml |
| Syrup | ad 100 ml |

Send 50 ml.

Dissolve citric acid in a portion of syrup, add Invert syrup, Lemon spirit. Then add sufficient syrup to produce the required quantity. Mix uniformly.

**Exercise 2 :**

R$_x$

| Strong ginger syrup | 5 ml |
|---|---|
| Syrup | to 100 ml |

Send 50 ml

Mix.

**Label :** Take 2.5 to 5 ml after meals.

**Exercise 3 :**

R$_x$

| Tolu solution | 10 ml |
|---|---|
| Syrup | to 100 ml |

Send 50 ml

Mix.

**Label :** Take as directed by the physician.

## Exercise 4:

Rx

| | | |
|---|---|---|
| Codeine phosphate | | 0.5 g |
| Purified water | | 1.5 ml |
| Chloroform spirit | | 2.5 ml |
| Syrup | to | 100 ml |

Send 50 ml

**Label :** Take as directed by the physician.

**Method of Preparation :**

Dissolve Codeine phosphate in purified water. Then add 75 ml of syrup, mix well. Chloroform spirit should be added to it and then syrup to produce the required volume.

### QUESTIONS

1. What are elixirs ? How are they prepared ? What are they used for ?
2. Define syrup. Describe the various methods of preparation of syrups.
3. Write a note on the uses, storage and preservation of syrups.

# CHAPTER 7

# MOUTH WASHES, GARGLES AND THROAT PAINTS

## (1) MOUTH WASHES

Mouth washes are simple aqueous solutions intended to wash oral cavity and impart a deodorising analgesic, astringent or antiseptic action. The vehicle may be water or a combination of water and alcohol.

**Containers :** These are dispensed in white fluted bottles.

**Labelling :** Proper directions for diluting the mouth wash before use should be clearly indicated on the label.

**Exercise 1 :**

$R_x$

| | |
|---|---|
| Liquified phenol | 1.5 ml |
| Peppermint oil | 0.5 ml |
| Purified water | ad 100 ml |

The mouth wash

**Method :**

Dissolve the phenol in water, add the peppermint oil and make up the volume.

**Label :** Dilute it with twice the warm water before use.

For external use only.

**Exercise 2 :**

$R_x$

| | |
|---|---|
| Potassium permanganate | 50 mg |
| Water | ad 100 ml |

The mouth wash.

**Label :** Warm and use the solution.

For external use only. Use freshly prepared.

**Method :**

Powder the potassium permanganate in a glass mortar. Add a little water. Transfer the solution to a measure. Repeatedly wash the mortar with water and add the washings to the measure. Finally, make up the volume by addition of more of the vehicle.

Use as directed by the physician. For external use only.

## (2) GARGLES

The aqueous solutions usually highly medicated and intended for administration only after dilution, in the treatment of an infection of throat.

**Containers :** White fluted bottles, to distinguish them from preparations for internal use. Coloured bottles are to be used if the gargle needs protection from light.

**Labelling :** Directions for proper dilution should be stated on the label. It should also include the words **"For external use only"**.

**Exercise 1 :**

R<sub>x</sub>

| | |
|---|---|
| Alum | 2.0 g |
| Purified water | ad 100 ml |

"The Alum gargle."

**Label :** Use as directed.

**Method**

Dissolve alum in purified water and dispense.

**Exercise 2 :**

R<sub>x</sub>

| | |
|---|---|
| Acetyl salicylic acid | 2.5 g |
| Amaranth solution | 1.0 g |
| Sodium citrate | 0.5 g |
| Water | ad 100 ml |

The gargle.

**Label :** Use as directed by the physician. It should be freshly prepared.

**Method :**

Dissolve the sodium citrate in about 50 ml of water and then add acetyl salicylic acid. Add the amaranth solution and then make up the volume.

### Exercise 3 :

Rx

| | |
|---|---|
| Phenol | 4.0 g |
| Glycerin of Tannic acid | 20 ml |
| Peppermint water | ad 100 ml |

**Label :** The gargle.

Dilute one tablespoonful with a pint of warm water and gargle, morning and night.

## (3) THROAT PAINTS

Throat paints are the liquid preparations for application to the mucous membrane of the buccal cavity.

Glycerine, liquid paraffin, propylene glycol or resinous substances like balsams are employed as bases.

Throat paints may be antiseptic, astringent or analgesic in action.

**Containers :**

Wide mouthed bottles are used where the paint is to be used with a brush or swab. If the paint contains a poison, vertically fluted bottle may be used in order to distinguish from ordinary medicines for internal use. A few of the glycerines are also used as throat paints.

Unless otherwise mentioned 25 ml of throat paint is to be prepared.

**Labelling :** Containers should be labelled **"For external use only."**

**Storage :** Throat paints should be stored in air-tight containers and in a cool place.

### Exercise 1 :

Rx

| | |
|---|---|
| Phenol | 1.5 g |
| Glycerine | ad 25 ml |

The throat paint.

**Label :** Use as directed, **"For external use only."**

**Method :**

Dissolve phenol by adding it to glycerine and gently warm until solution is obtained.

It should not be diluted with water.

### Exercise 2 :

R$_x$

| | |
|---|---|
| Iodine | 1.4 g |
| Potassium iodide | 5.0 g |
| Peppermint oil | 1.0 ml |
| Glycerine | 100 ml |

The throat paint.

**Label :** Apply with a swab.

*Shake well before use.*

**"For external use only".**

### Method :

Powder the iodine and potassium iodide crystals. Dissolve the powders in about 25 ml of glycerine. Transfer to a measure. Add the peppermint oil. Rinse the mortar with a little glycerine. Add this to the mortar. Make up the volume. Filter if necessary and then dispense.

### QUESTIONS

1. Define gargles, throat paints and mouth washes. Describe the way of labelling them along with suitable containers.
2. Differentiate the following :
   (a) Mouth wash and throat paint
   (b) Gargles and mouth wash.

# 8

## CHAPTER

# EAR DROPS, NASAL DROPS, DOUCHES AND SPRAYS

### (1) EAR DROPS

Ear drops are meant to be instilled into the ear. They are usually solutions or suspensions of drugs in water, diluted alcohol, glycerine, propylene glycol or ethylene glycol. The non-aqueous vehicles are more favourable than aqueous vehicles, since aqueous vehicles promote and enhance ear infections. If water is used as a vehicle purified water boiled and cooled must be used.

**Containers :** Ear drops must be dispensed in coloured fluted glass bottles fitted with a plastic screw-cap along with a glass dropper tube fitted with a rubber teat or a suitable plastic cap and a dropper device.

Unless otherwise directed, 15 ml of ear drops should be dispensed.

**Fig. 8.1 : Containers for ear drops**

**Labelling :** Label should indicate the words **"For external use only"**.

Prescribed instructions be included on the label. In absence of any instructions, 3 to 4 drops to be put into affected ear, should be stated on the label.

**Exercise 1 :**

R<sub>x</sub>  Phenol           0.5 g
    Glycerine        ad  100 ml
    Prepare ear drops.

**Label :** Place 5 drops in the affected ear.

**Note :** An additional warning may be put on the label.

*"Dilute with glycerine only"* or *"Not to be diluted with water."*

**Method :**

Dissolve phenol in glycerine, if necessary warm to dissolve.

**Label :** For external use only.

## Exercise 2 :

℞

| Sodium bicarbonate | 7.0 g |
|---|---|
| Phenol | 0.5 g |
| Glycerine | 50 ml |
| Purified water | ad 100 ml |
| The Ear drops | |

**Label :** Use as directed. For external use only.

**Method :**

Take about 60 ml of purified water, boil it for half an hour and cool it. Dissolve sodium bicarbonate in about 40 ml of water. Separately dissolve phenol in glycerine. Mix the two solutions, transfer to a measure and make up the required volume.

## Exercise 3 :

℞

| Amethocaine | 1.5 g |
|---|---|
| Phenol | 2.0 g |
| Glycerine | ad 100 ml |
| The Ear drops. | |

**Label :** Use as directed by the physician. For external use only.

Mix.

## Exercise 4 :

℞

| Picric acid | 1 g |
|---|---|
| Boric acid | 2 g |
| Alcohol 95% | 30 ml |
| Purified water | ad 100 ml |
| The Ear drops. | |

**Label :** Use as directed. For external use only.

**Caution :** Handle picric acid carefully. It explodes if triturated or heated.

**Method:**

Boil and cool excess of purified water. Dissolve boric acid and picric acid in 30 ml of boiled purified water. Add 30 ml of 95% alcohol. Transfer to a measure and adjust to volume with purified water.

**Exercise 5 :**

R̥

| | |
|---|---|
| Salicylic acid | 1 g |
| Alcohol 90% | ad 100 ml |

The Ear drops.

**Label :** Use as directed by the physician. "For external use only."

Mix.

**Exercise 6 :**

R̥

| | |
|---|---|
| Chloramphenicol | 250 mg |
| Propylene glycol | ad 25 ml |

The Ear drops.

**Label :** Use as directed. "For external use only."

Mix.

## (2) NASAL DROPS

These are the aqueous or oily preparations to be instilled into the nostrils by means of a dropper.

Since, the oil retards the ciliary action of the nasal mucous, oily nasal drops are not to be utilized for long periods.

**Containers :** Similar to the ear drops, nasal drops should be dispensed in coloured fluted glass bottles, fitted with plastic screw cap along with glass dropper tube, fitted with rubber teat or a suitable plastic cap and a dropper device.

**Exercise 1 :**

R̥

| | |
|---|---|
| Penicillin (Sodium salt) | 2,500 units |
| Normal saline | ad 100 ml |

The Nasal drops.

**Label :** Use as directed.

Mix.

**Exercise 2 :**

℞

    Ephedrine hydrochloride    100 mg

    Normal saline    ad 10 ml

The Nasal drops.

**Label :** Use as directed.

Mix.

**Exercise 3 :**

℞

    Atropine sulphate    50 mg

    Normal saline    ad 10 ml

    The Nasal drops.

**Label :** Use as directed.

**Note :** These drops are meant to lessen mucous production.

**Method :** Mix.

## (3) DOUCHES

Medicated solutions prepared for rinsing body cavity are known as douches. However, they are mostly used to irrigate vagina.

Solutions used for the treatment of bladder, rectum and nasal cavity though called irrigations are also douches.

Douches used for bladder and vagina are always sterile solutions, while for nasal and rectum their sterilisation is not essential. Douches are used for various purposes, such as

(i) Antiseptics

(ii) Cleansing agents

(iii) Astringents.

Usually, the douches are supplied as concentrated solutions and are required to be diluted before administrations.

**Containers :** Douches are supplied in narrow-mouth coloured fluted bottles.

Large quantities are supplied in douch-can (of PVC) for hospital purposes and are administered by gravity flow.

**Labelling :**

1. Being a concentrated solution, the method of dilution should be indicated on the label.
2. The words "For external use " should be included.
3. Be stored in cool place.

**Exercise 1 :**

R̥

        Potassium permanganate      0.1 gm
        Water                                 ad 100 ml

**Label :** Vaginal douch

Send 500 ml of 0.025 % solution for use on a vaginal douch.

Use freshly prepared.

**Exercise 2 :**

R̥

        Ephedrine hydrochloride      0.5
        Chlorbutol                        0.5
        Sodium chloride            0.5
        Purified water               ad 100

**Label :** The Nasal douch.

## (4) SPRAYS

These are the alcoholic, hydro-alcoholic, or glycerol containing solutions of medicaments, to be applied to the nose or throat by means of atomiser.

Sprays are intended for the treatment of asthma and also for similar conditions of the respiratory tract. Now-a-days analgesic sprays are also available.

Since, the oily sprays retard the cilial action of the nasal mucosa and may also enter the trachea causing lipoid pneumonia, it should be avoided.

**Containers :** These are provided in small, coloured fluted glass bottles. Plastic squeeze bottles, atomisers or pressurised aerosols are most suitable for administration.

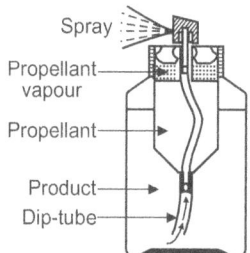

Fig. 8.2 : Aerosol

**Storage condition :** Sprays should be stored in well-filled air-tight containers and should be protected from light.

Only one spray "Compound Adrenaline and atropine spray" is official in BPC 1973.

R$_x$

| Borax | 2.5 g |
| Sodium benzoate | 1.0 g |
| Glycerine of phenol | 5.0 ml |
| Water | ad 100 ml |

Prepare spray, send 20 ml

**Label :** Use as directed by the physician.

### QUESTIONS

1. Define the following :
   (a) Douches, (b) Sprays, (c) Nasal drops and Ear drops.
   Write a note on containers for nasal drops and ear drops. How will you store them ?
2. Describe the therapeutic value of Ear drops and Douches.
3. What are aerosols ? Describe the working of aerosols.

❒❒❒

# 9
## CHAPTER

# LINIMENTS AND LOTIONS

## (1) LINIMENTS

*Liniments are solutions or suspensions or emulsions intended for external application. They are generally applied with massage.*

Therapeutic properties depend on the penetration of medicaments through the skin and layers below, and will depend on the nature of medication as well as on the degree of massage employed. They possess analgesic, rubefacient, soothing or stimulating properties.

**Containers of Liniments :**

The containers must be easily distinguishable by touch from those used for internal medicine. Coloured fluted bottles may be used. If poisonous substances are present, then the solution may be coloured by adding colouring agents such as amaranth, sulphan blue, etc.

Unless otherwise mentioned, 50 ml of liniments should be prepared and be supplied in coloured bottles.

Fig. 9.1 : Containers for liniments

**Labelling :** Labelling is similar to mixtures. It should include the words, 'For external use only.'

Should not be applied to broken skin.

**Storage :** Depending upon the nature of medicaments, these are to be stored in well-filled, well-closed, air-tight containers and in a cool place.

**Exercise 1 :**

R$_x$

| | |
|---|---|
| Soft soap | 9 g |
| Camphor | 5 g |
| Turpentine oil | 69 ml |
| Purified water | to 100 ml |

Prepare Liniment

**Label :** Use as directed. For external use only.

## Method :

Take the required quantity of soft soap in the mortar and add water in thrice the quantity as soft soap. Triturate to make a soapy solution. Take the required quantity of oil of turpentine in a dry measure glass and dissolve camphor in it. Add this solution drop by drop in the mortar, triturating continuously and rapidly, till the primary emulsion is formed.

Add a small quantity of water and transfer it to the previously calibrated, round, vertically ribbed and blue or amber coloured bottle. Adjust to the required volume by adding water. Cork and label it.

---

**LINIMENT**

30 ml

FOR EXTERNAL USE ONLY

FOR      MR. X. Y. Z.

**Direction :** To be applied externally on the affected part with friction

SHAKE WELL BEFORE USE

Date                Prepared by

Janata Hosptial, Main Road, SOLAPUR

---

## Use :

Liniment of turpentine is used externally in a patient suffering from arthralgia (joint pain), myalgia (muscular pain), fibrositis, and sprain.

## MECHANISM OF ACTION

It acts as an irritant and counter-irritant.

**Irritants and counter-irritants :** The practice of applying irritants to the skin in internal diseases was known long before, as it was originally believed that disease was a malignant entity which might be drawn from the deeper organs of the surface by irritating the skin.

*Irritants* are agents which produce more or less local inflammatory reactions when used locally.

The initial symptoms of irritation are congestion and redness of the part; such drugs producing only this degree of irritation are known as rubefacients. Stronger irritants cause blistering and are known as **vesicants** like cantherdin; while some drugs which cause irritation and small discrete suppurations are called **pustulants**.

Counter-irritants are the drugs or agents which are applied locally to irritate the intact skin for the purpose of relieving deep-seated pain.

Visceral disease is often accompanied by tenderness of the skin and underlying muscles, and pain arising in such cases may be referred to this area of the skin and not to the organ involved. For example in heart disease, pain is often felt in the left chest wall and shoulder extending down the left arm.

The physiological basis of counter-irritation is not precisely known but it is presumed to act by the following mechanisms :

**1. Local :** Counter-irritants cause vasodilation and redness of the part (rubefacient action) accompanied by sensory stimulation. This is associated with a feeling of warmth and comfort. The vasodilation is due to the axon reflex i.e. the vasodilator effect with all its accompaniments occurring without the impulse passing through a nerve cell.

**2. Focal :** Vasodilation may affect the more deep-seated tissues and permit the dispersal of pain producing substances. The vasodilation is produced by stimulation of sensory nerve endings in the skin and relay of afferent impulses in the cerebrospinal axis to efferent vasomotor fibres supplying the internal tissue.

Strong sensory irritation of a segment of the skin either alters or completely depresses the pain arising from an internal organ which is innervated by the same segment and following the common sensory pathway to the brain. This effect is due to cortical pre-occupation. There is a crowding of sensations which results in inability of brain to receive all impulses which are directed to it. This helps in relieving internal pain.

Counter-irritants can be either physical or chemical agents.

Physical counter-irritants are :

(a) Hot water bottles

(b) Short wave diathermy

(c) Radiant heat

(d) Galvanic electric current.

Chemical counter-irritants are :

(a) Volatile oils e.g. oil of turpentine, camphor, menthol, thymol, methyl salicylate, etc.

(b) Black mustard powder or oil.

**Exercise 2 :**

R$_x$

| | |
|---|---|
| Menthol | 4 g |
| Camphor | 4 g |
| Thymol | 4 g |

Let the liniment be made.

**Label :** Apply with camel hair brush to the affected part.

**Method :**

The above three substances when combined together form an oily liquid. Hence, triturate together in a dry mortar until a liquid is formed. Then transfer to a dry bottle.

## Exercise 3 :

Rx

| Salicylic acid | 1.2 g |
|---|---|
| Resorcinol | 3.6 g |
| Alcohol 70% | 120 ml |

Let the liniment be made.

**Label :** Use as directed.

**Method :**

Dissolve salicylic acid and resorcinol in about 100 ml of alcohol. Transfer to a measure and make up the volume by addition of 70% alcohol.

## Exercise 4 :

Rx

| Calamine | 1.0 g |
|---|---|
| Zinc oxide | 2.0 g |
| Olive oil | 15 ml |
| Solution of calcium hydroxide | 15 ml |

Make a liniment.

**Label :** To be used daily.

**Note :** The free fatty acids in olive oil react with the solution of calcium hydroxide forming a divalent soap giving a water in oil emulsion. The solution of calcium hydroxide must be freshly prepared.

**Method :**

Triturate calamine and zinc oxide in a mortar and continue trituration after adding the olive oil. Add calcium hydroxide solution and triturate briskly until a cream is formed.

## Exercise 5 :

Rx

| Triethanolamine | 1.0 ml |
|---|---|
| Oleic acid | 4.0 ml |
| Benzyl benzoate | 24 ml |
| Water | 120 ml |

Benzyl benzoate liniment

**Label :** Apply as directed.

This is a soap emulsion. The soap is formed due to interaction between triethanolamine and oleic acid (the fatty acid).

**Method :**

Mix triethanolamine with the required quantity of water, 120 ml. Mix oleic acid and benzyl benzoate. Add both mixtures and stir gently.

**Exercise 6 :**

R̥

| | |
|---|---|
| Camphor | 4.0 g |
| Oleic acid | 4.0 g |
| Alcohol 90% | 70 ml |
| Potassium hydroxide | q. s. |
| Flavour | 1.5 ml |
| Purified water | ad 100 ml |

Prepare Liniment

**Label :** Use as directed by the physician.

**Method :**

Dissolve the oleic acid in about 50 ml of alcohol and add potassium hydroxide solution until one drop of solution diluted with ten drops of carbon dioxide free water gives a full blue colour with one drop of bromothymol blue and a full yellow colour with thymol blue which indicates a pH between 7.6 and 8.0. Dissolve camphor and the flavour in the remainder of the alcohol and mix the two solutions. Make up the volume to 100 ml. Allow the liniment to stand for seven days, then filter and dispense.

**Exercise 7 :**

R̥

| | |
|---|---|
| Methyl salicylate | 13 ml |
| Arachis oil | ad 50 ml |

Mix. Prepare liniment

## (2) LOTIONS

*Lotions are aqueous suspensions intended for external application to the skin without massage* on lint, or other soft absorbent fabric (distinction from Liniments). A few are emulsions. Use of homogenisers serves to give a better dispersion of insoluble substances.

Lotions are used for their cooling, soothing anti-allergic, antiseptic, astringent or drying properties depending on the ingredients used.

## Differences between liniments and lotions :

| Liniments | Lotions |
|---|---|
| 1. Most of them are to be applied with a slight friction. | 1. These are to be applied without friction. |
| 2. These are used for application to the unbroken skin only. | 2. Lotions are used for application to skin (even broken or inflammed). |
| 3. Act as irritants and counter-irritants. | 3. Have antiseptic, anti-inflammatory and cooling properties. |
| 4. May contain camphor. | 4. Do not contain camphor. |

**Containers for lotions :** Lotions must be dispensed in coloured fluted bottles or in suitable plastic containers.

Unless otherwise directed, 100 ml of lotions be prepared.

**Fig. 9.2 : Containers for lotions**

**Labelling :** It should cover the words *'For external use only'*. Proper instructions for lotions, if diluted to use within one month of dilution.

**Storage :** In well-filled, well-closed containers in cool place.

**Classification :**
1. Simple lotions containing soluble ingredients i.e. potassium permanganate lotion (0.1%), Cetrimide lotion (1%), etc.
2. Lotions containing insoluble ingredients, e.g. Calamine lotion.
3. Lotions exhibiting intentional incompatibility, e.g. Lotion nigra (Black wash).

**Exercise 1 :**

R$_x$

| | |
|---|---|
| Prepared calamine | 3.50 g |
| Zinc oxide | 1.50 g |
| Bentonite | 0.90 g |
| Sodium citrate | 0.15 g |
| Liquified phenol | 0.15 g |
| Glycerine | 0.15 g |
| Rose water up to | 30 ml |

Mix and prepare a lotion.

**Direction :** To be applied externally on the affected part without friction.

## Method

Take the required quantities of calamine, zinc oxide and bentonite in the mortar, finely powder them and mix. Measure about three quarters (20 ml) of the vehicle and dissolve in it, the quantity of sodium citrate; pour a portion of it in the mortar and triturate to form a smooth cream; add the remaining amount of sodium citrate solution and mix well. Add the required quantity of glycerine and liquefied phenol into it, add more of the vehicle to produce the prescribed volume (30 ml). Transfer it into the bottle, cork and label it. The bottle should be round, vertically ribbed and blue or amber coloured.

## Label

| LOTION |
| --- |
| 30 ml |
| FOR EXTERNAL USE ONLY |
| FOR        MR. X. Y. Z. |
| **Direction :** To be applied on the affected part without friction |
| SHAKE WELL BEFORE USE |
| Date                             Prepared by |
| Pharmacy Laboratory, Address : |

**Note :** In addition to the direction **'For external use only'**, 'Shake well before use' should be written on the label.

## Uses :

1. To allay pain and swelling of sunburn.
2. In pruritus.
3. In any irritating skin disease e.g. dermatitis eczema, ringworm psoriasis, etc.

## Mechanism of action :

1. Astringent,   2. Antipruritic,   3. Antiseptic.

## Exercise 2 :

$R_x$

| | |
|---|---|
| Calamine | 8.0 g |
| Zinc oxide | 8.0 g |
| Sodium carboxymethyl cellulose | 2.2 g |
| Dioctyl sodium sulphosuccinate | 0.08 g |
| Glycerine | 0.4 ml |
| Purified water | ad 120 ml |

The calamine lotion, send 60 ml.

**Label :** Apply as directed.

**Method :**

Mix calamine and zinc oxide in a mortar. Add glycerine to levigate the mixed powders. The sodium carboxymethyl cellulose and dioctyl sodium sulphosuccinate are dissolved in sufficient water. This solution is added to the levigated paste. The volume is then made upto 120 ml pass through a homogeniser.

**Label :** 'For external use only', 'Shake well before use'.

## Exercise 3 :

R$_x$

| | |
|---|---|
| Precipitated sulphur | 5.0 g |
| Glycerine | 5.0 ml |
| Sodium lauryl sulphate | 0.25 gm |
| Alcohol | 15 ml |
| Rose water | ad 100 ml |

Let a lotion be made, send 50 ml

**Label :** Apply every night.

**Method :**

Triturate the sulphur with glycerine (glycerine is used to wet the sulphur), add 0.25 gm of sodium lauryl sulphate, and the alcohol. Finally, add the rose water to make up the required volume.

## Exercise 4 :

R$_x$

| | |
|---|---|
| Zinc sulphate | 4.0 g |
| Sulphurated potash | 4.0 g |
| Water | 100 ml |

Let a lotion be made.

Mop on face each night.

It should be freshly prepared.

**Note :** Sulphurated potash is a mixture of potassium sulphides and other potassium compounds. Zinc sulphate reacts with sulphurated potash forming zinc sulphide which is diffusible.

**Method :**

Mix sulphate with water to produce 50 ml and similarly mix sulphurated potash to produce 50 ml of mixture. Add the two mixtures together and dispense.

**Eye Lotions**

**Eye lotions are required to be used while warm.** It, therefore, follows that the eye lotion should be diluted with warm water before use. Consequently, they are issued in double strength and the patient is instructed to dilute it with equal volume of warm water before use. Eye lotions are not used for open wounds or damaged eye. There is always a danger of infection. The eye lotions are used for washing or bathing the eyes. Patient is required to be told to clean and wash the eye before use.

Eye lotions are sterilized products.

Following exercise represents preparation of eye lotion.

**Exercise 5 :**

$R_x$

Potassium permanganate solution 8 ounces
(1 in 5000)

**Label :** The eye lotion.

Use freshly prepared.

To be used thrice a day with equal volume of warm water.

**Calculations :** 35 grains in 8 ounces is 1 in 100 solution.

Therefore, number of grains required in 8 ounces to make 1 in 5000 solution will be

$$\frac{35 \times 100 \times 8}{5000 \times 8} = 0.7 \text{ grains}$$

will make 8.0 ℥ of 1 in 5000 solution.

This quantity (0.7 gr) is not directly weighable. Therefore, dissolve 1 grain in ten drachms of boiled distilled water. Seven drachms of this solution will contain 0.7 grains of potassium permanganate. Make up the volume of 8 ounces and dispense.

**Exercise 6 :**

$R_x$

| Chlorinated lime | 1.25 g |
| Boric acid | 1.25 g |
| Water upto | 100 ml |

Prepare a Lotion.

**Label :** Use as directed by the physician.

It should be recently prepared.

## QUESTIONS

1. Differentiate lotions and liniments. Write a note on containers for liniments and lotions.
2. Write the various purposes for which liniments and lotions are used. How liniments are prepared and dispensed ?
3. What are eye-lotions ? How are they labelled ?
4. What is the role of oil in lotions ? Why is camphor used in lotions ?

# 10
**CHAPTER**

# SUSPENSIONS

## INTRODUCTION

Suspension is the dispersion of particles of the insoluble liquid or of partially soluble or insoluble solids in liquid. Depending upon the particle size of dispersed solid, it may be further classified as coarse suspension, fine suspension and colloidal dispersion. Suspensions may be parenteral, external or for oral administration.

**Containers :** Depending upon the viscosity, suspensions can be dispensed either in narrow mouth fluted or wide mouth bottles.

**Labelling :** In case of liquid preparations, *"shake well before use" label* should be used. In case of dry-suspension powders, the specified amounts of vehicle to be used for dilution should be indicated clearly.

Many pharmaceutical preparations are prepared in the suspension form for one reason or the other. A good suspension

1. after shaking, should remain in suspension for long time, particle size of solid in suspensions vary from 0.5 to 5.0 μ;
2. should have easy redispersion of solids;
3. be pourable from the container;
4. be elegant in appearance;
5. have uniform small particles which on standing should not form aggregates;
6. should have solid particles with adequate stability in the vehicle used.

Solids in suspension are classified according to their wettability as under :

(a) Diffusible solids, and
(b) Indiffusible solids.

Diffusible solids remain in dispersed form for a sufficiently long time till they are consumed. Indiffusible solids settle down on standing. Indiffusibility depends on various factors such as

1. Wettability
2. Viscosity
3. Particle size.

Hence, use of surface active agents, thickening agents and fine powder helps to obtain good suspension.

**General method of preparation of suspensions containing diffusible solids :**

Grind all the ingredients of suspension to obtain a fine powder. Then mix the powders as per ascending order of their weights as under :

**Example :** If the suspension contains the following powders :

| Powder A | 1 g |
| Powder B | 3 g |
| Powder C | 4 g |
| Powder D | 8 g |

Mix 1 g of powder A with 1 g of powder B. Then mix the 2 g of the mixture with the remaining 2 g of powder B. Total mixture quantity becomes 4 g. Now, mix this 4 g mixture with 4 g of powder C and finally prepare homogeneous mixture of this 8 g powder with 8 g of powder D.

After mixing the powder, add a little amount of vehicle to form a paste. Then add the required amount of vehicle to obtain the volume. Observe the suspension for any suspended impurity and then transfer it in a bottle and rinse the mortar. Collect the rinse and transfer it to a bottle. Shake the bottle to obtain a uniform suspension. If any volatile ingredient is present in the formula, add in the bottle and shake it to disperse uniformly.

Thin suspensions (low viscosity) can be filled in a narrow mouth bottle. High viscosity suspensions require wide mouth bottle for storage. Temperature variations adversely affect the preparation, hence it is stored in a cool place.

Indiffusible solids, settle down quickly and it becomes difficult to maintain the uniformity of dose. However, preparation can easily be done but stabilised by incorporating thickening agent in the preparation. It increases the viscosity of the preparation and the rate of sedimentation is decreased.

Different types of thickening agents are given below :

**1. Acacia :** Dried exudate of Acacia Senegal. It forms colloid solution in water and increases the viscosity.

**2. Tragacanth :** Dried extract from Astragalus gummifer and certain other species of Astragalus. It forms a gel with water. The mucilage or gel is viscous and less sticky than acacia.

**3. Compound powder of Tragacanth :** It is a good thickening agent and used in the concentration of 2 g per 100 ml of final mixture. It is prepared by mixing acacia 20 per cent, tragacanth 15 per cent, starch 20 per cent and remaining sucrose. When tragacanth alone is used, then 0.2 gm per 100 ml suspension may be used.

**4. Starch :** Sometimes starch mucilage is used as a suspending or thickening agent. Maize, wheat or rice starch may be used.

**5. Sodium alginate :** It is a sodium salt of alginic acid. Alcohol 2 to 4 per cent is used while preparing the mucilage. Being an anionic compound, it is incompatible with many cationic substances. Hence, while using it its incompatibility with other ingredients should be ascertained.

**6. Methyl cellulose :** In the cellulose, there are three hydroxy groups in the monomers, one or more is replaced by methoxy group to give methyl cellulose. It can be used for internal as well as external preparations. High viscosity grade methyl cellulose is used as a thickening agent. Normally, 0.5 to 2 per cent is sufficient to give adequate viscosity.

**7. Hydroxy ethyl cellulose :** When hydroxy ethyl group is substituted for hydroxy group in the cellulose monomer, the compound formed is called hydroxy ethyl cellulose. It is soluble in hot and cold water.

**8. Sodium carboxy methyl cellulose (S.C.M.C.) :** It differs from methyl cellulose in having one of the hydrogen atom of methyl group is replaced by carboxy group ($-CH_2COOH$). Due to carboxyl group, salts can be produced. Various grades of S.C.M.C. are available with viscosity 6 to 4000 centipoises for 1 per cent solution. It is used in the concentration 0.25 to 1 per cent in the suspension.

**9. Microcrystalline cellulose :** Solution of high molecular weight polymer crystallizes to form microcrystals. These are separated microcrystals of cellulose and a molecular weight of around 36000. They are dispersible but not soluble. These produce colloidal dispersion. It is sometimes used in combination with S.C.M.C.

**10. Bentonite :** Formula of bentonite is $Al_2O_3, 4\ SiO_2 \cdot H_2O$ with a little magnesium, iron and calcium carbonate. It is a hygroscopic powder. About 2 per cent is used as a suspending agent in external preparations. When used on the broken skin it should be sterilised. *Clostridium tetani* spores are many a times seen associated with bentonite.

**11. Aluminium magnesium silicate :** It is also called as Veegum. 0.5 to 2 per cent is used in the suspension. Heat and presence of electrolytes, reduce the viscosity of solution.

**12. Hectorite :** It is used in the suspension for external use.

Bentonite, veegum and hectorite are of mineral origin and are used in the preparations to be used externally only.

**13. Aluminium hydroxide :** Colloidal hydrated aluminium hydroxide is sometimes used as a suspending agent. It assists wetting of unwettable substances.

**14. Carbomer (Carboxy vinyl polymer) :** It is a high molecular weight polymer of acrylic acid. In low concentration (0.1 to 0.5 per cent), it is effective as a suspending agent.

**15. Colloidal silicon dioxide :** Silicon compounds such as Silicon tetrachloride when hydrolysed in the vapour phase give Silicon dioxide.

In water, it forms a network and thus remains in a suspended form. It is used in the suspension in the concentration of 1.5 to 4 per cent.

Commonly used diffusible and non-diffusible substances are

**Diffusible solids :**

Powders for Internal use

    Light kaolin

    Light magnesium carbonate

    Calcium carbonate

    Magnesium trisilicate

    Rhubarb powder.

**Indiffusible solids :**

    Succinyl sulphathiazole

    Phenobarbitone

    Chalk

    Sulphadimidine

    Aspirin

    Aromatic chalk powder.

Following are used for External preparations only :

    Calamine

    Zinc oxide

    Precipitated sulphur

    Hydrocortisone.

**Wetting agents :** These are the substances which help the wetting process which is nothing but a spreading of liquid over a solid surface.

The surfactants having HLB value from 8-10 are satisfactory wetting agents and they are used to cause homogenisation where it is badly desired.

**Exercise 1 :**

    $R_x$

| | |
|---|---|
| Acacia | 40 g |
| Chloroform water | 60 ml |

    **Label :** A suspending agent.

**Method :**

Remove adhered impurities from acacia by washing with chloroform water. Put 40 g of acacia and add 60 ml of chloroform water, stirr slowly to obtain the solution.

### Exercise 2 :

℞

| | |
|---|---|
| Tragacanth | 0.2 g |
| Ethyl alcohol | 2 ml |
| Chloroform water to | 100 ml |

**Label :** A suspending agent.

### Method :

Put tragacanth in a beaker. Moisten it with alcohol and mix it with chloroform water to form mucilage.

### Exercise 3 :

℞

| | |
|---|---|
| Starch | 25 g |
| Water | to 1000 ml |

**Label :** A suspending agent.

### Method

Keep 25 g starch in a beaker and add $3/4^{th}$ of water. Mix it thoroughly and heat on a low flame to gelatinise the starch. Cool it under the current of water and then adjust the volume with water. It should be prepared freshly.

### Exercise 4 :

℞

| | |
|---|---|
| Eucalyptus oil | 10 ml |
| Menthol | 3 g |
| Water | ad 200 ml |

**Note :** When volatile oil or solid is to be incorporated in water, diffusible solid is used as a distributing agent.

In this prescription, light magnesium carbonate is used as a distributing agent. For 2 ml of volatile oil or 2 g of volatile solid, 1 gm of light magnesium carbonate give a good result. The preparation is used for adding the preparation in water at 65°C for inhaling purpose.

Final formula

| | |
|---|---|
| Eucalyptus oil | 10 ml |
| Menthol | 3 g |
| Light Magnesium Carbonate | 6.5 g |
| Water | ad 100 ml |

**Method :**

Dissolve finely powdered menthol in oil and add light magnesium carbonate powder. Mix it thoroughly. Slowly pour water with constant trituration to form a pourable paste. Transfer the paste in the bottle.

**Label :** As a inhaler or as directed by the physician.

**Exercise 5 :**

R$_x$

| | |
|---|---|
| Sulphadimidine | 12 g |
| Syrup of orange | 15 ml |
| Water | ad 160 ml |

Send 50 ml.

**Label :** Take twenty ml every four hours.

**Type :** Mixture containing indiffusible solid.

**Note :** Sulphadimidine is indiffusible and hence compound powder of tragacanth is used in the proportion of 2 g-200 ml of final suspension.

**Method :**

Sulphadimidine is powdered in the mortar. Then 3.2 g of compound powder of tragacanth is added. Both the powders are thoroughly mixed. Add water in small amount with constant trituration till the pourable paste is formed. Transfer it in a bottle. Rinse the mortar with water. Add the rinse in the bottle and finally add syrup of orange. Make up the required volume by water.

**Exercise 6 :**

R$_x$

| | |
|---|---|
| Strychnine hydrochloride | 0.4 mg |
| Chloroform water | 15 ml |

Prepare a mixture.

Send 180 ml.

**Label :** Take three times a day.

**Note :** This is a mixture containing a potent medicament in a fraction, non-weighable.

**Calculations :** Each dose contains 0.4 mg of strychnine hydrochloride. Total doses are twelve. Hence, quantity of strychnine hydrochloride is 0.4 × 12 = 4.8 mg which is not weighable.

Hence, accurately weigh 100 mg of strychnine hydrochloride.

Prepare 100 ml solution in chloroform water. Pipette out 4.8 ml of solution which contains 4.8 mg of drug.

### Method :

Take 4.8 ml of above solution and dilute it with chloroform water to make the volume 180 ml.

### Exercise 7 :

R̥

| | |
|---|---|
| Magnesium sulphate | 31 g |
| Magnesium carbonate | 4 g |
| Peppermint water    ad | 180 ml |

Send 60 ml

**Label :** Take two tablespoonful half an hour before breakfast.

**Type :** Mixture containing diffusible solid.

Shake well before use, label is necessary.

### Method :

Magnesium sulphate and magnesium carbonate are powdered. Three fourth of the vehicle is then added slowly with trituration to form a cream. Cream is then transfered to a measure. The volume is then adjusted with a vehicle and labeled.

### Exercise 8 :

R̥

| | |
|---|---|
| Bismuth carbonate | 1.0 g |
| Sodium bicarbonate | 0.7 g |
| Tincture of belladonna | 0.4 ml |
| Water | ad   30 ml |

**Label :** Take 30 ml before each meal; Shake well before use.

Send 60 ml.

**Type :** Mixture containing diffusible solids.

### Method :

Powder bismuth carbonate and sodium bicarbonate and mix. Add a small amount of water to it, form pourable paste. Transfer it in a bottle. Then add tincture of belladonna and adjust the volume with water.

**Exercise 9 :**

R$_x$

| | |
|---|---|
| Quinine sulphate | 1.6 g |
| Potassium iodide | 0.8 g |
| Water | ad  180 ml |

**Label :** Take 15 ml every four hours.

(Quinine sulphate is diffusible) 'shake well before use' label is necessary.

Follow the method for mixtures containing diffusible solids.

Magnesium hydroxide mixture B.P. and Aluminium hydroxide gel B.P. are some of the official suspension preparations.

## SUSPENSIONS PRODUCED BY CHEMICAL REACTION

In this method, the reacting constituents in dilute solutions are reacted to produce a suspension of active constituent. In this method, the reactants are dissolved separately in half volumes of the vehicle and then the two solutions are mixed. The advantage of this method is that, we get diffusible precipitate.

**Exercise 10 :**

R$_x$

Sulphurated Potash

Zinc sulphate

Concentrated Camphor Water

Water

**Use :** Scabicide.

**Direction :** To be applied as directed.

Sulphurated potash is a mixture of potassium polysulphides and other sulphur compounds. It reacts with zinc sulphate to form diffusible precipitate of zinc sulphide.

**Method :**

Dissolve sulphurated potash and zinc sulphate separately in 40 ml water. The sulphurated potash solution is slowly added to the zinc sulphate solution with constant stirring. Camphor water is added slowly with vigorous shaking. Volume of solution was made up.

Other suspensions prepared by chemical reaction include Magnesium hydroxide gel, Aluminium hydroxide gel, etc.

## FLOCCULATED AND NON-FLOCCULATED SUSPENSION

At the same concentration of the added ion, the electrical forces of repulsion are lowered sufficiently so that the forces of attraction predominate. Under these conditions, the particles may approach each other more closely and form loose aggregates which are called flocs. Such a system is said to be flocculated system.

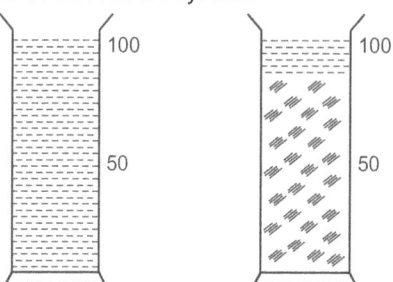

(a) Deflocculated suspension    (b) Flocculated suspension

Fig. 10.1

Electrolytes, polymers and surfactants are commonly used as flocculating agents. In a deflocculated system containing a distribution of particle sizes, the larger particles naturally settle faster than the smaller particles. The very small particles remain suspended for a considerable length of time with the result that no distinct boundary is formed between the supernatant and the sediment.

When the same system is flocculated, two effects are immediately apparent. First, the flocs tend to fall together so that a distinct boundary between the sediment and the supernatant is readily observed and second the supernatant is clear, showing that the very fine particles have been incorporated into the flocs. The initial rate of settling in flocculated system is determined by the size of the flocks and porosity of the aggregated area.

Frequently, the pharmacist needs to assess a formulation in terms of the amount of flocculation in the suspension and to compare this with that found in other formulations. The two parameters commonly used for this are

    (i)  Sedimentation Volume    (ii)  Degree of Flocculation

**I. Sedimentation Volume :** The sedimentation volume F, is the ratio of the equilibrium volume of the sediment $V_u$ to the total volume of the suspension $V_o$.

Thus, $$F = \frac{V_u}{V_o}$$

As the value of F, which normally ranges from nearly 0 to 1, increases the volume of suspension that appears occupied by the sediment increases. In the system where F = 0.75 for example, 75% of the total volume in the container is apparently occupied by the loose, porous flocs forming the sediment. In a particular suspension therefore, if F can be made to approach the value of unity, the product becomes more acceptable. When F = 1 no sediment is apparent even though the system is flocculated. This is the ideal suspension, under these conditions, no sedimentation will occur and caking will be absent.

**II. Degree of Flocculation :** A better parameter for comparing flocculated system is the degree of flocculation, β.

Degree of flocculation relates the sedimentation volume of the flocculated suspension, F to the sedimentation volume of the suspension when deflocculated, $F_\alpha$. It is expressed as

$$\beta = \frac{F}{F_\alpha}$$

The degree of flocculation is, therefore, an expression of the increased sediment volume resulting from flocculation. If for example, β has a value of 5.0, this means that the volume of the sediment in the flocculated is five times that in the deflocculated state. The flocs are quite porous and the desirable scaffold-like structure is present.

**Relative Properties of Flocculated and Deflocculated Particles in Suspension :**

| Deflocculated | Flocculated |
|---|---|
| 1. Particles exist as separate entities. | 1. Particles form loose aggregates. |
| 2. Rate of sedimentation is slow because each particle settles separately and particle size is minimum. | 2. Rate of sedimentation is high because particles settle as floc, which is a collection of particles. |
| 3. A sediment is formed slowly but the sediment eventually becomes very closely packed and hard cake is formed which is very difficult to redisperse. | 3. The sediment is formed rapidly but the sediment is loosely packed. Particles are not bonded tightly to each other and a hard dense cake does not form. The sediment is easily redispersible. |
| 4. The suspension has a pleasing appearance since the suspended material remains suspended for a relatively long time. | 4. The suspension is somewhat unsightly due to rapid sedimentation and the presence of an obvious clear, supernatant region. |

## QUESTIONS

1. Define the following :
   (a) Suspensions,
   (b) Flocculated and non-flocculated solutions.
2. What are the requirements of a good suspension ? How good suspensions can be prepared, explain with suitable examples ?
3. Write notes on various suspending and thickening agents known to you with their merits and demerits.

# 11
CHAPTER

# EMULSIONS

## INTRODUCTION

Oil and water if taken together, the two phases remain separated. This is because oil is immiscible with water. Now, shake the mixture rigorously, small globules of one phase get formed. These globules disperse in the other phase. The globules are called dispersed phase and the medium is called continuous phase. The mixture formed is called as an *emulsion*. Still this mixture is unstable and the globules come together to form a big globule. Thus, the immiscible phase separates. In order to obtain a stable emulsion, third substance which keeps the globules separated is used. This substance is called as an emulsifying agent (Emulgent).

Hence, emulsion can be defined as a mixture containing two immiscible liquids, in which one liquid is dispersed in the form of small globules in the other liquid (continuous phase) and stabilized by the third substance called as an emulsifying agent.

In general, two immiscible liquids form an emulsion. However, in pharmaceutical emulsions, one of the liquids is water and the other is an oil. Therefore, we get two types of emulsions :

1. Oil globules in water (o/w type emulsion)
2. Water globules in oil (w/o type emulsion).

In o/w type, oil is in the dispersed phase and water in a continuous phase. While conditions are reversed in w/o type of emulsion.

However, in Pharmaceutical practical, the term "emulsion" is used to indicate oil in water (o/w) type of emulsion only for internal use. An emulsion for external use may be water in oil (w/o) type. Normal globule size of macroemulsion is 100 to 1,00,000 nm and in case of microemulsion 10 to 100 nm.

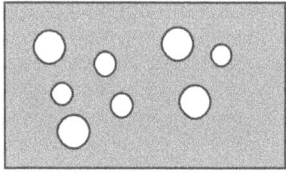 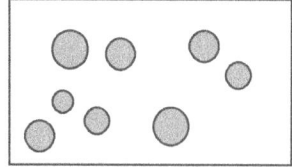

(a) O/W Type          (b) W/O Type

**Fig. 11.1 : Types of emulsion**

**Examples :** Natural emulsions such as milk and latex of plant. Artificial emulsions as liquid paraffin emulsion, castor oil emulsion, cod liver oil emulsion etc.

**Containers :** Emulsions are dispensed in wide mouthed glass bottles, since normally they are viscous preparations.

Unless otherwise mentioned, 100 ml emulsion can be dispensed.

**Labelling :** Bottles containing emulsions must be labelled as "Shake Well before Use." Emulsion intended for external use must be labelled as "For External use Only."

Identification of type of emulsion can be done by the following methods :

1. **Dilution test :** If continuous phase is added in the emulsion it will not crack or separate into phases. For example, if water is added in o/w type of emulsion, it will remain stable.

2. **Staining :** Add oil soluble dye such as scarlet red in oil and prepare an emulsion with water and emulsifying agent. Observe a drop of emulsion under a microscope. You will see red globules dispersed in water. Background will be colourless and globules will appear red. The test can be carried out by using water-soluble dyes such as methylene blue.

3. **Electrical conductivity :** Dip the electrodes in an emulsion. Put an electric bulb in the circuit. Switch on, if the bulb glows the emulsion is o/w type because continuous phase water conducts the charge and circuit is completed. If water is in the dispersed form, the bulb will not glow or it may flicker.

**Concentration of Dispersed Phase :**

Theoretically, all the globules are spherical and of a uniform size. They do not occupy more than 75 per cent of the total volume of an emulsion. In reality, the globules are not of a uniform size and shape, hence it is not possible to have emulsion containing more than 75 per cent of dispersed phase. Such emulsions are prepared by machine.

Emulsion containing less than 10 per cent of dispersed phase is also not stable. If it is required to prepare an emulsion of medicinal oil of less than 10 per cent then the volume of the oil can be increased by using inert fixed oil to obtain stability for the preparation.

Concentration less than 10 per cent of dispersed phase leads to creaming which is not desirable.

The type of product that is formed is dependent to some extent on characteristics of oil, but it is much more dependent on the emulsifying agent used. However, when the oil phase is less than 2 per cent without an emulsifying agent, it is o/w type.

**Phase Inversion - Dual Emulsions :**

In the phase inversion process, the internal (disperse) phase and external (dispersion medium) phase interchange. The inversion in the emulsion may take place by mechanical or chemical action. If the emulsion contains 10 to 45 per cent of water and it is agitated or pumped, then phase inversion may occur. The chemical reaction between one of the phases and emulsifying agent may change the emulgent to give phase inversion. Change in pH or change in solubility of phases on ageing also causes a phase inversion. An emulgent (emulsifying agent) with adequate solubility in both the phases causes such a change.

When the emulsion is partially converted into the other type, it is called as dual emulsion. Small amount of continuous phase is present in the droplet of the globules in the dual emulsion.

Lecithin forms dual emulsion with cresol, linseed oil, light petroleum, chloroform and hexalin. Albumin, casein and gelatin also form dual emulsions.

Monovalent soaps such as sodium and potassium form o/w type and divalent soaps such as calcium give w/o emulsion. If both are present in the emulsion, then phase inversion occurs on standing.

**Emulsion Stability :**

An emulsion may be considered as stable when it retains its colour, appearance, consistency, odour, chemical nature etc. at the time of manufacture till consumed or on ageing. Instability of an emulsion may be of the following types :

(i) Creaming    (ii) Cracking.

**Creaming :**

Creaming may be defined as formation of a layer of dispersed phase in relatively concentrated form at the surface. Such an emulsion on vigorous shaking results in homogeneous emulsion. On standing again, the cream forms on the surface. It is undesirable because this leads to cracking of emulsion resulting in an inaccurate dose.

Intensive study has been carried out to find the factors responsible for creaming on emulsion. Stoke's law explains the rate of creaming.

**Stoke's Law :**

$$V = \frac{2r^2 (\Delta P) g}{g n}$$

where,

$V$ = rate of creaming.
$r$ = radius of globules.
$n$ = viscosity of continuous phase.
$\Delta P$ = density difference between two phases.
$g$ = gravitational constant.

Rate of creaming can be decreased by reducing the globule size and increasing the viscosity. Use of unstable thickening agent may form lumps on standing and increase the globule diameter with increasing rate of creaming.

**Cracking :**

Separation of dispersed phase from the emulsion is referred as cracking. Once the emulsion is cracked it is difficult to correct it. The following are the reasons for cracking of an emulsion :

1. Decomposition of an emulsifying agent.
2. Precipitation of a thickening agent.
3. Addition of opposite type of an emulgent.
4. Increase in temperature.

5. Microbial attack.
6. Excessive creaming, and
7. Addition of a solvent which dissolves both phases.

**Miscellaneous Instabilities :**

Deterioration of emulsion in the presence of light and extreme low or high temperature is a common feature. Hence, it is to be stored in a coloured bottle and air-tight bottles at moderate temperatures. Phase inversion is another physical instability of the emulsion.

**Evaluation of Emulsions :** This can be done by using the following parameters :

**1. Globule size :** Increase in globule size by coalescence rate on ageing is the indication of physical instability of the emulsion. Microscopic and coulter counter measurement at a frequent interval of time gives indication of the rate of coalescence of globules. If these studies continue to show increase in globule size, it indicates poor emulsion.

**2. Temperature :** Exposure to high (60°C) and low (0 to 4°C) temperature alternatively gives an indication of emulsion stability. However, effect of thermal stresses on different emulsions vary from formulation to formulation.

**3. Flow properties :** Flow property is the manifestation of globule size, concentration of emulgent and phase volume ratio. So the study of flow property over an extended period of time gives a clue for emulsion stability. Any suitable instrument for the measurement of viscosity can be used for such studies.

**4. Phase separation :** The rate at which coalescence of globule occurs definitely indicates the stability pattern of emulsion. The test can be carried out by keeping the emulsion in the measuring cylinder and observing the rate of separation of the phase. This is a lengthy process and can be accelerated using a high speed centrifuge. If emulsion stands such stress, it can be considered as a stable emulsion.

Good emulsion should possess the following characteristics :

(i) Dispersed globules should not separate or coalescence;
(ii) Should maintain flow property throughout its shelf life;
(iii) No phase inversion; and
(iv) Should stand to mechanical and physical stresses.

**Additives in the Emulsion :**

**1. Preservatives :** Preservatives act as an antimicrobial agent. The growth of microorganism is in the aqueous phase. Hence, preservative should have adequate solubility in water. If it has more solubility in lipid phase, the activity reduces. Concentration of preservative should be adequate to retard the growth of microbes. Some of the preservatives used in emulsion are benzoic acid, formic acid, salicylic acid, p-chlorobenzoic acid, benzalkonium chloride, hexachlorophene, phenyl mercury nitrate, hexamine, etc.

2. **Thickening agents :** Viscosity plays a major role in stability of emulsion. Thickening agents are sometimes included in the formulation to get adequate consistency. Hydrocolloids in aqueous phase or long chain waxes serve the purpose. Selection depends on the type of emulsion formulation and actual amount of substance needed for the required consistency.

3. **Elegance :** In order to improve the taste, flavour and colour of the emulsion, different additives are included in the preparation. These are normally vanillin, raspberry, rose etc. for flavour, sweetner for taste and permitted colours.

4. **Antioxidants :** Butylated hydroxytoluene, $\alpha$-tocopherol are the common antioxidants used in emulsion. Oily constituent of emulsion may get rancid on standing, inclusion of antioxidant preserves the preparation from such deterioration.

## THEORIES OF EMULSION

Extensive research has been carried out to study the mechanism of emulsification and role of emulgent. Outcome of the work is the postulation of theories of emulsion formation. However, no single theory is sufficient to explain the nature of emulsification because of the various factors such as pH, proportion of water and oil, effect of electrolyte on the stability of an emulsion.

All the liquids possess force at its surface and assume a shape having minimum surface that is a sphere. When two drops come in contact, they combine to form a bigger drop occupying less surface area than did the two smaller individual drops. The force (energy) at the surface is known as surface tension of the liquid when it is in contact with its own vapour or air. However, it is called as interfacial tension when one liquid is in contact with another liquid. Surface active agents or wetting agents reduce the interfacial tension at the boundary of the liquids. The interfacial tension can be overcome to form the globules of the liquid. Hence, some mechanism should be present to keep these globules separate; otherwise they coalescence and the emulsion breaks. In order to stabilize emulsion, any one of the following mechanisms is useful :

1. Formation of a thin film of a substance around the globule to separate it from other globules.
2. Substance should orient in such a way that its ends separate the globules from dispersion medium.
3. Substance that lowers down the interfacial tension between the liquids.

Basically, all these mechanisms are physical phenomenon and hence the action of emulsification in the presence of emulgent is also physical.

Some theories of emulsification are discussed here.

### 1. Surface Tension Theory :

The substance which lowers down the interfacial tension between two immiscible liquids and thereby reduces the tendency of the globules to coalescence, gives a stable emulsion. Surface active agent lowers down the surface tension and thus acts as an emulsion stabilizer.

## 2. Oriented - Wedge Theory :

In this theory, it is presupposed that the emulsifying agent has two groups with affinity for two immiscible liquids and it forms a monomolecular layer at the surface of one liquid (globule). It orients in such a way that the other group projects towards the continuous phase forming a wedge. Oil in water or water in oil emulsion formation depends on the quantity of oil-soluble portion or water-soluble portion in the molecule. The main drawbacks of this theory are :

(i) Improbability of the formation of monolayer;
(ii) Absence of definite polar groups in many of the common emulsifying agents; and
(iii) It does not explain why some substances, not themselves emulsifying agents, favour the formation of emulsion and others do not.

## 3. Plastic Film Theory :

According to this theory, the emulgent forms a plastic thin film around the globules and thus hinder the coalescence. This effect is purely mechanical and is not dependent on the surface tension. The formation of oil in water and water in oil emulsion can be explained on the basis of selective solubility of the emulsifying agent. Water soluble emulgent will give o/w type and oil-soluble emulgent will form w/o type emulsions. The plastic film formed around the globule will keep the globules away from each other. If the viscosity of the continuous phase is increased by the addition of emulgent or any other substance, it will restrict the movement of the globule and thus stabilize the emulsion. On the other hand, the substance which reduces the viscosity, if added to the emulsion, reduces the stability of the emulsion.

This theory is in agreement with most of the observed facts concerning emulsion formation, but does not explain the effects of pH, particle size and electrical charge developed on the globules.

## EMULSIFYING AGENTS

In order to obtain a stable emulsion, it is necessary to choose a suitable emulsifying agent or a suitable combination of emulsifying agents. This is a difficult task considering a wide variety of emulsifying agents. This is simplified by Griffin who introduced Hydrophile-Lipophile Balance system (HLB system). The HLB is weight per cent of the portion of the hydrophilic surfactant divided by five. The HLB of an oil-soluble substance will be low i.e. between 2 to 10, and for water-soluble substance it will be high i.e. 10 - 20.

Oils can also be classified on this scale by the HLB required by a surface active agent to emulsify them. The HLB can be calculated for most polyol fatty acid esters as

$$HLB = 20\left[1-\left(\frac{S}{A}\right)\right]$$

where,

$S$ = saponification number of ester.
$A$ = the acid number of the recovered acid.

Once the required HLB of oils is determined; the HLB of emulsifying agent(s) should equal this figure for best stability. For a blend of emulsifying agent, the HLB is assumed to be an additive quantity.

Substances with 3-6 HLB value produce w/o emulsion and 8 to 18 LHB value produces o/w emulsion.

The following are the HLB values of few important emulsifying agents.

| Emulsifying agent | HLB value |
|---|---|
| Sorbitan trioleate | 1.8 |
| Glyceryl monostearate | 3.8 |
| Sorbitan mono-oleate (span 80) | 4.3 |
| Sorbitan mono-palmitate (span 40) | 6.7 |
| Acacia | 8.0 |
| Gelatin | 9.8 |
| Triethanolamine oleate | 12.0 |
| Tragacanth | 13.2 |
| Tween - 20 | 16.7 |
| Potassium oleate | 20.0 |
| Sodium lauryl sulphate | 40.0 |

**Classification of Emulsifying agents :**

Emulsifying agents are classified in two ways. The first method is based on the ionizing characteristic of the substance.

**(A) Non-ionizing substances :** These are esters of high fatty acids. If the polar group dominates, it is useful as o/w emulsifying agent and in pressure of dominance of non-polar group, w/o type of emulsion is formed. Polyethylene glycol esters of higher fatty acids and polyethylene glycol ethers of higher fatty acids under the trade name span 20, Tween 40, span 40, span 60, span 80 and Tween 20, Tween 80 are examples of this type.

**(B) Ionizing substances :**

**(a) Anionic Emulsifiers :** Substances which ionize and the emulsifying property lies in the anion are called anionic emulsifiers. Sodium and potassium soaps belong to this group. Monovalent soap forms o/w type of emulsion. Divalent soap (calcium, aluminium soap) forms w/o type of emulsion. Organic sulphates and sulphonates also belong to this group. Examples are sodium lauryl sulphate, Lanette wax Sx (mixture of cetyl and stearyl alcohol and sulphate) and sodium cetyl sulphonate.

**(b) Cationic Emulsifiers :** Quaternary ammonium compounds such as cetyl trimethyl ammonium bromide and benzalkonium chloride are the representatives of this group.

## Second method of classification of Emulsifying agents :

In this method, the agents are divided into the following groups :

### 1. Carbohydrates :

**Acacia :** Gum acacia is used as an emulsifying agent; for o/w type, this gives good extempore preparation of emulsion. The proportion of acacia used as an emulsifying agent is 1/4 for fixed oil, 1/2 for volatile oil and equal for oleo resin. Incompatibilities are found with alcohol, solution of ferric chloride and lead acetate. Being a carbohydrate, it undergoes bacterial decomposition.

**Tragacanth :** This is another gum with comparatively weak emulsifying action. One part with forty parts of fixed oil is used in combination with acacia. Tragacanth being viscosity builder, stabilizes the emulsion.

Other emulsifying agents of this group are agar, condrus, gum, resins, methyl cellulose, etc.

### 2. Proteins :

**Gelatin :** Gelatin is prepared from bones, skin of an animal. Homogeniser is normally used when gelatin is used as a emulgent. Two forms of gelatin are available, pharma gel A is used at pH 3 to 3.5 and gel B is used in alkaline medium. It undergoes slow hydrolysis loosing the viscosity. Hence, the emulsion requires a preservative.

**Egg yolk :** This gives an excellent emulgent property to form o/w type of an emulsion with nutrient value. An average egg yolk emulsifies 120 ml of fixed oil and 60 ml of volatile oil. The only disadvantage of this type of emulsion is that it undergoes purification.

### 3. Soaps and Alkalies :

Monovalent soaps form o/w type of emulsion while divalent soaps give w/o emulsion. These are generally used in emulsion for external use. It is incompatible with acids.

### 4. Wetting agents (Surface active agents) :

Sodium lauryl sulphate, benzalkonium chloride, Tweens, Spans, and the sorbiton esters belong to this group.

### 5. Finely divided solids and colloids :

The type of emulsion formation depends on whether these agents are wetted by oil or water. If the solid is wetted more by water than oil, an o/w emulsion will form. A w/o emulsion results, if the solid is wetted by oil. Some agents belonging to this category are magnesium trisilicate giving o/w emulsion. Bentonite, a clay is used as an emulsifying agent for both types of emulsions depending on the order of mixing. For o/w emulsion, oil should be added last. For w/o type, bentonite is dispersed in water and then gradually added to oil. Bentonite is used in dermatological preparations. It swells to the extent of eight times its own volume in water.

Synthetic emulsifying agents such as carbopols are included in this group.

## Preservatives :

Simple refrigeration is sufficient for extempore emulsions. Those which are stored for prolonged period require inclusion of preservatives.

Preservatives used should be compatible with other ingredients of emulsion, non-toxic and tasteless. In acidic medium, 2.0 per cent benzoic acid may be used. Sodium benzoate (0.5%) with 0.25% chloroform also gives a good result. Chlorocresol 0.1 per cent in aqueous cream is preferred to chloroform in the preparation impact little sweet taste. Vanillin and other essential oil may be added for flavour.

## Laboratory Method of Preparation of Emulsion :

It is very difficult to prepare an emulsion taking the required quantities of water, oil and emulsifying agent and mixing it in one operation. However, if part or total quantity of oil with portion of water and emulsifying agent is mixed to form a primary emulsion and diluting it either with water or oil to form the required volume is the best method for preparation of an emulsion.

While preparing an emulsion by trituration method, copper or porcelain is recommended over glass mortar which is too smooth for the operation. The mortar should have relatively a flat bottom. Trituration should be continuous and rapid. Slow trituration will not give effective emulsion formation.

There are three methods for preparation of an emulsion :

1. Dry gum method (Continental method)
2. Wet gum method (English method)
3. Bottle method.

**1. Dry gum method or continental method :** In this method, proportion of the ingredient is four parts of fixed oil, one part of emulgent and two parts of water. Emulgent powder is added in the dry mortar and oil is poured on it. It is mixed to form an uniform mixture then required quantity of water is added and mixture is triturated rapidly to form a primary emulsion. Primary emulsion is white, creamy, homogeneous and gives a characteristic crackling sound when the pestle is moved in it. Then by adding a continuous phase with vigorous shaking, required volume is prepared.

**2. Wet gum method or English method :** The portion of gum, water and fixed oil is one, two, four to form a primary emulsion.

In the mortar, one part of gum (emulgent) powder is added and two parts of water is poured on it with trituration to form a homogeneous mixture. Then oil is added in small succession with continuous trituration to emulsify each portion before addition of the next. If the preparation becomes too thick to triturate then add little quantity of water and then complete the addition of oil with constant trituration. Finally, adjust the volume with the required quantity of water.

**3. Bottle method :** Volatile oil gets readily emulsified by shaking in a bottle with gum and water. As the volatile oil is less viscous, the quantity of gum required is more. The proportion of ingredient is two parts of volatile oil, one part of gum and two parts of water. While preparing emulsion by the bottle method, one part of gum is placed in the bottle and two parts of the volatile oil is added. It is vigorously shaken to form a uniform mixture. Then two parts of water is added and mixture is shaken continuously to form an primary emulsion. Shaking at irregular intervals is more effective than regular shaking. Then add remaining water in small portion with agitation to form the required quantity of an emulsion.

This emulsion can also be formed in the mortar. Water soluble substance (medicament) if present in the formula is dissolved in the water required for the preparation. Resinous tincture is added to the primary emulsion and then the volume is made up. Oil soluble drug present in the formula is dissolved in oil of emulsion and then emulsion is prepared by any of the above methods. Insoluble substances in oil and water are incorporated in primary emulsion. If medicinal oily phase is less than ten per cent then it is increased by addition of any inert oil such as olive oil suitable to form an emulsion.

In most of the laboratory emulsion preparation, it is necessary to prepare primary emulsion and then dilute it with dispersion medium. The explanation is simple. If all the oil and water is mixed together the volume of liquid is quite large and the force required to cut the dispersed phase into suitable size of globules is difficult to attain. In the preparation of primary emulsion, the volume of liquid to be emulsified is considerably reduced and the force required is also reduced.

In the preparation of acacia emulsions, it is better to have gum tears, powder them and then use the powder. It saves the cost of powdering, commercially available powdered acacia is adulterated with fine clay and is dirty coloured.

**General method of Preparation, using acacia as an emulgent :**

Measure the oil using dry measuring cylinder and add it to a clean dry mortar and triturate it with corresponding quantity (depending upon the type of oil) of powdered acacia. Add twice as much water as gum and tritutrate the contents until a crackling sound is heard and the mixture assumes a white colour. At this stage, primary emulsion is complete. Add the portion of the remaining vehicle to complete the required volume with constant trituration. Transfer the emulsion to measure. Rinse the mortar with some more of water and add this to the measure. Finally adjust the volume, stir the emulsion and bottle it.

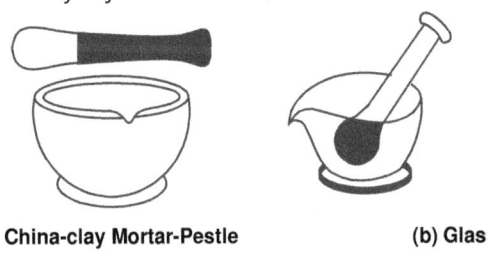

(a) China-clay Mortar-Pestle        (b) Glass

**Fig. 11.2 : Mortar pestles**

In Acacia emulsion, the quantity of acacia to be used must be in the following proportions.

| For Fixed oils : | |
|---|---|
| Castor oil, almond oil, olive oil and liquid paraffin though not an oil chemically, it is considered under fixed oil for emulgent concentration. | Use one fourth the quantity of gum as the oil. |
| **For Volatile oils :** | |
| Oil of turpentine, Sandal wood oil, oil of cubeb etc. | Use half as much gum as the oil. |
| **For Oleo resins :** | |
| Balsam of Tolu, Copaiba etc. | Use an equal amount of gum. |

## MACHINES USED FOR PREPARATION OF EMULSION

Hand emulsifier is used for small-scale work. This is also called as hand homogeniser. It works on the principle that when a jet of coarsely prepared emulsion is forced against a plate, the globules are further split in smaller globules to form a stable emulsion.

**Silverson Emulsifier :**

For large scale production, this emulsifier is used. It consists of fan shaped blades with a shaft. The shaft is rotated by a motor. The blades are surrounded by a sieve with a fine mesh. The blades are immersed into the liquid to be emulsified. When rotated the liquid is sucked into the sieve and expelled through the sieve, breaking the dispersed globules into still smaller size. Thus, giving stable emulsion.

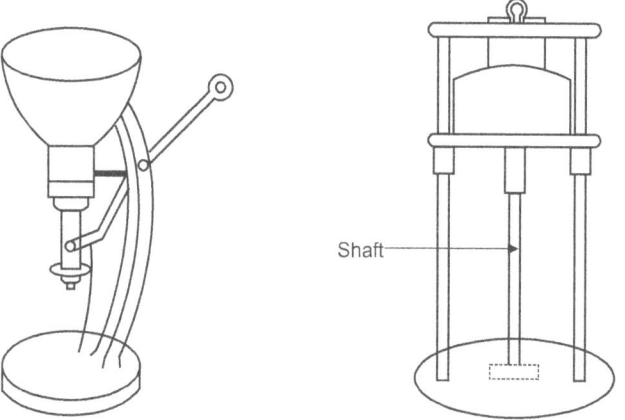

Fig. 11.3 : Hand homogeniser        Fig. 11.4 : Silverson emulsifier

Simple household mixer can also be used for preparation of the stable emulsion.

## Formulation of an emulsion :

*Factors to be considered.*

The various factors affecting the emulsion are :

1. Choice of emulgent
2. Method of emulsification
3. Use of preservative.
4. Use of flavour.
5. Inclusion of other agents such as thickeners, viscosity builders, etc.

For any of the above type of preparation, calculate the quantity of gum for any individual type and use the calculated quantity of gum.

### Acacia o/w emulsion

**Exercise 1 :**

$R_x$

| | |
|---|---|
| Olive oil | 30 ml |
| Water | ad 120 ml |

Prepare an emulsion

Send 60 ml

**Label** : Take a tablespoonful twice a day.

Primary emulsion

| | | |
|---|---|---|
| Olive oil | 30 ml | Fixed oil formula for emulgent |
| Powdered acacia | 7.5 g | |
| Water | 15 ml | |

Prepare as per general method.

**Exercise 2 :**

$R_x$

| | | |
|---|---|---|
| Oil of turpentine | 08 ml | Volatile oil formula for emulgent |
| Cinnamon water | ad 40 ml | |

Prepare a draught.

**Label :** Take at once.

Primary emulsion

| | | |
|---|---|---|
| Oil of turpentine | | 8 ml |
| Powdered acacia | | 4 g |
| Water | | 8 ml |

Prepare as per general method.

## Acacia o/w emulsion

**Exercise 3 :**

R<sub>x</sub>

| | | |
|---|---|---|
| Terbene | 6 ml | Volatile oil |
| Almond oil | 16 ml | Fixed oil |
| Tincture of Ipecacuanha | 8 ml | Take gum quantity 1/2 for terbene and 1/4 for almond oil |
| Water | ad 180 ml | |

Prepare an emulsion, send 90 ml.

**Label :** Take a tablespoonful every four hours.

Primary emulsion

| | |
|---|---|
| Terbene | 6 ml |
| Almond oil | 16 ml |
| Powdered acacia (3 + 4) | 7 g |
| Water | 14 ml |

Prepare a primary emulsion. Dilute the tincture with required quantity of vehicle and add to the primary emulsion and complete the emulsion.

**Exercise 4 : Acacia o/w emulsion**

R<sub>x</sub>

| | | |
|---|---|---|
| Terbene | | 6 ml |
| Almond oil | | 16 ml |
| Tincture of tolu | | 8 ml |
| Water | ad | 180 ml |

Make an emulsion.

**Label :** Use as directed.

Primary emulsion

| | |
|---|---|
| Terbene | 06 ml |
| Almond oil | 16 ml |
| Powdered acacia (3 + 4) | 7 g |
| Water | 14 ml |

**Method of Preparations :**

Prepare primary emulsion. Tincture of tolu is a resinous tincture and resins will be precipitated, hence it is added after the completion of primary emulsion. Gum in the preparation gives it protection and make it diffusible. After the primary emulsion is prepared, measure the tincture of tolu in a dry measure, add it with constant trituration. Then complete as per general procedure.

### Acacia o/w emulsion

**Exercise 5 :**

R$_x$

| | |
|---|---|
| Cod liver oil | 30 ml |
| Syrup | 12 ml |
| Ferric ammonium citrate | 04 g |
| Cinnamon water | ad 90 ml |

Prepare an emulsion.

**Label :** Take a tablespoonful twice a day.

Primary Emulsion.

| | |
|---|---|
| Cod liver oil | 30 ml |
| Powdered acacia | 7.5 g |
| Cinnamon water | 15 ml |

Prepare primary emulsion. Dilute the syrup to the remaining required volume. Dissolve ferric ammonium citrate in it and complete the emulsion as per general procedure.

### EMULSION CONTAINING SUBSTANCES INSOLUBLE IN OIL OR WATER

**Exercise 6 :**

R$_x$

| | |
|---|---|
| Liquid paraffin | 30 ml |
| Phenolphthalein | 1 g |
| Agar | 5 g |
| Syrup | 7 ml |
| Water | 90 ml |

Prepare an emulsion.

**Label :** Take three teaspoonful twice a day.

Formula for primary emulsion

| Liquid paraffin | 30 ml |
|---|---|
| Phenolphthalein | 1 g |
| Acacia | 7.5 g |
| Water | 15 ml |

**Method :**

Phenolphthalein is insoluble in water and oil. Hence, powder it along with acacia and then add liquid paraffin and prepare primary emulsion in hot mortar.

The volume of primary emulsion is 53.5 ml. Separately heat agar in about 25 ml of water in a tarred dish over a small flame until a solution is formed. Add the syrup to agar solution and mix. Gradually add this solution to the warm primary emulsion to measure and make up the volume.

## EMULSION CONTAINING OIL SOLUBLE SUBSTANCES

**Exercise 7 :**

$R_x$

| Salol | 2 g |
|---|---|
| Castor oil | 10 ml |
| Peppermint water    to | 60 ml |

Prepare an emulsion.

**Lable :** Take 15 ml four times a day.

Castor oil is a fixed oil. Take the proportionate quantity of gum plus 50 per cent additional gum for salol in the formulation.

Formula for primary emulsion

| Castor oil | 10 ml |
|---|---|
| Powdered acacia (2.5 g + 1.25 g) | 3.75 g |
| Peppermint water | 7.5 ml |

**Method :**

Dissolve salol in castor oil by warming the mixture. Triturate the mixture with gum acacia, add the vehicle and continue the trituration until primary emulsion is formed. Then proceed in the manner given in the earlier exercise and dispense.

## Exercise 8 :

℞

| | |
|---|---|
| Salol | 4 g |
| Camphorated opium tincture | 8 ml |
| Cinnamon water | q.s. 60 ml |

Prepare an emulsion.

**Label** : Take as directed.

Here oil is not included in the prescription. Pharmacist should include sufficient amount of oil such as olive oil and then proceed.

Formula for primary emulsion

| | |
|---|---|
| Salol | 4 g |
| Olive oil | 8 ml |
| Powdered acacia (2 + 1) | 3 g |
| Cinnamon water | 6 ml |

**Method :**

Dissolve salol in warm olive oil and finish the preparation of primary emulsion, calculate the quantity of cinnamon water (cinnamon water minus volume of tincture) and add to it the tincture and complete the emulsion.

## IRISH MOSS EMULSION

### Exercise 9 :

℞

| | | |
|---|---|---|
| Cod liver oil | | 30 ml |
| Creosote | | 0.6 ml |
| Glycerine | | 16 ml |
| Mucilage of Irish moss | | 90 ml |
| Water | ad | 180 ml |

Prepare an emulsion, send 30 ml.

**Label :** Take as directed.

The mucilage is prepared as follows - Wash the seaweed with water. The seaweed is then heated with 40 times as much water on a water bath and finally strained. It is done by using cotton wool in a hot water funnel. It is used in the preparation of cod, for satisfactory results liver oil emulsion. Emulsifier is essential for this preparation.

## Method :

Irish Moss mucilage is placed in a bottle. The creosote is then dissolved in cod liver oil. This mixture is added to the bottle and agitated vigorously. Then glycerine is added. This forms a coarse emulsion. It is then passed through a homogeniser. Finally the volume is adjusted and the preparation is transferred in the bottle and label.

## METHYL CELLULOSE EMULSION

### Exercise 10 :

R$_x$

| | |
|---|---|
| Methyl cellulose 20 | 4 g |
| Liquid paraffin | 50 ml |
| Vanillin | 0.1 g |
| Syrup | 25 ml |
| Chloroform water   ad | 200 ml |

Prepare an emulsion. Send 100 ml.

**Label :** Take as directed.

## Method :

40 ml of boiling water is added to methyl cellulose 20. Then vanillin is dissolved in 65 ml of chloroform water and added to methyl cellulose solution. It is then stirred. Liquid paraffin and syrup is added with vigorous shaking. Pass it through a homogeniser. Then make up the required volume and transfer in the bottle and then label it.

## O/W EMULSION CONTAINING AN OLEO RESIN

### Exercise 11 :

R$_x$

| | |
|---|---|
| Copaiba | 08 ml |
| Infusion of buchu   ad | 60 ml |

Prepare an emulsion.

**Label :** Take half tonight and remaining half tomorrow night.

Formula for primary emulsion.

| | |
|---|---|
| Copaiba | 8 ml |
| Powdered acacia | 8 g |
| Infusion of buchu | 16 ml |

If infusion is concentrated then dilute one volume with seven volumes of water. Calculate and take required quantity.

Prepare primary emulsion and then finish the emulsion using the process described earlier.

## O/W EMULSION USING SODIUM ALGINATE AS A SECONDARY EMULSIFYING AGENT

Sodium alginate forms a viscous solution in water. One per cent solution of sodium alginate is sufficient to produce an emulsion.

### Exercise 12 :

R$_x$

| | |
|---|---|
| Liquid paraffin | 60 ml |
| Acacia | 02 g |
| Sodium alginate | 2.5 g |
| Water | ad 250 ml |

'Liquid Paraffin Emulsion'. Send 125 ml.

**Label :** Use as directed by the physician.

### Method :

Triturate liquid paraffin with acacia, dissolve sodium alginate in a portion of water and add it to liquid paraffin-acacia mixture. Make up the volume and pass through an homogeniser.

## O/W EMULSION PREPARED WITH EGG YOLK

Yolk of egg has twice the emulsifying property, compared to acacia. An average yolk emulsifies four ounces (120 ml) of fixed oil or two ounces (60 ml) of a volatile oil. It is useful as an emulsifying agent with acid substances. It also has nutritive properties, only the yellow portion of egg should be used.

### Exercise 13 :

R$_x$

| | |
|---|---|
| Olive oil | 60 ml |
| Egg yolk | 08 ml |
| Water | ad 150 ml |

Prepare an emulsion. Send 75 ml.

**Label :** Take a tablespoonful after meals.

### Method :

Separate the egg yolk from the white of the egg. Place it in a measure and add equal an volume of water. Stir the mixture thoroughly. Take 8 ml of this egg yolk in a mortar and gradually add the oil with constant stirring. When all the oil is added, add a little more water with trituration. Then strain through muslin cloth. Transfer to a measure, make up the volume and transfer in the bottle. Then label it.

## PAEDIATRIC EMULSIONS

Emulsion containing less than 10% dispersed phase.

### Exercise 14 :

R$_x$

| | |
|---|---|
| Solution of calciferol | mii |
| Glycerine | mv |
| Water | ad ℥ i |

Make an emulsion.

**Label** : Give as directed. Send two ounces.

### Calculation :

Two ounces = 960 minims

The oily liquid present in two ounces = 32 minims

32 minims in two ounces of final volume is less than 10 per cent.

10 per cent of 960 minims is 96 minims so 96 – 32 = 64 minims of fixed oil such as olive oil may be added to raise the percentage to 10 per cent of dispersed phase.

Formula for primary emulsion.

| | |
|---|---|
| Solution of calciferol | 32 minims |
| Olive oil | 64 minims |
| Acacia (16 + 8) | 24 grains |
| Distilled water | 48 minims |

Mix calciferol and olive oil and then complete the primary emulsion and proceed as usual after mixing glycerine with water.

### Exercise 15 :

R$_x$

| | | |
|---|---|---|
| Castor oil | | 10 ml |
| Cinnamon oil | ad | 25 ml |

Prepare an emulsion.

**Label :** Use as directed by the physician.

This is a preparation for a child, 25 ml is to be dispensed unless otherwise directed.

Formula for primary emulsion.

| | |
|---|---|
| Castor oil | 10 ml |
| Acacia | 2.5 g |
| Cinnamon water | 5 ml |

Make a primary emulsion and complete the emulsion as per general method.

## QUESTIONS

1. What are emulsions ? How they are classified and tested ?
2. What are emulsifying agents ? Write a note on each type of emulsifying agents known to you.
3. Describe the various methods of preparing emulsions.
4. What is creaming and cracking of emulsions ? How are stable emulsions prepared ?
5. Describe the containers for storing the emulsions. How emulsion is to be labelled ?
6. Write notes on :
   (a) HLB value  (b) Preservatives in emulsion
   (c) Emulsifier  (d) Paediatric emulsions.

# 12

**CHAPTER**

# OINTMENTS AND PASTES

## (1) OINTMENTS

**INTRODUCTION**

Ointments are semi-solid preparations consisting of a medicament or mixture of medicaments dispersed in a suitable anhydrous base.

**Containers :** Ointments and pastes are dispensed in glasses or plastic jars provided with screw caps with impermeable liners or even with close fitting slip on lids. More conveniently now-a-days these preparations are supplied in metallic collapsible tubes (squeeze-tubes) or plastic tubes. (Unless otherwise mentioned, 25 g of ointment is to be prepared.)

**Storage :** These should be stored in well closed container so as to prevent the loss of volatile constituents, and be placed in a cool place.

**Labelling :** The words *"For external use only"* should be incorporated on the label.

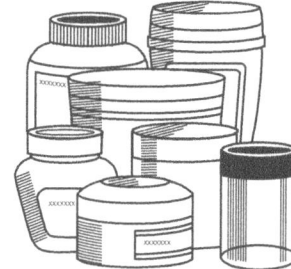

Fig. 12.1 : Bulk containers for ointments and creams

**Classification of Ointment Bases :**

Ointment bases are broadly classified in four groups :

**(1) Hydrocarbon Bases (Oily Bases) :** Hydrocarbon bases are sticky, water immiscible, inert and give occlusive film when applied to the skin. Soft paraffin, hard paraffin, liquid paraffin are commonly used in this type of base. As these substances are hydrophobic in nature, these restrict the loss of moisture from the skin surface. The occlusive layer formed on the skin retains the body heat giving an uncomfortable feeling. Some persons do not like the greasy feeling of this base. About 5 to 10 per cent water can easily be incorporated in this base.

**(2) Absorption Bases :** Absorption bases are hydrophilic and hence a considerable amount of water can be incorporated in these bases. Wool fat can absorb water about 50 per cent of its own weight. It assists absorption of active ingredients. Simple ointment B.P.

and eye ointment B.P. contain wool fat as an essential ingredient. Hydrous wool fat and wool alcohol gives w/o emulsion. Sometimes, aqueous part gets separated from the base but it can easily be redistributed in the base by stirring.

**(3) Water Miscible Bases :** Absorption bases, though hydrophilic in nature, are difficult to wash from the skin. Hence, water miscible bases are developed. Emulsifying ointment B.P. (an ionic), cetrimide emulsifying ointment B.P. (cationic), cetomacrogol emulsifying ointment B.P. (non-ionic) are the unhydrous water-miscible bases. These bases contain white soft paraffin and liquid paraffin as other ingredients. General formula for the preparation of these bases is 30 per cent of emulsifying wax with 50 per cent of soft paraffin and 20 per cent of liquid paraffin. Other advantages of these bases are miscibility with body exudate, no interference with skin functioning, adherance to the skin, cosmetic acceptability, and easy removal from the hair.

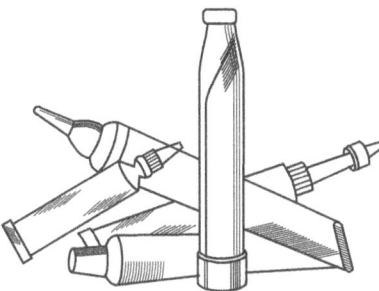

**Fig. 12.2 : Collapsible tubes**

**(4) Water Soluble Bases :** Complete water-soluble bases of ointment can be prepared from macrogols (polyethylene glycols). It is a mixture of polycondensation product of ethylene oxide. A variety of grades of macrogols from viscous liquid to waxy solid having miscibility with water are available. They are non-toxic, non-irritant to skin. Suitable consistency can be obtained by mixing the various grades in different proportions. These bases give the following advantages to the preparation :

(a) Water solubility

(b) Good absorption by the skin

(c) Good solvent property

(d) Freedom from greasiness

(e) Compatibility with many dermatological medicaments.

Few disadvantages associated with the bases are

(a) Reduction in antibacterial activity of certain antibacterial agents, solvent action on polythene and bakelite.

(b) Limited uptake of water.

### Requirements of an Ideal Ointment Base :

1. Base must not interfere with normal functions of the skin.
2. Must have low sensitivity index and must be non-irritating.
3. Must not stain clothes.
4. Must be compatible with other ingredients of the preparation.
5. Must release the drug at the site of action.
6. Must be washable i.e. must be easy to remove.
7. Must not become rancid quickly.

### Selection of the base for Ointment :

The following factors are taken into consideration when choosing an ointment base.

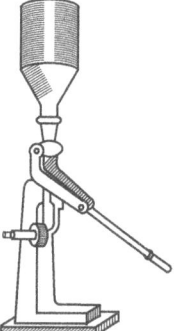

Fig. 12.3 : Collapsible tube filling machine

**1. Absorption and Penetration :** Absorption indicates actual entry of medicament in the blood stream. Absorption is the property of the medicament itself. Penetration means passage of the base (together with medicament) into the deeper layers of skin. This is the property of base. Water miscible bases have the property of deeper penetration. The paraffins do not penetrate deeply. Vegetable oils and wool fat when combined with water penetrate the skin.

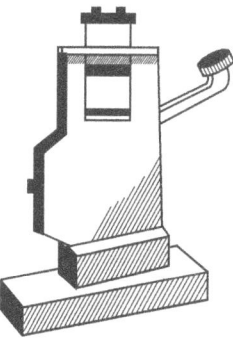

Fig. 12.4 : Collapsible tube sealing and crimping machine

**2. Effect on Normal Functions of Skin :** Greasy bases interfere with heat radiation and normal aspiration. Oil in water emulsions are devoid of these defects and therefore more useful.

**3.** Oil in water emulsion bases mix freely with fatty and aqueous secretions of the skin and therefore medicament contained in such bases is released satisfactorily.

**4.** Greasy bases are irritant to the skin and also stain clothes.

**5.** Greasy bases such as paraffins and ointments containing wool fat keep the skin soft and moistened, hence such bases are useful where skin is required to be softened and brittleness and dryness of the skin is to be avoided.

**6.** Water miscible bases can be easily removed. Mixtures of ethylene glycols have this property.

**7.** Animal and vegetable fats become rancid on storage. If these are used as bases, it is better to include preservatives. Free acids in vegetable oils may react with monovalent or divalent metals to form soaps and reverse the emulsion type. The consistency of any ointment be such as to withstand the room temperature and remain solid; where necessary substances such as hard paraffin and bees wax be included in the ointment base to raise the melting point.

From what has been discussed above, there is no ideal ointment base. On the other hand, it is possible to choose an ointment base approaching ideal requirements after considering the purpose for which an ointment base is required.

**Note :** In case if foreign particles are present in the melted base they must be removed by filtering through muslin cloth. The yellow soft paraffin is usually a source of foreign particles.

In big hospitals, where a same prescription is repeated several times in a day (such as sulphur ointment, salicylic acid ointment, etc.), the bulk quantities of medicaments required can not be weighed satisfactorily with dispensing balance. Normally, a torsion balance is used to weigh such quantities.

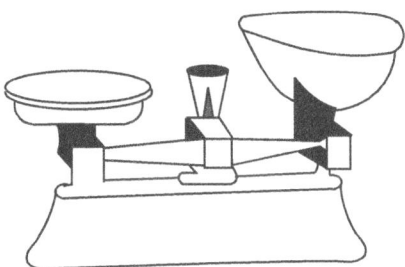

**Fig. 12.5 : Torsion balance**

When an ointment is to be removed from a container, never dig into the ointment but scape off the ointment from the surface.

## Additives of Ointment Bases :

In order to obtain proper consistency and other required characteristics, some ingredients are added to the ointment bases. They are arachis oil, coconut oil, olive oil, isopropyl myristate, and other isopropyl esters such as lanoleate, palmitate, palmitate-stearate, cetyl alcohol, stearyl alcohol, cetostearyl alcohol, silicones are also used in the ointment bases.

Ointments are prepared by using the following methods :

**(1) Fusion Method :** By melting the ingredients for mixing.

**(2) Trituration :** Incorporating the solid fine powder in the base by grinding or on laboratory scale using pestle and mortar.

**(1) Fusion Method :** When the ingredients of ointment bases possess different melting points, the mixing is carried out by melting it in a vessel and mixing it with the use of a stirrer. Mixing of ingredients is carried out by following the descending order of the melting points of the ingredients. Mixing is carried out till the base is cooled to room temperature. Other miscible medicaments are incorporated in the base by simple mixing.

**(2) Trituration Method :** Once the base is prepared by fusion method, insoluble ingredients are incorporated by the trituration method.

Solid insoluble medicament is powdered to obtain a fine powder. This powder is levigated using two to three times weight of powder with base. After thorough levigation remaining part of the base is mixed. When the powder is completely mixed, the ointment is tested for grittiness. If gritty particles are observed, the whole mass is passed through an ointment mill (tripple roller mill) to get a smooth ointment.

If required on a small scale or for use in the laboratory, mixing of powder is carried out using a pestle and mortar or on a plain, clean tile with the help of a spatula.

**Some examples of ointment preparations are given below.**

**Exercise 1 :**

### Simple Ointment

$R_x$

| | |
|---|---|
| Wool fat | 50 g |
| Hard paraffin | 50 g |
| Cetosteryl alcohol | 50 g |
| White soft paraffin | 850 g |
| Prepare an ointment. | Send 100 g |

**Method :**

Melt hard paraffin on water bath. Then add cetosteryl alcohol followed by wool fat and white soft paraffin. Mix it thoroughly until it solidifies.

**Use :** As a base.

**Exercise 2 :**

Paraffin Ointment

R<sub>x</sub>

| | |
|---|---|
| White bees wax | 20 g |
| Hard paraffin    30 g | |
| Cetosteryl alcohol | 50 g |
| White or yellow soft paraffin | 900 g |

**Method :**

Melt hard paraffin on a water bath. Add cetosteryl alcohol followed by beeswax and soft paraffin. Mix it.

**Label :** An ointment base.

**Use :** As a base.

**Exercise 3 :**

Emulsifying Wax

R<sub>x</sub>

| | |
|---|---|
| Cetosteryl alcohol | 900 g |
| Sodium lauryl sulphate | 100 g |
| Purified water | 40 g |

**Method :**

Heat cetosteryl alcohol to melt. Add sodium lauryl sulphate to it and mix. Add purified water and continue heating to 115°C with stirring till frothing ceases and the product is translucent, then cool quickly.

**Label :** An ointment base.

**Use :** As a base.

**Exercise 4 :**

R<sub>x</sub>

| | |
|---|---|
| Emulsifying wax | 300 g |
| White soft paraffin | 500 g |
| Liquid paraffin | 200 g |

**Method :**

Melt together and stir until cold. Send 100 g.

**Label :** An emulsifying ointment base.

**Use :** As a base.

**Exercise 5 :**

Rx

| Wool alcohol | 60 g |
| Hard paraffin | 240 g |
| White or yellow soft paraffin | 100 g |
| Liquid paraffin | 600 g |

**Method :**

Melt together and stir until cold. Send 100 g.

**Label :** An ointment base.

**Exercise 6 :**

Rx

| Wool alcohol ointment | 500 g |
| Purified water | 500 g |

Send 100 g.

**Method :**

Melt wool alcohol ointment. Add purified water stirring slowly. Continue stirring till it solidifies.

**Label :** Hydrous ointment base.

**Exercise 7 :**

Rx

| Wool fat | 700 g |
| Purified water | 300 g |

Send 100 g.

**Method :**

Melt wool fat and add purified water slowly with constant stirring till the mass becomes homogeneous and cool.

**Label :** An ointment base.

## Exercise 8 :

℞

|  |  |
|---|---|
| Sublimed sulphur | 100 g |
| Simple ointment | 900 g |

Send 100 g.

**Method :**

Triturate the sulphur to obtain fine powder. Mix this powder with a small portion of the ointment until homogeneous mass is obtained. Then add the remaining quantity of base and mix it.

**Label :** As directed by the physician.

## Exercise 9 :

℞

|  |  |
|---|---|
| Salicylic acid finely sifted | 20 g |
| Wool alcohol ointment | 980 g |

Send 100 g.

**Method :**

Melt wool alcohol ointment, add salicylic acid and stir until cold.

**Label :** Apply on affected area.

## Exercise 10 :

℞

|  |  |
|---|---|
| Dithranol | 1 g |
| Yellow soft paraffin | 999 g |

Send 100 g.

**Method :**

Triturate dithranol with a small portion of yellow soft paraffin. Add the remaining portion of the paraffin gradually and mix it to obtain a homogeneous ointment.

**Use :** As directed.

**Label :** As topical antisporiatic.

## Exercise 11 :

℞

|  |  |
|---|---|
| Tannic acid | 2.5 g |
| Distilled water | 3.5 ml |
| Wool alcohol ointment | 4.09 g |

## Method :

Melt wool alcohol ointment and transfer it in a hot mortar. Dissolve tannic acid in distilled water and warm it. Add the solution to the melted base with trituration until cool.

### Exercise 12 :

R̥

| | |
|---|---|
| Iodine | 2.5 g |
| Oleic acid | 2.0 g |
| Castor oil | 2.5 g |
| Methyl salicylate | 12 ml |
| Yellow soft paraffin | q.s. 50 g |

Send 50 g.

**Label :** Non-staining iodine ointment.

## Method :

Powder the iodine crystals. Place them in a closed bottle. Add castor oil and oleic acid and heat it on a water bath below 60°C with occasional stirring. Then remove it from the flame and add melted soft paraffin with agitation to form a homogeneous mixture.

### Exercise 13 :

R̥

| | |
|---|---|
| Mephenesin | 2.5 g |
| Methyl salicylate | 0.1 ml |
| Polyethylene glycol 4000 | 10 g |
| Polyethylene glycol 400 | 15 g |

**Label :** Rub on the affected part.

## Method :

Melt both the glycols. Add mephenesin and mix it. Cool down to 40°C and add methyl salicylate with agitation. Allow it to solidify.

### Exercise 14 :

R̥

| | |
|---|---|
| Salicylic acid fine powder | 0.5 g |
| Benzoic acid fine powder | 1.25 g |
| White soft paraffin | ad 25 g |

**Label :** Prepare an ointment. Apply as directed by the physician.

**Method :**

Melt the paraffin. Mix salicylic acid and benzoic acid in it with trituration. Allow it to cool.

**Exercise 15 :**

R<sub>x</sub>

| | |
|---|---|
| White bees wax | 20 g |
| Borax | 1 g |
| Almond oil | 60 ml |
| Rose oil | 0.2 ml |
| Water | 25 ml |

**Label :** Cold cream.

**Method :**

Melt bees wax and mix almond oil in it. Dissolve borax in water and warm it. Mix the solution gradually in the melted wax with trituration. Allow it to cool.

**Exercise 16 :**

R<sub>x</sub>

| | |
|---|---|
| Cetrimide | 600 mg |
| Cetosteryl alcohol | 6.5 g |
| Soft paraffin | 8.5 g |
| Liquid paraffin | 10 g |
| Purified water | 25 ml |

Send 50 g.

**Label :** Antiseptic cream.

**Method :**

Melt cetosteryl alcohol, add soft and liquid paraffin to it. Dissolve cetrimide in water and warm it. Add warm solution to the melted mixture with trituration and allow it to cool.

**Exercise 17 :**

R<sub>x</sub>

| | |
|---|---|
| Lenette wax | 3 g |
| Liquid paraffin | 3.2 g |
| White soft paraffin | 10 g |
| Wool fat | 3 g |
| Propyl paraben | 0.3 g |
| Glycerine | 6 ml |
| Water | 25 ml |

Send 25 g.

**Label :** Cold cream.

## Method

Melt lanette wax, soft paraffin and wool fat on a water bath. Add liquid paraffin to it. Dissolve propyl paraben in water. Add glycerine to it and warm it. Mix both the solutions with trituration to form a cream.

**Use :** Skin protection.

### Exercise 18 :

R$_x$

| Boric acid | 25 g |
|---|---|
| Cold cream | ad 50 g |

Send 25 g.

**Method :**

Powder boric acid in the mortar. Add a small amount of cold cream to it and matrix. Then incorporate the remaining quantity and mix it thoroughly.

**Label :** Antiseptic cream.

### Exercise 19 :

R$_x$

| Bees wax | 1 g |
|---|---|
| Spermaceti | 1 g |
| Stearic acid | 10 g |
| Glycerine | 2.5 g |
| Methyl paraben | 0.1 g |
| Perfume | 0.1 ml |
| Purified water to | 30 ml |

Send 25 g.

**Label :** Vanishing cream.

**Method :**

Melt bees wax, spermaceti and stearic acid together. Dissolve methyl paraben in water, add glycerine and warm it. Add the solution to melted base with trituration. Cool it and add perfume.

**Use :** Protective and as a base for other cosmetics.

## (2) PASTES

These are semi-solid and non-greasy preparations consisting of high proportion of finely powdered medicaments for external use.

Pastes contain normally soft or hard paraffin with glycerine, mucilage or soap. These are meant for protection, antiseptic or soothening properties.

In the water-miscible base, emulsifying ointment is of a prime importance. As this is miscible with water, it facilitates easy removal from the skin after use. Examples of this type are resorcinol and sulphur paste, magnesium sulphate paste, BPC, titanium dioxide paste etc.

Macrogol bases are water-soluble bases, which can be used for pastes. Example is a dental paste with neomycin.

Most of the pastes contain jelling agents and hence such preparations are discussed.

**Classification of pastes :**

Class I : Pastes with a gelatin base e.g. Zinc gelatin paste (Unna's paste)

Class II : Pastes with a starch base

Class III : Pastes with a tragacanth base

Class IV : Pastes with a soap base

Class V : Pastes with a cellulose ether base

Class VI : Pastes with a pectin base

Class VII : Pastes with a solid colloidal base.

**Exercise 20 :**

$R_x$

| | |
|---|---|
| Zinc oxide finely sifted | 25 g |
| Starch finely sifted | 25 g |
| White soft paraffin | 50 g |

**Method :**

Melt white soft paraffin and add zinc oxide and starch with constant stirring to form a paste.

Prepare a paste. Send 20 g.

**Label :** Protective and astringent.

℞

| Chalk | 39.5 g |
| --- | --- |
| Water | 32.5 g |
| Glycerol | 20 g |
| Hard soap | 6.3 g |
| Sodium alginate | 1.4 g |
| Saccharin | 0.1 g |
| Peppermint oil | 1.2 ml |

Prepare a tooth paste. Send 50 g.

**Method :**

Triturate chalk, hard soap, sodium alginate, and saccharin sodium to form a fine powder. These powders be mixed and glycerine added with trituration. Finally, add water to form a paste. The paste be flavoured with peppermint oil.

**Exercise 22 :**

℞

| Sodium sulphide | 4 g |
| --- | --- |
| Calcium hydroxide | 4 g |
| Glycerol | 1 g |
| Kaolin | 32 g |
| Water | 59 g |
| Perfume | q.s. |

Prepare Depilatory paste. Send 20 g.

**Method :**

All the solid ingredients be triturated to form a fine powder. All the powders be mixed with glycerine and water to form a paste. The paste be then transferred to a collapsible tube to prevent drying.

The character of the base forms a useful basis for classification.

**Exercise 23 :**

℞

| Zinc oxide, finely sifted | 1.5 g |
| --- | --- |
| Gelatin (cut-small) | 1.5 g |
| Glycerine | 3.5 g |
| Distilled water | 3.5 ml |

Mix and prepare a paste. Send 10 g.

**Label :** To be applied externally on a piece of lint and then to place that lint on the affected part.

## QUESTIONS

1. What are ointments ? How do they differ from pastes ?
2. What are the ideal requirements of an ointment base ? How are ointments and pastes classified ?
3. Write a note on oil and water soluble ointment base.
4. Describe the various methods of preparation of ointments with a note on storage and containers for ointments.

# 13
CHAPTER

# JELLIES AND POULTICES

## INTRODUCTION

Jellies are transparent, non-greasy, semi-solid preparations mainly for external use prepared by using jelling agents and water. Their water proportion is normally considerable and hence medicated preparations with water-soluble drugs are given in this form.

Antiseptics, anti-inflammatory, muscle relaxants, spermicides and anaesthetics are generally prepared in jelly forms. Since, jelly gives a thin film on application, it imparts protection to the surface.

Jellies are used as a lubricant for catheters, electrodiagnostic equipments and rubber gloves. In the patch testing of allergens on the skin, it is used as a vehicle.

**Containers :** Jellies are normally dispensed in wide mouth glass bottles, for hospital purposes they are supplied in glass jars fitted with plastic screw-caps. Collapsible tubes are the most ideal containers for jellies.

**Labelling :** Jellies are for local application and hence words "*For external use only*" be mentioned on the label.

## GELLING AGENTS

These are natural or semisynthetic compounds.

**Starch :** Gelatinised starch and glycerine provides a water-soluble base. When glycerine is used in a large quantity (50 per cent and above), it acts as a preservative and humectant.

**Gelatin :** 2 to 15 per cent aqueous solution of gelatin is used as a gelling agent. A larger concentration of jel gives a stiff layer to protect the affected part. Zinc gelatin (Unna's paste) is one of such preparations.

### Cellulose Derivatives :

Jellies with cellulose derivatives are a very stable viscous preparations. The film formed on the skin after drying has better strength. It is not easily attacked by micro-organisms. Methyl cellulose, sodium carboxy methyl cellulose, hydroxy-propyl methyl cellulose are some of the derivatives which are frequently used in the jelly preparation.

### Polyvinyl Alcohol :

It is used in the percentage of 10 to 20 as a jelling agent. When applied on the skin, it gets quickly dried. The film obtained is strong, plastic, and gives protection to the affected part.

**Carbomer :**

Carbomer has a high jelling capacity. It is used in varying concentrations in the preparations ranging from 0.3 to 5 per cent.

**Bentonite :**

It is used in the proportion of 7 to 20 per cent as jelling agent. Although gel is not attractive, it facilitates incorporation of solid in the preparation.

**Tragacanth :**

The hydrophilic component of tragacanth responsible for gel formation is bassorin. 2 to 5 percent is used as a lubricant and in the preparation as a dermatological vehicle. While preparing a jel with tragacanth, alcohol is used as a distributing agent. This avoids lump formation.

**Pectin :**

It is used with glycerol in gel preparation. Preservative is necessary in the preparation to avoid microbial attack.

**Sodium alginate :**

Sodium alginate in 1.5 to 2 per cent is used as a lubricant and 5 to 10 per cent as dermatological base, calcium ion facilitates gel formation. Glycerine is used as a humectent in the preparation.

**Preservatives :**

As most of the gelling agents are of natural origin, they are susceptible to microbial attack. Hence, preservatives are used in the preparations. Preservatives for jellies are methyl hydroxy benzoate (0.1 to 2%), propyl hydroxy benzoate (0.05%), chlorocresol (0.1 to 0.2%), phenyl mercuric nitrate (0.001%), benzalkonium chloride (0.02%), chlorhexidine acetate (0.02%), benzoic acid (0.2%), etc.

**Exercise 1 :**

$R_x$

| | |
|---|---|
| Resorcinol | 12 g |
| Ichthammol | 20 g |
| Starch glycerine | to 100 g |

Prepare a jel.

**Label :** Use as directed.

**Method :**

Formula for starch-glycerine is

| | |
|---|---|
| Wheat starch | 08.5 g |
| Water | 17.0 ml |
| Glycerol | 74.5 g |

Prepare starch-glycerine by adding wheat starch in water. Heat glycerol on sand bath at 140°C and add starch water suspension. Continue stirring till the starch gelatinises. Use this paste for the above preparation.

Incorporate finely sifted resorcinol and ichthammol in the base on a plain tile with the help of a spatula.

Transfer the preparation in to a wide mouth container or collapsible tube.

**Exercise 2 :**

$R_x$

| | |
|---|---|
| Zinc oxide | 15 g |
| Gelatin | 15 g |
| Glycerol | 35 g |
| Water | 35 g |

**Label :** Use as directed. For external use only.

**Method :**

Prepare the base by adding gelatin in water and then incorporating it in hot glycerol to form a glycerol-gelatin paste.

Powder zinc oxide by trituration to obtain a fine powder and incorporate it in the above base on a plain tile using spatula. Transfer the preparation into a wide-mouth bottle and label it.

**Exercise 3 :**

$R_x$

| | |
|---|---|
| Sodium carboxy methyl cellulose (Medium viscosity grade) | 5 g |
| Glycerol | 15 g |
| Methyl hydroxy benzoate | 0.1 g |
| Purified water | 100 g |

Let a gel be prepared

**Label :** Use as directed. "For external use only."

**Method :**

Dissolve the preservative in half the quantity of water with the aid of heat. In another container, mix sodium carboxy methyl cellulose in glycerine. Add preservative solution to form a jel with continuous stirring. Transfer it in a final container.

**Exercise 4 :**

Rx

| | |
|---|---|
| Ephedrine sulphate | 1 g |
| Carbopol 934 | 2 g |
| Triethanolamine | 1.65 ml |
| Purified water | to 100 ml |

**Method :**

Dissolve ephedrine sulphate in water. Add carbopol 934 in the solution with stirring. Then incorporate triethanolamine successively with agitation to form a jel. Agitation should be slow to avoid incorporation of air in the jel which is very difficult to remove. Transfer it into a nasal tube with nasal applicator.

**Label :** Applied to nostril for broncho-dilatation.

**Exercise 5 :**

Rx

| | |
|---|---|
| Sodium alginate | 0.7 g |
| Glycerol | 0.7 g |
| Methyl hydroxy benzoate | 0.2 g |
| Calcium glyconate | 0.05 g |
| Purified water | 100 g |

**Method :**

Mix sodium alginate in glycerol. Dissolve preservative and calcium glyconate in water with the aid of gentle heat (60°C). Allow it to cool. Add sodium alginate-glycerine mixture to the above solution with stirring. Transfer it into a wide-mouth container.

**Label :** Use as directed.

## POULTICES (CATAPLASMA)

Poultices are thick pasty products prepared fresh for the application to the skin, meant for counter-irritant, rubefacient, analgesic and anti-inflammatory action. Only kaolin poultice is official in BPC.

**Containers :** Poultices are supplied in glass or plastic jars fitted with screw caps along with impermeable liners or close fitting slip-on lids.

**Labelling :** Spread on Lint and then apply. For external use only.

**Storage :** Well-closed containers preventing the evaporation of volatile contents are used for their storage.

## Exercise 1 :

Rx

| Linseed meal (ground linseed) | 120 g |
|---|---|
| Boiling water | 300 ml |

Prepare poultice.

**Label :** Use as directed by the physician. For external use only.

### Method of Preparation :

Linseed meal is poured in boiling water and mixed thoroughly. It is then spread on a piece of cotton or linen cloth and applied on the skin. In order to prevent sticking, the skin should be lubricated with oil. Repeated applications one after the another are given till the desired effect is obtained.

## Exercise 2 :

### Mustard Poultice :

Pure mustard meal is used when prompt and strong action is desired. But this may give blister on the skin. So pure mustard is diluted with the flour. Dilution is dependent on the type of skin to which it is applied. For robust skin of men one part mustard with one part of flour, for delicate skin of woman one part mustard with two parts of flour and for children one part of mustard with four parts of flour. Paste of this mixture is prepared using warm water. Boiling water is never used because it inactivates the enzyme myrosin which is necessary to catalyse the reaction to evolve volatile oil from mustard. This volatile oil in presence of moisture acts as a counter-irritant and rubefacient. Action is seen within 15 to 20 minutes. However, it may be observed from 10 minutes to one hour or even more. Mustard poultice is also called as sinapisms.

## Exercise 3 :

Rx

| Heavy kaolin (dried at 110°C) | 565 g |
|---|---|
| Boric acid | 045 g |
| Glycerine | 387 g |
| Thymol | 0.5 g |
| Methyl salicylate | 02 ml |
| Peppermint oil | 0.5 ml |

Prepare poultice.

### Method :

Kaolin and Boric acid are mixed with glycerine. The mixture is heated at 120°C for one hour on a sand bath. This removes the moisture present in glycerine and kills *Bacillus tetani* organisms which are often seen in kaolin. The moisture is cooled and the remaining ingredients incorporated to form a poultice.

**Label :** Poultice for inflammations of chest, joints and muscles. For external use only.

**Storage :** As glycerine is hygroscopic, keep the container well closed to avoid absorption of moisture.

## QUESTIONS

1. What are jellies, how are they prepared ?
2. Write a note on any five jelling agents known to you.
3. What are poultices ? How are they prepared. Write a note on labelling of poultices.
4. How Kaolin - poultice is prepared and applied ?

# 14

**CHAPTER**

# SUPPOSITORIES AND PESSARIES

## INTRODUCTION

Suppositories are solid dosage forms intended for insertion into body cavities such as the rectum and vagina. Those intended for vagina are called *pessaries*. The medication is carried out through the use of a base. The base should melt at the body temperature and release the medicament.

**Suppositories :**

Suppositories are meant for local action but some are prepared for systemic action. Suppositories are prescribed for antiseptic, astringent, local anaesthetic, emmolient or antispasmodic treatments.

**Shape :**

Normally, torpedo shaped suppositories are prepared which facilitate easy insertion in rectum. Vaginal pessaries are spherical or balloon shaped.

**Fig. 14.1 : Various shapes of suppositories**

**Advantages of Suppositories :**

Advantages of suppositories are :

1. The drugs absorbed in large intestine from suppositories reach the site of action directly and do not undergo portal circulation and their biotransformation in liver is prevented.
2. Drugs are more rapidly absorbed in rectal mucosa without ionization.
3. Drugs sensitive to acidic pH can be administered safely.
4. Non-sedating and bitter drugs can be given in this form without difficulties.

**Fig. 14.2 : Shapes of suppositories**

## Disadvantages :

1. Irritant drugs can not be administered by this route.
2. Large volume of liquids can not be administered.

Depending upon the method of preparation, there are two types of suppositories :

1. Suppositories prepared by cold compression in the moulds.
2. Suppositories prepared by machine.

Suppositories may be prepared by any method.

They should

1. have a melting point of not more than 37°C.
2. have a maximum disintegration time of 30 minutes.
3. have uniformity in weight.

## Pessaries :

Similar to suppositories, there are two types of pessaries :

1. Moulded pessaries.
2. Compressed pessaries.

Moulded pessaries have a maximum disintegration time of 1 hour while compressed pessaries have a disintegration time of 15 minutes or as stated under the individual monograph of pesssary.

**Fig. 14.3 : Various shapes of pessaries**

Unless mentioned, 10 pessaries are to be dispensed.

## Containers :

Wide mouth bottles are commonly used for dispensing suppositories. Cardboard boxes with compartments may also be used. Such boxes with compartments are lined with impervious material like wax paper. If the suppository contains volatile ingredients, it should be wrapped in metal foil and the container should be tightly closed.

Unless otherwise directed, 1 g mould size suppositories are be dispensed.

## Storage :

Suppositories and pessaries should retain their shape at the room temperature. If the room temperature is high, then they must be stored at 10 to 25°C temperature.

## PROPERTIES OF BASES USED

Suppository base should possess the following properties :

1. It must melt at the body temperature with an easy release of medicament.
2. It must be inert and chemically stable.
3. It should be compatible with medicament.
4. It must not turn rancid, and
5. Some bases dissolve or disintegrate in presence of mucous secretion. This property of the base should be retained during ageing and in the presence of medicament.

## SUPPOSITORY BASES

**1. Cocoa butter or Oil of theobroma :** Cocoa butter almost fulfils the requirements of an ideal suppository base. However, it possesses few disadvantages. If it is heated above 60°C, its physical properties are temporarily changed and the base melts at the room temperature. Certain medicaments such as phenol lower its melting point while other chemicals may raise the melting point of finished suppositories. This can be avoided by not heating the base above 60°C and by addition of wax when melting point is lowered and by addition of oil, when melting point is raised.

**2. Glycero gelatin base :** This base is quite satisfactory for preparation of vaginal suppositories and for nasal bougies.

**3. Polyethylene glycol polymers :** Solid polymers of polyethylene glycol are marked as carbo-waxes. These are available in several forms depending on the molecular weight. Although these substances are waxy in nature, the solid forms are soluble in water and their ability to mix in mucous secretion makes them useful as suppository bases. Each base is followed by a number which indicates mean molecular weight; e.g. polyethylene glycol 1000 indicates its mean molecular weight. All polyethylene glycol polymers above the average molecular weight of 1000 are waxy solids.

**4.** Fractionated *palm kernel oil* or other suitable *hydrogenated vegetable oil* may also be used provided the melting point of suppositories is not more than 37°C.

## Moulds :

Moulds are used to prepare suppositories. They are of glass, aluminium, or stainless steel. While cleaning the mould, it should not be scraped, otherwise it gives unevenness to the surface. It must be washed with cleansing solution followed by hot water. Moulds are in two halves and fixed with a tight screw. There are various capacity moulds ranging from 1 g to 8 g. After receiving the new set of mould, it must be calibrated first and then used.

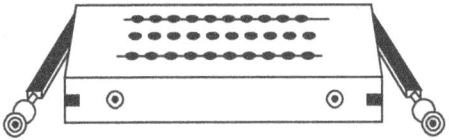

Fig. 14.4 : Large size suppository mould

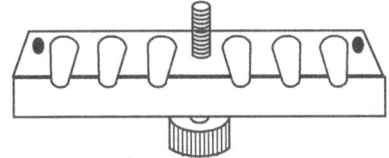

Fig. 14.5 : Suppository Mould opened to show two halves

**Displacement value :**

The volume of suppository for a particular mould is fixed and uniform. But the weight of suppositories from the same mould differs from substance to substance. This is because of the difference of densities. Hence, it becomes necessary to calculate displacement value of a base for medicament.

*The quantity of medicament that displaces one part of cocoa butter or any other base is called the displacement value of that medicament with respect to cocoa butter or that base.*

The capacity of mould is determined by using the base alone. The capacity and weight of the suppository (with base alone) is permanently recorded. The suppositories are weighed and average weight recorded. The approximate volume of liquid base is found out by melting the suppository. Approximate volume is calculated from the weight and density of the medicament.

The displacement value of liquids may be taken as one for practical purposes. When medicament for each suppository is less than 30 mg, there is no point in calculating displacement value and making correction, since no serious error occurs.

**Table 14.1 : Displacement values of some medicaments with respect to cocoa butter**

| Substance | Displacement value |
|---|---|
| Alum | 2.0 |
| Boric acid | 1.5 |
| Chloral hydrate | 1.5 |
| Hydrocortisone | 1.5 |
| Ichthammol | 1.0 |
| Iodoform | 4.0 |
| Resorcinol | 1.5 |
| Tannic acid | 1.0 |
| Zinc oxide | 5.0 |
| Zinc sulphate | 2.0 |

Mould may be calibrated in imperial or metric system. 15 grain mould may be considered as equivalent to 1 g mould.

To calculate the quantity of base required, the following procedure is followed :

Suppose the suppositories of zinc sulphate are to be prepared in a 15 grain mould. The displacement value of zinc sulphate is 2. Each suppository is required to contain 5 grains of zinc sulphate.

i.e.  $10 \times 5 = 50$ grains of zinc sulphate

$\frac{50}{2} = 25$ gr  Cocoa butter will be displaced, by zinc sulphate.

The mould capacity is 15 grains for 10 suppositories. The total quantity of cocoa butter would be

$10 \times 15 = 150$ grains

But zinc sulphate displaces 25 grains of cocoa butter.

Therefore, the actual quantity of cocoa butter required would be $150 - 25 = 125$ grains.

Actual weight of each suppository will be

$125 + 50 = 175 / 10 = 17.5$ grains

**To Determine the Displacement value :**

Prepare and weigh 10 suppositories containing cocoa butter (base) alone.

Let this weight be 'a'

Prepare and weigh 10 suppositories containing medicament.

Let this weight be 'b'

$b - a = c$ grains weight of drug

$a - c = d$ will be weight of cocoa butter displaced c grains of drug.

Displacement value $= \frac{c}{d}$

**Example :**

Prepare 10 suppositories each containing 30 per cent of iodoform.

Let the weight of 10 suppositories of cocoa butter be

$= 108$ gr (a)

Let the weight of 10 suppositories containing 30% iodoform be

$= 140$ gr (b)

Quantity of cocoa butter in 140 gr

$= 70 \times \frac{140}{100} = 98$ gr (c)

Quantity of iodoform

$$= 30 \times \frac{140}{100} = 42 \text{ gr (d)}$$

Cocoa butter displaced by 42 grains of iodoform

$$= 108 - 98 = 10 \text{ gr}$$

Therefore, the displacement value of iodoform

$$= \frac{42}{10} = 4.2$$

**Preparation of Suppositories or Pessaries :**

Lubricate the mould with a liquid or mixture of liquids different from the base i.e. any lubricating fluid that will not be absorbed by the mass.

| Soft soap | 14.3 g |
|---|---|
| Glycerine | 14.3 g |
| Alcohol rectified | 71.4 ml |

This solution may be used for lubrication of mould. For cocoa butter or gelato-glycerine base suppositories, liquid paraffin, olive oil or arachis oil may be used as lubricant for mould.

While preparing suppository mass, calculate the ingredients sufficient to produce one or two extra number of suppositories.

**Exercise 1 :**

℞

    Alum                0.35 g

Send 4 suppositories.

Use : One gramme mould.

    Quantity for 5 suppositories

Alum 0.35 × 5 = 1.75 g

The displacement value of Alum is 2.

Thus, 1.75 / 2 = 0.875 g of cocoa butter will be displaced.

Total quantity of cocoa butter will be (1 g mould)

    1 g × 5 = 5 g − 0.875 g = 4.125 g

**Method of Preparation :**

Keep the mould in ice or freezer for cooling. Lubricate the mould with soap glycerine and alcohol mixture.

Melt the calculated quantity of cocoa butter in a dish. When 3/4th of the base melts, remove the dish from water bath. Pour half of the base on the required alum powder placed on the clean tile. Mix with spatula. Transfer it to dish and stir. If necessary, warm and stir to make the mass pourable. Fill each cavity to overflowing level.

Keep the mould in ice or freezer for half an hour. Remove the mould. Scrape off the excess mass by a sharp razor. Open the mould and remove the suppositories. Wipe off the excess of lubricant and wrap in butter paper. Keep the suppositories in a box and label it.

**Exercise 2 :**

℞

Bisacodyl                          10 mg

Send 8 suppositories.

**Label :** Use one suppository before radiographic examination of the abdomen.

Since, bisacodyl is less than 30 mg per suppository, there is no need to calculate displacement value. Use 1 g mould.

Use cocoa butter as base

Calculate for two extra amount of bisacodyl for 10 suppositories

$$10 \times 10 = 100 \text{ mg}$$
$$(10 \times 1 \text{ g}) - 100 \text{ mg} = 9.9 \text{ g of cocoa butter}$$

**Method :**

Follow the method given in exercise 1 above.

**Exercise 3 :**

℞

Indomethacin                     100 mg

Send 4 suppositories.

**Label :** Insert one in the morning and night.

Use 2 g mould.

Use a combination of polyethylene glycol 1540 (7 parts) and polyethylene glycol 6000 (3 parts) as a base.

Calculate for 5 suppositories.

Indomethacin                     500 mg
Polyethylene glycol 1540         7 g
Polyethylene glycol 6000         3 g

## Method :

Melt over a water bath polyethylene glycols in a dish. When about 3/4$^{th}$ of the base is melted, remove from water bath, add indomethacin and stir to make a homogeneous mass. Pour into previously cooled mould. Allow it to remain in ice or freezer for half an hour. Remove the suppositories and wipe off the lubricant. Wrap in butter paper and keep the suppositories in a box.

## Exercise 4 :

$R_x$

Eucalyptus oil             0.5 ml

Send five suppositories using cocoa butter as a base.

Use 2 g mould.

Calculate for one extra

$0.5 \times 6$ = 3 ml eucalyptus oil

$(6 \times 2) - 3$ = 9 g cocoa butter

## Method :

Lubricate the mould. Cool it in ice or freezer.

Melt 9 g of cocoa butter over a warm water bath. Remove the cocoa butter from water bath when 3/4$^{th}$ of the base is melted. Cool a little. Add the oil and stir to make a homogeneous mass. Fill the cavities of the mould and then place in ice for thirty minutes. Remove the suppositories and wipe off the lubricant. Wrap in butter prepare and keep in suppository box.

## Glycerinated Gelatin :

This is used as a base for vaginal pessary. The vaginal pessaries weigh from 4 to 8 g. This base dissolves slowly in mucous secretion and releases the medicament.

The following formula is used to prepare glycerinated suppository base :

| Purified water | 10 g |
|---|---|
| Gelatin | 20 g |
| Glycerine | 70 g |

Prepare 25 suppositories.

## Method :

Add gelatin in water and allow it to soak for ten minutes. Then mix glycerine with the above mass and heat it on a water bath until the gelatin is dissolved. Pour the material in 4 g mould. Cool in ice for thirty minutes. Remove the suppositories and wrap in butter paper. Keep it in suppository box.

### Exercise 5 :

Rx

    Tetracycline               100 mg

    Amphotericin - B       50 mg

    Glycerinated base      q.s.

Send 8 vaginal suppositories.

**Label :** Insert one every six hours.

Calculate for ten.

Tetracycline        $100 \times 10 = 1000$ mg

Amphotericin - B   $50 \times 10 = 500$ mg

Purified water            4 g

Gelatin                     8 g

Glycerine                28 g

### Method :

Mix tetracycline and amphotericin - B and add water to produce 4 g. Mix gelatin and glycerine to above and heat at 40°C on water bath till the gelatin dissolves. Stir the mixture and fill the cavities of 4 g capacity mould. Cool by placing the mould in ice. Remove the suppositories. Wipe off the lubricant and wrap in butter paper. Keep the suppositories in a box.

### Exercise 6 :

Rx

    Dibucaine hydrochloride   150 mg

    Glycerinated gelatin       q.s.

Send 5 pessaries.

Calculate for seven.

    Dibucaine hydrochloride   1050 mg

    Water                         3.5 g

    Gelatin                       7 g

    Glycerine                  24.5 g

Use 4 g mould.

**Method :**

Dissolve dibucaine hydrochloride in a little water. Add more water to weigh 3.5 g. Mix glycerine and gelatin with the above mixture and heat it on a water bath to dissolve gelatin. Then stir the mixture and pour it in the previously cleaned lubricated mould. Keep it on ice for half an hour. Remove wrap in butter paper. Keep the pessaries in a box. Put a label with a direction 'Use as directed'.

## QUESTIONS

1. What are suppositories ? How do they differ from pessaries ? What are the advantages and disadvantages of suppositories ?
2. Write a note on the various bases and methods used for preparation of suppositories.
3. What do you know about
   (a) Various shapes of suppositories,
   (b) Displacement values of medicament,
   (c) Lubricants for suppository mould ?

# 15 CHAPTER

# DENTAL AND COSMETIC PREPARATIONS

**INTRODUCTION**

Cosmetic science is a very ancient science, it is changing as per the need of the society. The cosmetic consumption in India is growing at a very fast rate. Thus, the cosmeticology is focussed in the pharmacy curriculum.

*Cosmetic is defined as an item intended to be rubbed, poured, sprinkled or sprayed on, introduced into, or otherwise applied to the human body or any part thereof for cleansing, beautifying, promoting attractiveness, or altering the appearance; but soap is excluded from the definition.*

On the basis of physical form, cosmetics are classified as :

| | | | |
|---|---|---|---|
| (a) | Oils | : | Brilliantine, hair oils. |
| (b) | Emulsions | : | Cold cream, cleansing cream, vanishing cream, all purpose cream, etc. |
| (c) | Suspensions | : | Liquid powder, cosmetic stockings. |
| (d) | Pastes | : | Toothpaste, deodorant paste. |
| (e) | Sticks | : | Lipstick, deodorant stick. |
| (f) | Jellies | : | Brilliantine jelly, wave set jelly. |
| (g) | Cakes | : | Rouge compacts, make-up compacts. |
| (h) | Powders | : | Face powder, tooth powder. |
| (i) | Solutions | : | After shave lotions, astringent lotions. |

On the basis of part of the organ where they are applied, cosmetics are classified as :

[A] Cosmetics for the skin :

(i) Powders
(ii) Creams
(iii) Lotions
(iv) Deodorants
(v) Suntan preparations
(vi) Make-up
(vii) Bath and cleansing preparations.

[B] Cosmetics for hairs :
(i) Shampoos
(ii) Hair tonics
(iii) Hair dressings
(iv) Shaving media
(v) Depilatories.

[C] Cosmetics for the nails :
(i) Nail polishes and polish removers
(ii) Manicure preparations.

[D] Cosmetics for teeth and mouth :
(i) Dentifrices
(ii) Mouth washes.

[E] Other cosmetics
(i) Eye preparations
(ii) Foot powders
(iii) Miscellaneous.

## DENTIFRICES

A dentifrice is a preparation which aids in cleaning, abrasion and polishing of teeth. Cleaning of teeth involves removal of plaque and sugary food remains from the teeth and gums.

The dentifrices are used for the following purposes :

(i) For pleasing mouth-freshening sensation.

(ii) As an ideal carrier of topical therapeutic treatments in the mouth.

(iii) To inhibit the reformation and growth of plaque colonies.

Thus, dentifrice should have abrasion, polishing and stain removal power. The minimum requirements of dentifrice are as follows :

(i) It should be efficient in the removal of debris.

(ii) It should give a fresh and clean sensation.

(iii) It should be stable during storage.

(iv) It should not be expensive.

(v) It should satisfy all the prophylactic claims which are made.

(vi) It should be harmless and convenient to use.

**Dentifrice Formulations :** Dentifrices can be in the form of paste, powder or liquid; but paste and powders are widely used. The functional ingredients of a dentifrice include

(i)  Abrasives
(ii) Detergent
(iii) Humectant
(iv) Gelling agent
(v) Flavouring agent
(vi) Anticorrosive
(vii) Preservatives
(viii) Colours
(ix) Active ingredients.

**(i) Abrasives :** Abrasives or fricating agents due to friction remove the debris from the tooth surface without damaging it. The abrasiveness of the dentifrice should not be more than that necessary to clean the teeth. Cleaning power of an abrasive depends on the size, shape, hardness, crystallinity and brittleness.

The commonly used abrasives are precipitated calcium carbonate, dicalcium phosphate dihydrate, tricalcium phosphate, calcium pyrophosphate, sodium metaphosphate, sodium aluminium silicates, zirconium silicate, etc.

Precipitated calcium carbonate normally used has an orthorhombic or rhombohedral form. The particle size of these crystals vary between 2 - 20 µm. Particle size above 20 µm may cause scratching of enamel surface. Although precipitated calcium carbonate has a good cleansing power, it does not produce good lustre on teeth. Zirconium silicate if used in small quantities may produce good lustre. Of the various calcium phosphates, dicalcium phosphate dihydrate is commonly used in dentifrice. It is preferred over calcium carbonate as it gives toothpaste of better quality and good flavour stability than calcium carbonates. Anhydrous dicalcium phosphate is used in smaller quantities in fluoride containing pastes. Calcium pyrophosphate is used in products containing sodium and stannous fluoride.

Recently, formulation of transparent dentifrices need an abrasive having same refractive index as that of liquid medium. Sodium aluminium silicates, hydrated xerogel are abrasives in transparent toothpastes.

**(ii) Detergents :** Detergents lower the surface tension, penetrate and loosen surface deposits and emulsify or suspend the debris, which the toothbrush removes from the tooth surface. Initially, soaps were used as detergents; but they give high pH, bad taste and incompatibility problems with other components. Therefore, soaps were replaced by synthetic detergents. The detergent selected should be tasteless, non-toxic and non-irritant to the oral mucosa. In addition, they should have good foaming properties. The commonly used detergents are sodium lauryl sulphate, sodium ricinoleate, sodium sulphoricinoleate, alkane sulphonates, etc. Sodium lauryl sulphate is widely used as a detergent as it satisfies most of the requirements. Recrystallised grade sodium lauryl sulphate is superior but expensive.

**(iii) Humectants :** Humectants are used so as to prevent drying of tooth pastes. Glycerine (50% solution) was used initially. It is stable, sweet, non-toxic with some solubilizing properties. But now 70 per cent sorbitol syrup is used as it is less expensive than glycerine. Propylene glycol may also be used as a humectant.

**(iv) Gelling Agents :** Gelling agents are necessary in tooth pastes so as to maintain the stability. These are hydrophilic colloids. They change dispersibility, foaming and feel of the tooth paste in the mouth. It should be non-toxic, colourless, tasteless. Cellulose derivatives like, carboxymethyl cellulose (CMC) sodium carboxymethyl cellulose (SCMC), hydroxy ethylcellulose, methylcellulose etc. Sodium CMC is widely used in toothpaste. It forms anionic gels, stable over a wide pH range and in presence of electrolytes and calcium ions. But it is not suitable for tooth pastes containing cationic antibacterials. For such formulation, non-ionic cellulose derivatives like methyl or hydroxyethyl ethers of cellulose are used. A synthetic clay laporite is recently widely used.

**(v) Flavouring agents :** It usually includes oils of spearmint, peppermint, clove, eucalyptus and aniseed, etc. Menthol gives a cooling effect also.

**(vi) Anticorrosive agents :** Precipitated chalks give alkalinity to the toothpaste and make it corrosive to the aluminium tubes. Sodium silicate is used as anticorrosive an agent in such toothpastes.

**(vii) Preservatives :** Gelling agents may be suitable for microbial growth. Formalin, sodium benzoates, parahydroxy benzoates are the preservatives used.

**(viii) Colours :** Colours are sometimes added in toothpastes.

**(ix) Therapeutic agents :** These therapeutic agents are anti-plaque agents or used in dental caries (a tooth disease where acids produced attack tooth enamel). Such therapeutic agents include fluorides, antibiotics, proteolytic enzymes, surfactants, crystal growth inhibitors, chlorophyll, essential oils etc.

Fluoride reduces plaque and gingivitis. Antibiotics like vancomycin are effective. Proteolytic enzymes reduce mucin deposition and inhibit or soften calculus. Disodium etidronate and zinc acetate are crystal growth inhibitors which prevent calcification of plaques* in calculus** . Chlorophyll, prevents dental caries***, gingivitis has deodorising properties. Formalin, strontium chloride and potassium nitrate are also used.

---

\*  **Plaque :** Several hours after cleansing of the teeth and gums, colonies of bacteria in the order of 1 mm across will be accumulating. Such colonies comprise the major part of the soft loosely adhering film known as plaque.

\*\*  **Calculus :** If plaque is allowed to remain in mouth for long periods, it may gradually calcify to form calculus.

\*  **Dental caries :** It is a disease of the calcified tissues of the teeth. It is caused by acids framed by the action of micro-organisms on carbohydrates.

## FACIAL COSMETICS

### Introduction :

Necessity or Importance of facial cosmetics :

1. Cleansers – cleansing creams.
2. Emollients and Moisturizers – cold cream, moisturizing cream, night creams.
3. Bleaches – skin lightening agents (opaque covering agents, oxidising agents).
4. Sunscreen, suntan and anti-sunburn preparations.
5. Make up – Face powder, rouge (red powder for cheeks). Mascara (eyelash cosmetic), Eye shadow, Eye liner, Eyebrow pencils, Beauty spots, Lipstick.
6. Remedies for dryness, wrinkles, freckles (spots on skin), white spots, scars.

### 1. CLEANSERS (CLEANSING CREAMS)

Cleansing creams are used to improve the healthy and good appearance of the skin which requires frequent cleansing to remove grime, sebum and other secretions, dead cells, crusts and applied make up.

Water is a very cheap and effective cleansing agent for certain types of facial oil but is ineffective on its own against oils.

By the process of emulsification, soaps and other detergents are able to improve the cleansing properties of water dramatically. However, this combination suffers from disadvantages; it is inconvenient to use outside the bathroom and it may remove too much oil from the surface, leaving it feeling dry and rough, and because of alkalinity of soap the outermost cells get lifted and separate from their neighbours.

While using cleansing cream or lotion is spread on the skin, using the finger-tips and massaged onto the surface.

Related to cleansing creams is a group of emulsions known collectively as 'cold creams'.

Most formulae were composed of natural waxes and vegetable oils. The inclusion of borax into the formulae imparted increased stability since, by reaction with the free fatty acids in the natural waxes, it was able to form sodium soaps, thus producing an emulsifier.

Cleansing creams may be thickened by the use of cellulose derivate alginates and other hydrocolloids.

Generally, pH of cleansing creams is buffered acidic which allow a more rapid return to normal skin pH.

The non-emulsified cleansing lotions are usually just simple aqueous or aqueous-alcoholic solutions of mild detergents with or without a humectant.

### Requirements of a Cleansing Cream :

1. It should liquify at body temperature.
2. Its viscosity should be low enough to permit easy spreading, but high enough to retain in suspension particles of dirt and insoluble foreign matter.
3. It should penetrate the epidermis.

4. It should be an emulsion with a small percentage of water.
5. It should possess a mild bleaching action.
6. It should leave the skin smooth, relaxed, refreshed, non-greasy and clean.
7. It should contain no chemical that would be quickly absorbed by the skin.

## 2. EMOLLIENTS AND MOISTURISERS

Of all the beneficial properties claimed for cosmetic creams, 'moisturising' is possibly the most widely used. Water is the only material which will plasticize the outer dead layers of the epidermis to maintain a soft, smooth skin.

If water is lost more rapidly from the stratum corneum than it is received from the lower layers of the epidermis, the skin becomes dehydrated and loses its flexibility, oil alone will not restore flexibility.

There are two basic types of dry skin. The first is due to prolonged exposure to low humidity and air movement, which modifies the normal hydration gradient of the stratum corneum. The second is due to physical or chemical changes in the skin due to processes such as ageing, continual degreasing, etc.

The approach to restoring water to dry skin has taken three different routes-occlusion, humectancy and restoration of deficient materials which may be combined.

Occlusion consists in reducing the rate of trans-epidermal water loss through old or damaged skin or in protecting otherwise healthy skin from the effect of a severely drying environment. Occlusive substances e.g. non-water permeable substances such as mineral and vegetable oils, lanolin and silicones.

A second approach to the moisturising problem is the use of humectants to attract water from the atmosphere, so supplementing the skin's water content, their action is doubtful as it as demonstrated that externally applied water will not increase the flexibility of the stratum corneum. e.g. glycerol, ethylene glycol, propylene glycol and sorbitol.

### EMOLLIENTS

These are the preparations which impart smoothness and a general sense of well-being to the skin, as determined by touch. Emollients may also cause flattening of the surface contours of the skin, plumping of individual corneocytes and general smoothing and diminishing of facial lines. e.g. hydrocarbon oils and waxes, silicone oils, vegetable oils and fats, alkyl esters, fatty acids and alcohols.

The choice is determined by personal preference, data on potential skin irritation, the degree of greasiness, and apparent residual film on the skin, cheapness and availability.

### VANISHING CREAMS

As the name indicates these are the creams which easily vanish after application i.e. these are emulsions with low percentage of oil phase is usually chosen. In order to have their rapid rub in effect, vanishing creams are composed in the oil phase, of emollient esters which leave little apparent film on the skin.

## Purpose or application of vanishing cream :

These are more generally applied to the skin as foundation creams to hold face powder and improve adhesion (i.e. for make up).

The consistency of vanishing cream is governed by the amount of stearic acid saponified or neutralised and also by the alkali used. These are all oil in water type products with stearic acid or one of its fat like hydrophilic esters as the major emulsified ingredient and with comparatively little other fat or oil constituents.

## Significance or Role of ingredients :

Glycerine or other humectants prevent excessive drying out of the cream, which takes place because the product is of the oil in water type with water in the external phase, while sufficient glycerine prevents rolling.

Alkalies use potassium hydroxide, sodium hydroxide, potassium carbonate, aqueous ammonia, triethanolamine, borax.

Potassium hydroxide is most generally used because it makes a cream of fine texture and excellent consistency without excessive harshness.

Glycerine also prevents any harsh reaction from the alkalies or the free stearic acid and to keep the cream from drying out and cracking.

Preservatives should always be present if the cream contains substances likely to deteriorate under bacterial or fungal action. e.g. methyl, propyl and butyl hydroxy benzoate, phenyl mercuric nitrate, bronopol.

Perfumes either as they come or dissolved in alcohol or a perfume solvent.

Foundation creams are prepared by milling pigments e.g. titanium dioxide, aluminium silicate.

## COLD CREAMS

Cold cream is one of the oldest of cosmetics. Its discovery is attributed to Galen, a physician of the second century A. D.

Preparation is called as cold cream, may be because of the cooling sensation caused by evaporation of the water in the cream after it is applied to the skin.

The latest creams are non-alkaline, therefore, this cream will not dry or dissolve out the natural lubricant of the skin.

The emulsifying agent used in the cold cream is a soap formed by the interaction of borax with the free acid of bees wax.

Cold creams may be oil in water or water in oil. In the preparation when a borax solution is mixed with molten bees wax, the sodium salts of the wax acids will be formed at the oil-water interface. It is unusual to use rather less than the theoretical quantity of borax since this gives a more stable, textured cream. Usually, 5-6% of the weight of beeswax is used. The borax neutralised bees wax in a cold cream can vary from 5 to 16%. The lower levels produce softer creams which can be stiffened by incorporating other waxes.

Bees wax borax system can prepare both water in oil and oil in water creams without the use of secondary emulsifiers.

Non-ionic emulsifiers can be used to supplement bees wax borax emulsions, adding increased flexibility and stability to the emulsion.

Cold creams are most popular as its modifications are all purpose creams, cleansing creams, astringent creams and emollient creams.

Preservatives such as methyl or propyl parahydroxy benzoate 0.15% are added to the formulation.

## NIGHT AND MASSAGE CREAMS

These are the creams designed to be left on the skin for several hours or to remain mobile on the skin even after vigorous rubbing. The occlusive layer of these creams slows the rate of trans-epidermal water loss, thus having a moisturizing effect, also makes the skin surface feel smooth by the action of lubricating the surface.

These creams are also nutritive in property, the fat-soluble as well as water-soluble vitamins are capable of being taken up through the skin. e.g. pantothenic acid, and its related materials panthenol, pantethine and pangamic acid. These are water soluble.

Vitamins D, A, E and H are oil-soluble and essential for skin health.

### 3. BLEACHES

**Skin lighteners or Bleaches :**

These are agents which lighten the skin colour used for make up, protection of skin against ultraviolet radiation. The lightening of the skin colour may be by reducing pigmentation : decolourize the melanin present or prevent new melanin from being formed. Sunscreening agent in a skin lightening preparation which prevents reoxidation by UV light the leuco or reduced form of melanin.

**Skin lightening agents :**

1. Opaque covering agents

    Titanium dioxide, zinc oxide, talc, kaolin.

2. Oxidising agents

    Creams containing hydrogen peroxide, sodium hydrochlorite solution.

3. Mercury compounds

    Red mercuric oxide, mercurous chloride.

4. Hydroquinone.

5. Catechol and its derivatives.

6. Other - 2 – mercaptoethylamine.

**Natural way :**

Materials used – Cucumber juice, lemon juice, buttermilk, crushed strawberries and fresh horseradish.

## 4. SUNSCREEN, SUNTAN & ANTI-SUNBURN PREPARATIONS

Exposure to sunlight can have both beneficial and harmful effects on the human body, depending on the length and the frequency of exposure, the intensity of the sunlight and the sensitivity of the individual.

**Adverse effects of sunlight :**

Short term effect temporary damage of the epidermis, slight erythema (Reddening of the skin) to painful burns, in more severe cases shivering, fever and nausea and sometimes pruritus (itching), swelling of the skin.

Chronic exposure causes degenerative changes in the connective tissue of the corium and result in the so called premature ageing of the skin, thickening of the skin, loss of natural elasticity, appearance of wrinkles, skin diseases from dermatitis to skin cancer.

**Sunscreen and suntan preparations :**

These are the preparations which prevent or minimize the harmful effects of solar radiation or to assist in tanning the skin without any painful effects.

**Classes of Sunscreens :**

1. Sunburn preventive agents.
2. Suntanning agents.

Para-amino benzoic acid and its derivatives, anthranilates, salicylates, cinnamic acid derivatives, stilbene, quinine bisulphate, quinine chloride, uric and violuric acids, tannic acid and its derivatives are examples of sunscreens.

## 5. MAKE UP

### FACE POWDER

**Functions of face powder :**

1. to impart a smooth finish to the skin.
2. masking minor visible imperfections and any shine due to moisture or grease.

**Desired properties of face powder :**

1. **Covering powder :** It is used to conceal various defects of the facial skin, to cover more area. e.g. titanium dioxide, zinc oxide, kaolin, magnesium oxide.
2. **Slip :** To increase the flow and ease for spreadability, these substances are added. e.g. talc, magnesium stearate.

3. **Absorbency :** These agents eliminate shiny skin in certain facial areas by absorbing sebaceous secretions and perspiration.

   e.g. colloidal kaolin, starch, micro-crystalline cellulose, magnesium carbonate.

4. **Adhesiveness :** To cling powder well to the face.

   e.g. talc, zinc and magnesium stearate

5. **Bloom :** Requirement as per fashion, trend.

   e.g. chalk, rice starch, prepared starch, powdered silk.

6. **Colour :** Iron oxides, inorganic and organic pigments.

7. **Perfume :** Increases the cosmetic acceptability, alcoholic solution of floral bouquets.

## Coloured make up preparations :

**LIPSTICK :** It is preparation (cosmetic) moulded into sticks, essentially dispersions of colouring matter in a base consisting of a suitable blend of oils, fats and waxes.

It is used to

1. impart an attractive colour.
2. narrow bad tempered lips may be widened.
3. broad sensual lips made to appear narrower by its use.
4. emollient action.
5. decrease in cracked and chapped lips.

## Desired/Required characteristics :

1. Should have an attractive appearance, smooth surface of uniform colour, free from defects such as pinholes or grittiness or crystal aggregates, and should be retained during shelf life, should not exude oil, develop a bloom, flake, cake, harden, soften, crumble nor become brittle over the range of temperatures.
2. Should be safe both dermatologically and if ingested.
3. Should be easy to apply, reasonably permanant film of stable colour.

## Ingredients of Lipstick :

## Colouring materials :

Colour is imparted to the lips in two ways :

(a) By staining the skin, requires dye in solution, capable of penetrating the outer surface of the lips.

(b) By covering the lips with a coloured layer which hide any surface roughness and give a smooth appearance.

   e.g. insoluble dyes and pigments.

**Staining Dyes :**

e.g. water soluble eosin and other halogenated derivatives of fluorescein - tetrabromo fluorescein.

Pigments - titanium dioxide, calcium lakes, barium lakes.

**Base -** castor oil, fatty alcohols.

**Other base ingredients :**

Carnauba wax, candelilla, amorphous hydrocarbon waxes, petroleum - based waxes, bees wax, cocoa butter.

**Perfumes :** Rose alcohols and esters.

## ROUGE

This is the preparation used to apply colour to the cheeks.

It is of four types :

1. Dry rouge (compact rouge)
2. Wax-based rouge
3. Cream rouge
4. Liquid rouge.

**1. Dry rouge :** These are similar to ordinary compact powder, must be smooth, free from grittiness and should be easy to apply, should have good adhesion to the skin, good covering power.

Raw materials/ ingredients :

Talc, kaolin, precipitated chalk, magnesium carbonate, titanium dioxide, zinc stearate, inorganic oxides, certified colourants and perfumes.

Zinc oxide : It imparts adhesive property.

Titanium oxide : It gives stable colour shades.

Metallic stearates : It increases spreadability, imparts adhesiveness.

**2. Wax-based rouge :** Base used is waxy candelilla wax, carnauba wax, bees wax.

**3. Cream rouge :** It gives a natural effect and better results.

**4. Liquid rouge :** These are aqueous preparations prepared by dissolving the requisite amount of a suitable water soluble dye, adding a gum or synthetic thickener to increase the viscosity of the solution and including a small proportion of a suitable wetting agent to promote easy spreading.

## EYE MAKEUP
### MASCARA (Eyelash cosmetic)

Mascara is a black pigmented preparation for application to the eyelashes or eyebrows to beautify the eyes, used to darken the eyelashes and to increase their apparent length, the brightness and to enhance the expressiveness of the eyes.

### Cake (Black) Mascara :

It is prepared by melting together waxy materials, adding the colour. e.g. lamp black.

### Cream Mascara :

Prepared by milling the pigment into a vanishing cream base or by the use of a suitable oil-soluble dye. e.g. ivory black.

### Liquid Mascara :

Alcoholic solution of a resin in which carbon black is suspended.

### Eye Shadow :

These are the preparations used to produce an attractive 'moist looking background for the eyes.'

### Cream Eye Shadow :

Prepared by mixing selected colours with petroleum or other waxy material.

### Stick Eye Shadow :

Contains a high proportion of waxes. e. g. carnauba.

### Pressed Powder Eye Shadow :

These are compact rouge with a different colour system.

### Liquid Eye Shadow :

These are either liquid suspension or a liquid dispersion of pigments.

**Eye liner :** It is used to increase the expressiveness of eyes available in liquid, cake and pencil form. Brown colour is considered a good colour for daytime wear.

**Eyebrow pencils :** In these, the pigment is dispersed in a wax base to form a firm pencil. e.g. brown stick contains black iron oxide.

## ANTIPERSPIRANTS

'Antiperspirants' are the agents which reduce sweating. They are generally used to reduce the axillary wetness. Antiperspirants are classified as drugs because they affect the body function. i.e. closure of sweat ducts by protein precipitation. This leads to decrease in perspiration.

The body secretions are sweat and sebacious secretions. Sebum is an oily secretion containing cholesterol and its esters, palmitic and stearic acid, their esters, etc. but it is odourless. Sweat is a secretion of sweat glands. There are two types of sweat glands viz.

Endocrine and apocrine glands. Endocrine glands are present all over the body surface, whereas apocrine glands are few and present in axillae, pubic region, abdomen and near nipples. The sweat from both the types of glands is sterile and odourless at the time of secretion.

Odour develops due to decomposition of these secretions by microbial flora of skin. Odour from axillary region is pungent and resembles that of caprylic acid and its homologues, therefore, described as caprylic odour. The odourous mixture consists of caproic andbutyric caprylic acid, indoxyl and scatoxyl sulphate, macrocyclic compounds, steroid, lactones, etc. The apocrine sweat in the axillae is due to the axillary hair, at the collection site. Therefore, the antiperspirants act by reducing apocrine sweat secretion, or inhibiting the bacterial growth.

Metal salts having astringent action are commonly used as antiperspirants. Aluminium and zirconium salts are the main antiperspirants.

Aluminium chlorhydrates, aluminium chloride, aluminium zirconium chlorohydrates and buffered aluminium sulphate are the antiperspirants in use. Aluminium chlorhydroxide is five times effective in inhibiting bacterial growth than aluminium chloride. Aluminium chloride in presence of water hydrolyses to aluminium chlorhydroxide and hydrochloric acid.

$$AlCl_3 + 2H_2O \rightarrow Al(OH)_2Cl + 2HCl$$

This hydrochloric acid can cause skin irritation and damages clothing. Therefore, aluminium chlorhydroxide is perferred over aluminium chloride. Aluminium chloride should not be applied where skin is broken or irritated.

Aluminium chlorhydroxide is applied in 2.5 per cent in cream, lotion or spray. Zirconium aluminium complexes are used more than zirconium salts.

**Antiperspirant Formulations :** They are available as aerosols, sticks, creams and roll-on antiperspirants. The formulation should have maximum antiperspirant action with minimum staining.

Antiperspirant aerosols are suspensions of 3-5% micronised aluminium chlorhydrate powder in oil base. Antiperspirant sticks consist of a waxy matrix containing aluminium chlorhydrate powder and volatile silicone. These sticks are easy to apply without staining or corrosive effect on fabric and have high antiperspirant action. Antiperspirant creams are o/w emulsions, but many times in anhydrous form. Roll-on formulations are emulsions or aqueous alcoholic solutions thickened with cellulose gums.

## DEODORANTS

These are the agents which reduce the body odour mainly the axillary odour.

Deodorants reduce axillary odour without affecting any body function and act by neutralising the odours after secretions and therefore they are classified as cosmetics and not as a drug.

### Mechanism of Deodorants :

Bacterial decomposition of the apocrine secretions in axillae is responsible for axillary odour. Any agent which will inhibit the growth of these micro-organisms can act as a deodorant. Volatile acidic compounds are responsible for axillary odour and some agents may form stable odourless salt.

**Deodorant Ingredients :** Antibacterial agents like trichlorocarbonilide (TCC), hexamethylene tetramine, zinc ricinoleate are used as deodorants. Ethyl alcohol is used as a vehicle in deodorant products and also has antibacterial activity. The essential oils like thyme and clove oils which have high eugenol and thymol show good antibacterial activity and deodorant activity.

**Deodorant Formulations :** Deodorants are available as aerosol, deodorant sticks and soaps. Deodorant aerosols are the alcoholic solutions of bactericide. Deodorant soaps contain antimicrobial agents trichlorocarbanilide (TCC), triclosan, cloflucarban. Triclosan is effective against both gram-positive and gram-negative organisms but in soap formulation it is effective only against gram-positive organisms. Deodorant sticks are sodium stearate based.

## SHAMPOOS

Shampoos are the formulations used for cleaning hair and conditioning effects. The shampoos are used for removal of accumulated sebum, scalp debris and residues of hair grooming preparations. The shampoo should be selective in the coat of natural oil on hair and scalp i.e. it should only remove excessive oil from the hair. Hair conditioning is necessary to give hair life, softness, volume, body sheen, a silky touch, fly-away control and ease of styling.

The shampoos should have the following properties :

(i) It should spread easily over the hair and should not immediately sink into the hair.

(ii) It should produce easily a lather having sufficient stability.

(iii) It should efficiently remove excess oil and scalp debris.

(iv) It should rinse away easily.

(v) It should not give roughness and tangling tendency to hair.

(vi) It should make hair feel and smell clean and fresh. There should not be loss of lustre of hair.

(vii) It should not affect ease of combing and setting of the dry hair.

(viii) It should be for use. It should not produce irritation or reddening of the scalp.

**Ingredients of Shampoos :** The common ingredients in shampoos are classified as follows :

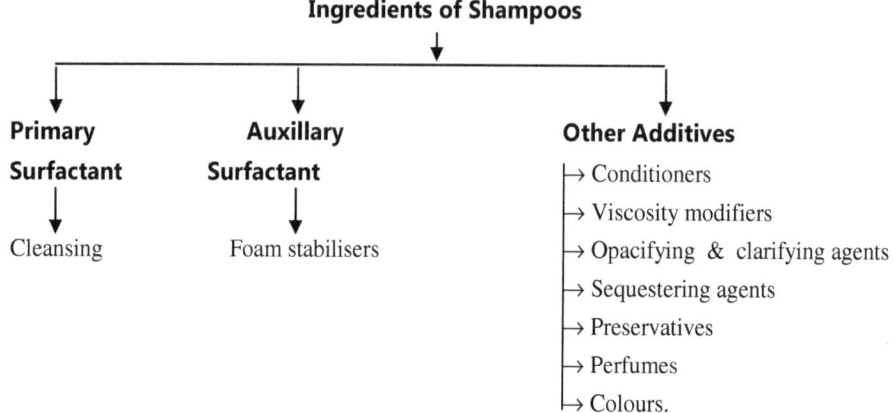

### (A) Primary Surfactants :

Anionic surfactants are widely used as detergents in shampoos. Triethamine dodecyl benzene sulphonate is used in shampoos for oily hair. Lauryl sulphates are also used in combination with myristyl sulphate. Sodium lauryl sulphate is a popular foaming agent. It is used in concentration 7-15. It is most suitable for powder or cream shampoos. Ammonium lauryl sulphate is preferred over sodium salt due to its stability at lower pH.

Alkyl ether sulphates show stability over a wide pH range, less irritancy, mildness, reduced keratin degradation and are suitable detergents in shampoos for dry hair. Sulphosuccinates are suitable for mild shampoos like baby shampoos.

**Amphoteric Surfactants :** Amphoteric surfactants are used as primary surfactants for mild shampoos. They are β-amino acid derivatives, asparagine derivatives, long chain betains and long chain imidazoline derivatives. Amphoteric surfactants allow large flexibility in their use.

**Cationic Surfactants :** Cationic surfactants have low cleansing and foaming properties as compared to anionics. Cetylpyridinum salts, distearyl dimethyl ammonium salt etc. are used as additives in small quantities.

### (B) Auxiliary Surfactants :

Non-ionic surfactants are used in combination with surfactants. Lauric monoethanoimide and diethanoamide is commonly used. They form complexes with lauryl sulphate ions at air-water interface and improve lather qualities.

Ethylene oxide and propylene oxide derivatives are common auxillaries, emulsifiers and opacifying agents.

### (C) Additives :

**(1) Conditioners :** Conditioners smooth, soften texturize and restore the protective sheath on hair. The agents used as conditioners are lanolin, mineral oil, polypeptides, herbal additives, egg derivatives and some synthetic resins.

**(2) Viscosity modifiers :** Various thickeners used are 1-4% w/w ammonium and sodium chloride, alginates, karaya gum, tragacanth, carboxymethyl cellulose, hydroxyethyl cellulose and carboxyvinyl polymers.

**(3) Opacifying and clarifying agents :** Opacity and opalescence is provided by finely dispersed zinc oxide, titanium oxide, glycerol monostearates and palmitates, magnesium, calcium or zinc salts of stearic acid, latexes, magnesium aluminium silicate, etc.

**(4) Preservatives :** Milder surfactants are not effective against bacteria. Natural additives make shampoos prone to microbial attacks. Therefore, preservatives like hydroxybenzoate esters, quaternary ammonium surfactants, formaldehyde, etc.

**(5) Sequestering agents :** These are required to prevent the formation and deposition of calcium and magnesium soaps onto the hair; while rinsing with hard water. EDTA and pyrophosphates are generally used.

### Formulations of Shampoos :

Different types of formulations on the basis of physical properties are :

(i) **Clear liquid shampoos :** Which contain amine (TEA), lauryl sulphate or lauryl ether sulphate as detergent.

(ii) **Liquid cream shampoos :** Where opacifiers like glycol distearate and magnesium stearates are used to make the liquid shampoo a creamy one.

(iii) **Solid cream shampoos :** Which are packed in jars, tubes and are gelled with sodium stearate.

(iv) **Oil shampoos :** Contain sulphonated oils.

(v) **Powder shampoos :** Consists of detergent powder with easily soluble non-hydroscopic substances. But they are not popular as they do not have good conditioning power.

(vi) **Aerosol shampoos :** Are clear liquid shampoos with medium viscosity mixed with the propellant.

(vii) **Dry shampoos :** Are powders which are sprinkled on greasy hair, leaving it for about ten minutes and then brushing it off. They do not involve use of water. But they are not efficient. These contain boric acid, starch, finely divided silica, talc, etc.

According to their functions, shampoos are classified as :

(i) **Conditioning shampoos :** Conditioning shampoos are aimed at cleansing hair and shampoo conditioners are for improving manageability and to promote desired feel and appearance of hair. Synthetic cationic polymers deposit a thin film on hair surface.

Conditioning shampoos may incorporate oils like olive oil, mineral oil in concentration 0.5 - 1.5% with amphoteric surfactants and quaternary ammonium compounds.

**(ii) Baby shampoos :** It is a shampoo employing a very mild detergent. It mainly includes amphoteric imidazole derivatives, fatty sulphosuccinate esters and amides. It should have no action on eye and skin. It is completely free from irritation.

**(iii) Anti-dandruff and medicated shampoos :** Dandruff is a chronic, non-inflammatory scaling of the scalp caused due to microbial proliferation. The common micro-organism associated with dandruff is *Pityrosporum ovale*. Thus, these shampoos contain germicides like thymol, quaternary ammonium surfactants, chlorinated phenols, zinc undecylenate, PVP-iodine complex. Selenium oxide and selenium sulphide are also effective against dandruff.

**(iv) Acid-balanced shampoos :** Low pH shampoos are used to minimize damage to the hair and skin. The low pH shampoos are acid-balanced shampoos. Low-acidity shampoos seem to improve sheen of hair. But many surfactants are not stable at low pH. Lactic acid and citric acid are commonly used.

## HAIR DRESSINGS

Hair dressings are the cosmetic formulations that are intended (i) to impart lustre, (ii) to maintain hair style, (iii) to improve control and manageability of hair. Hair dressings for women are less oily or greasy whereas men's hair dressings are oily.

**Women's Hair Dressings :**

**Hair setting lotions** which are used to strengthen and maintain the deformation given to the hair during waving. They deposit a polymeric film on the hair surface which remains unaffected by external environment for a sufficient period. It is applied on wet hair. These are available as clear lotion or aerated gel. They contain film forming polymers, plasticizers, perfumes, colouring agent, other additives to increase sheen, soften and decrease ageing of hair. All these components are present in a hydroalcoholic solution. Cationic polymers are widely used.

**(a) Hair curlers :** These formulations are used for curling the hair. This requires some special devices like brushes, blow combs. Along with these special formulations which will promote disentangling and manageability of hair when waves are introduced in the hairstyle.

**(b) Hair sprays :** These are the preparations which quickly dry when sprayed on hair and impart rigidity to the set. This helps to keep the set hair in place and control the loose ends during activities. These are sprayed once combing is complete. The spray should be fine and gentle. It should dry the wide area. The film formed by the spray should not be sticky and should keep the hair free to move. The polymers include shellac PVP-vinyl acetate co-polymers, etc. Spraying systems include hydrocarbons (liquifiable and compressible gases) and carbon dioxide.

**(c) Men's Hair Dressings :** These are required to set the hair and to enhance hair lustre. Men's hair setting involves initial setting and then to keep it in the same style for longer period of time. For the initial setting, water can be used but as water will be lost, the hair will get disturbed again. If only oil is used a large amount of oil is needed for initial setting of hair. Therefore, pomades or Brilliantines are used. Sometimes a mixture of oil and water is also suitable. It is used in emulsion form where water will cause initial setting and oil will help to maintain it.

Different hair dressing formulations for men use vegetable oils, mineral oils, deodorised kerosene, kaolin, cationic compounds, lecithins, vitamins, propylene glycol, etc.

**Brilliantines** is the oldest type of men's hair dressing. They may be : (a) Solid brilliantines or pomades; (b) Liquid brilliantines; (c) Alcoholic brilliantines; (d) Separable brilliantines.

Solid brilliantines are stiffened or thickened and perfumed mineral or vegetable oil. The stiffening agents used are different waxes such as bees wax, ceresin, carnauba wax, paraffin wax, spermaceti, etc. Aluminium tristearate is used as gelling agent for transparent brilliantines.

Liquid brilliantine consists of a mineral oil with deodorised kerosene or isopropyl myristate.

Alcoholic brilliantine is an alcoholic solution of oils. It spreads easily, gives the feeling of freshness and stimulating effect for the scalp. Castor oil, almond oil etc. Instead of castor oil, isopropyl myristate may be used.

Separable brilliantines are two layer systems prepared by addition of a perfume in alcohol to non-miscible mineral or vegetable oil. This mixture may be shaken vigorously before applying to the hair. The non-oily fixative preparations use gums like tragacanth, or sodium CMC etc. but they are not widely used. Aerosol sprays containing resins are used.

Creams are used as hair dressings. The emulsions may be o/w or w/o type. The brilliantine gels which are microgels (o/w type emulsion) or true gels which are aqueous solution of PEG thickened with cellulose derivatives.

## HAIR REMOVERS

Unwanted hair from skin can be removed by (i) Epilation, (ii) Electrolysis and (iii) Chemical depilation.

Depilatories are the preparations used to remove the unwanted hair mainly occurring on the face, legs and axillae; without causing injury to the skin. Removal of hair mechanically by plucking or embedding in adherent material and pulling it is known as epilation. Electrolysis is a new method of destruction of hair and then it's removal.

**(i) Epilation :** In the process of epilation, hair is removed by mechanical means. This removes the hair with hair bulbs. After a long gap, hair starts growing in the follicle and reaches the surface of the skin. But the method is painful and may cause skin damage and increase chances of subsequent infection.

The epilatory preparations contain rosin, bees wax along with mineral oil or vegetable oil. Other ingredients are (i) Cooling agent e.g. Camphor, (ii) Local anaesthetic like benzocaine and (iii) an antibacterial.

**(ii) Electrolysis :** It involves inserting a needle into the hair follicle and hair root is completely destructed by means of weak DC current. It is advantageous as it removes the hair permanently. But the method is expensive and time consuming.

**(iii) Chemical depilatories :** It involves chemical breakdown of the hair without injury to the skin. An ideal depilatory should remove the hair in about one minute without any irritation and preparation should be odourless.

An ideal depilatory should have the following properties :

(i) It should be non-toxic and non-irritant to the skin.

(ii) It should be harmless to clothes.

(iii) It must be elegant.

(iv) It should remove hair efficiently and quickly.

(v) It should be odourless.

(vi) It must be stable during storage.

Depilatory should act quickly because the composition of hair shaft and skin is similar, therefore if contact is prolonged it may damage the skin to a greater extent.

Active component in the depilatory preparations is an alkaline reducing agent. This agent causes swelling of hair fibre and breaks the cystine bridges between the adjacent polypeptide chains leading to complete degradation of hair.

The depilatory agents are classified as :

**(a) Sulphides :** Strontium sulphide is a commonly used sulphide. But sulphides on application produce the odour of hydrogen sulphide. In the preparation, sulphide contains along with it a humectant like glycerins or sorbitol and a thickening agent like methyl cellulose.

**(b) Stannites :** Sodium stannite is used.

**(c) Substituted Mercaptans :** Substituted mercaptans are used in presence of alkaline reacting material e.g. calcium thioglycollate alongwith calcium hydroxide. These preparations have less odour and are safer than sulphides. These thioglycollate depillatories are non-toxic and stable. The concentrations used are 2.5 to 4. At concentrations less than 2, it will act very slowly and show no significant increase in activity above concentration 4. The pH of the preparation is kept between 10 – 12.5. It produces depilation in 5 – 15 minutes. So as to reduce this depilation time melamine, sodium metasilicate with thiourea are added. Lithium salts of thioglycollic acid carry out fast depilation but is an irritant to the skin.

**(d) Enzymes :** Keratinase enzymes are used in depilatories.

Depilatories are generally used as creams.

## QUESTIONS

1. Define the following :
   (a) (i) Hair dressings, (ii) Hair removers, (iii) Shampoos.
   (b) (i) Antiperspirants, (ii) Deodorants and Dentifrices.
2. What are cosmetic products ? How are they classified ? What is the role played by Emollients, Moisturisers.
3. What are creams ? How cold creams and vanishing creams are prepared ?
4. What you know about :
   Mascara, Rouge, Lipsticks, Preservatives.

# SECTION - III
# STERILE DOSAGE FORMS

# 16
**CHAPTER**

# PARENTERAL DOSAGE FORMS

## INTRODUCTION

The term parenteral is derived from the Greek words *'para'* means outside and *'enteron'* the 'intestine'. Thus, it includes those dosage forms which are administered by routes other than the oral route. It refers to the route of administration of drugs by injection under or through the one or more layers of the skin or mucous membrane.

In the process of administration by this route as we disturb the most protective barrier of the body i.e. skin and mucous membrane, the product must have a very high degree of purity and it must be sterile.

## GENERAL REQUIREMENTS

General requirements of dosage forms to be administered parenterally are as follows :

**(a) Sterility :** A parenteral product must be sterile i.e. free from all micro-organisms. Thus, proper sterilisation of product must be carried out. Aseptic techniques must be observed during preparation and administration of the dosage form. Parenteral product must pass the sterility test.

**(b) Freedom from particulate matter :** It must be free from any particulate matter i.e. mobile, undissolved substances unintentionally present in the product. Thus, the parenteral product must pass the clarity tests.

**(c) Freedom from Pyrogens :** Pyrogens are the metabolic products of living micro-organisms, or the dead micro-organisms themselves which cause increase in body temperature after injection. Parenteral product must be completely free from pyrogens. It must pass the pyrogen test.

**(d) Stability :** The stability in a given parenteral dosage form is most important. The physical as well as chemical stability of the parenteral product must be maintained during storage.

The conditions which are to be observed during preparation of parenteral products include :

(i) The person responsible for preparation of the product must have high moral and ethics.
(ii) There must be complete utilization of the knowledge and training received.
(iii) The techniques and skills utilized for the preparation must be critically reviewed and improved.
(iv) The ingredients which are used must be of highest quality.
(v) The product must be checked for stability and effectiveness.

(vi) The ingredients, production procedures and finished products must undergo strict quality control tests.

## TYPES OF PARENTERAL FORMULATIONS

Parenteral formulation is a sterile drug solution or suspension that is packaged in a manner suitable for administration by injection below the skin. It is in the form prepared or following the addition of a suitable solvent or suspending agent.

'Small volume parenteral' is defined as an injection that is packaged in containers labelled as containing volume 100 ml or less.

'Large volume parenterals' are defined as the terminally sterilised aqueous drug solution intended for intravenous injection and is packaged in containers having 100 ml or more.

Various types of parenteral preparations are as follows :

**(a) Solutions or emulsions** of medicaments are suitable for injection. These are commonly referred as Injection. Injection may be defined as a drug in solution in a suitable vehicle, with or without added substances intended for parenteral administration. It may be packaged as a single dose or multiple dose units. It's volume varies from half millilitre to a litre. e.g. Atropine Sulfate Injection, Dextrose Injection.

**(b) Sterile solids :** Drugs which do not have stability in solution are prepared as dry sterile solids which upon the addition of a suitable solvent at the time of the use will yield solutions or suspensions confirming in all respects to the requirements for injections.

e.g. Benzyl Penicillin,

Amphotericin B for Injection;

Sterile Sodium Nafcillin.

**(c) Sterile suspensions :** It is a sterile suspension of solids in a suitable medium which are not injected intravenously or into the spinal column.

e.g. Sterile Hydrocortisone Acetate Suspension;

Sterile Chloramphenicol for Suspension.

**(d) Infusion fluids :** These are single dose injections for intravenous infusion. They are generally used for nutrition, restoration of electrolyte balance. e.g. Ringer's Injection, Dextrose Injection, Sodium Chloride Injection.

**Formulation of Parenteral Products :**

The formulation of a parenteral product involves the proper selection of

1. Suitable vehicles : Aqueous,
   Non-aqueous.
2. Adjuvants : Anti-oxidants, buffers, tonicity contributors, antimicrobial agents and chelating agents.
3. Method of manufacture : Compounding septic-area, quantitative and packaging.

## 1. VEHICLES

A vehicle is a non-toxic, non-therapeutic component of the injection. It is generally present in the highest proportion in the injections.

**(A) Aqueous Vehicles :** Water is the commonly used vehicle for parenteral products. Water has the following advantages as a vehicle.

(i) It is the vehicle for all natural body fluids, therefore, it is more compatible with it.

(ii) It has a high dielectric constant, therefore, dissolves ionisable electrolytes.

(iii) Due to its hydrogen bonding, it is a good solvent for alcohols, aldehydes, ketones and amines.

(iv) It is non-therapeutic and non-toxic.

But many drugs are unstable in presence of water.

Water for injection is the water specially prepared, collected and stored in such a way that it is sterile, free from pyrogens and particulate matter. It must be clear, colourless and odourless. It's pH is between 5.0 to 7.0.

**Preparation of water for injection :** There are two official methods for the preparation of water for injection : (a) Distillation method, (b) Reverse osmosis.

**(a) Distillation method :** In this method, the vapours are generated in a separator or by using baffles, the entrained liquid droplets are separated from the vapours. The distillation still is made up of high quality stainless steel or glass. The water produced has conductivity between high quality stainless steel or glass 0.1 µS/cm to 5 µS/sec. Limitations of distillation method include very low yield i.e. only 10% of the total water is collected as a product and the method is very expensive. The input water supply to the distillation still should be of high purity, otherwise development of scales takes place.

For some injections water must be free from dissolved carbon dioxide and dissolved air e.g. aminophylline injection, apomorphine injection. In such cases, freshly prepared water for injection is boiled in the final container.

**(b) Reverse osmosis :** In the process of osmosis, there is flow of water between two aqueous solutions of different dissolved solid concentration separated by a semipermeable membrane. This flow of fluid continues from a solution with lower concentration to higher concentrations until the equilibrium is achieved. In this process, the pressure exerted by the second liquid is known as osmotic pressure. If the pressure greater than the osmotic pressure of feed water is applied, the direction of flow will be exactly reverse. This is the principle of reverse osmosis.

Reverse osmosis is carried out using cellulose acetate membrane, with a size 100 A°. Cellulose acetate membrane sheet in the form of a spiral configuration is placed on a metallic cylinder. The feed water flows under pressure in one direction and the permeate flows out through the centre in another direction. The pressure applied is between 200 – 400 psi. Particles, micro-organisms, dissolved organic compounds with molecular weight over 200 are rejected due to their molecular size; hence it will be eliminated due to repulsion of ions from the surface of the membrane. This method is cheaper than distillation method. Output from this method is much higher as compared to distillation method.

Apart from water, other water miscible vehicles which are used are ethyl alcohol, propylene glycol, polyethylene glycol. Ethyl alcohol is used for cardiac glycosides and propylene glycol for barbiturates.

**(B) Non-aqueous Vehicles :** Drugs that are insoluble in aqueous systems are incorporated in oils which can be easily metabolised. e.g. steroids, hormones and oil-soluble vitamins are formulated as injections using vegetable oils like peanut oil, sesame oil, olive oil and cotton seeds oil. These oils should be pure and meet official standards as to the quantities of free acids present. Oily injections are only administered by intramuscular route. Some patients may exhibit allergic reactions to certain vegetable oils. Mineral oils or paraffins should not be used as they are not metabolised by the body.

## 2. ADJUVANTS

So as to provide safety, elegance and efficacy, adjuvants are added to the parenteral preparation. It includes antioxidants, buffers, antimicrobials, solubilisers, surfactants, tonicity adjusters, etc.

The adjuvant must be non-toxic and should not interfere with therapeutic efficacy or assay of the therapeutic compound.

**(a) Antibacterial agents :** They are required in a multi-dose container because product in such containers may become contaminated as successive doses are withdrawn. But antimicrobial agents should not be used for preparation to be used by intraocular, intracardiac route or into cerebrospinal fluid. As larger quantities of antimicrobials will be required in larger quantities they may become toxic at that quantities, therefore, antimicrobials should not be added in injections with a dose volume more than 15 ml. Such injections should be packed as a single dose.

For aqueous injections, phenol (0.5%), cresol (0.3%), phenylmercuric acid (0.002%), benzyl alcohol (1%) are common antimicrobials. Chances of growth of micro-organisms are less in oils; phenol, cresol are used in oily injections.

**(b) Antioxidants :** Antioxidants for aqueous parenteral are ascorbic acid, sodium metabisulphate, sodium thiosulphate and dextrose. For oily injections, propyl gallate, butylated hydroxyl anisole (BHA), butylated hydroxy toluene and alpha tocopherol are common antioxidants.

**(c) Chelating agents :** Chelating agents in parenterals are citric acid, calcium edetate and tartaric acid; which chelate the metal ions. Metal ions act as a catalyst for oxidative decomposition.

**(d) Buffers :** Buffers are required to avoid the changes in pH of the formulation during storage. Thus, a buffer should maintain the pH of the preparation. The pH of injections for intravenous administration should be between 3 to 10, whereas for parenterals given by other routes it should be between 4 to 9. But buffers should not be included in injections for intracardiac or intraocular route. Buffer systems commonly used are acetates, citrates, phosphates and glutamates.

**(e) Tonicity Contributors :** Aqueous solutions having osmotic pressure same as that of blood plasma are called isotonic with plasma. Parenteral aqueous solutions should be isotonic with plasma so as to avoid any adverse effects. Solutions which are not isotonic (i.e. are paratonic) may cause adverse effects. Hypotonic solutions if injected cause haemolysis. Hypertonic solution if injected may cause irritation to vein and lead to thrombosis. Sodium chloride and dextrose are the commonly used tonicity contributors. The amount of tonicity adjuster is calculated by various methods like freezing point depression, serum osmolity, sodium chloride equivalents.

### 3. MANUFACTURE OF PARENTERALS

Manufacture of parenterals requires special precautions and special facilities so as to maintain sterility and freedom from particulate matter. Thus, environmental control is an important aspect of parenteral manufacture.

The production area for parenterals is divided into five sections : (i) Clean-up area, (ii) Compounding area, (iii) Aseptic area, (iv) Quarantine area and (v) Packaging area.

From the stockroom the formula ingredients are transferred to the compounding area while containers, equipments etc. are passed to the clean-up area. Clean-up area is not aseptic. In the clean-up area, preparations are carried out for filling operations. It may involve assembling of equipments, containers, etc. The compounding area must be aseptic. From the compounding area, the formulation will be transferred to the aseptic filling area. Personnel will enter the aseptic area through an airlock. In this filling area the formulation is packed in the final container. This area should be completely dust free. Air entering this area should pass through high efficiency particulate air (HEPA) filters. This filter removes particles greater than 0.3 µm. Thus, this air is free from dust particles as well as microbial contaminants. This air is supplied under positive pressure; which prevents particulate contamination from sweeping from adjoining areas. The walls must be of stainless steel or regular wall with epoxy resin paint. Ultraviolet lights are fitted for the purpose of maintenance of sterility. There is a strict control over the movement within the filling area or in or out from the filling area when the filling is in progress. The flow in the parenteral section is as shown in Fig. 16.1.

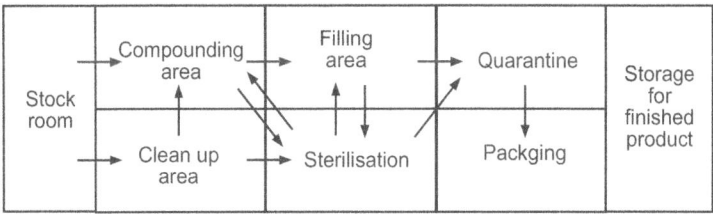

**Fig. 16.1 : Flow Diagram in the Parenteral Section**

### (a) Environmental Control :

Environmental control is necessary in the parenteral section. The environmental control in different areas of parenteral production varies in strictness.

The entry in aseptic area must be restricted. While entering this area one must wash the hands, and use gowns, hats, shoes, face mask etc. so as to avoid contamination. Frequent cleaning and disinfection of room is recommended. U.V. lamps should be used to reduce the microbial count. Air control requires special attention.

### (b) Air Control :

So as to obtain good quality air, various measures are taken.

(i) Fresh air undergoes preliminary cleaning by passing through spun glass, cloth etc.

(ii) Final filtration of air takes place by passing through high efficiency particulate air (HEPA) filter.

(iii) Most critical operations are carried out very close to laminar flow unit. Laminar flow is defined as "the air flow in which the entire body of air within a confined space moves with a uniform velocity along parallel lines with a minimum of eddies". The velocity of air in the laminar flow is 90 ± 20 feet per minute. Laminar flow units are placed above the filing machines.

### (c) Personnel :

Personnel is an important source of contamination. Thus, it is necessary to take control measures to minimize the contamination from personnel. The following measures should be considered :

(a) Operating personnel selected should have good health and should undergo periodic medical checkups.

(b) Personnel should be given complete training and they should undergo periodic retraining.

(c) Clean room garments should be used. The garments will filter out all contaminants carried by personnel. The garments should be of proper size.

(d) Manufacturing procedures should be subjected to routine verification.

(e) The training program for production personnel should include responsibilities of their position, growing techniques, cleaning and disinfection procedures for their bodies, equipments and rooms, the operation of laminar flow system, operation of sterilisation equipments, monitoring microbial count, etc.

## PROCESSING OF PARENTERALS

Manufacture of parenterals involves the following steps :

(i) Procurement and selection of components

(ii) Cleaning of equipments and containers

(iii) Sterilisation of equipments

(iv) Compounding the products

(v) Filtration of solutions

(vi) Filling of products

(vii) Sealing

(viii) Sterilisation of products.

### (i) Procurement and Selection of Components :

First step in processing involves selection and procurement of acceptable components. The components include vehicles, solutes, adjuvants, containers and closures.

The vehicles like water for injection are generally manufactured as per the required specifications. The best quality solutes should be selected. It is necessary to check the microbial and pyrogen contamination, freedom from dirt and solubility characteristics of the drug.

The container for injection is based on the composition of the container and the solution as well as treatment for which it is used. The materials which are commonly used for the container are plastic and glass. The closures for the container should be such that it should allow the needle of the syringe into the multiple dose vials and should provide re-sealing. Rubber closures are widely used. Compatibility of these closures with the product must be tested. Physicochemical and toxicological tests for evaluation of rubber should be carried out. These tested and approved components may be subjected to further processing steps.

### (ii) Cleaning of Equipments and Containers :

The new equipments and containers are also contaminated with dirt, fibres and other debris. Similarly, used containers and equipments are contaminated. Thus, these containers and equipments to be used must be carefully cleaned. The cleaning procedures are as follows :

**(a) Glass Containers :** Glass containers are subjected to many cleaning cycles in the washing equipment. The containers are subjected alternatively to the rinse by cold water and then with steam. This thermal shock sequence causes contraction and expansion; leading to loosening of the debris that is adhered to the container. The washing will now start which involves (i) rinse the outside of containers with filtered water followed by inside rinse with steam, (ii) outside is again rinsed with filtered water and inside with steam.

Detergents are not generally used because they may remain as a residue and contaminate the product.

Sometimes fluoride treatment is given in washing cycle to make it more effective. In this, treat the container with dilute hydrofluoric acid for 30 sec. After washing, containers are placed in stainless steel boxes and sterilised by dry heat.

For plastic containers usually filtered air is passed to remove particulate matter. It is then wrapped and sterilised with ethylene oxide.

**(b) Rubber Closures :** These are gently agitated in hot solution of a mild detergent. The next step is to rinse away the detergent. The closures are then immersed in water for injection; it is repeated several times. This step remove the water soluble extractive from the rubber closure. The closures are then autoclaved and dried at low heat.

**(c) Equipments :** First all the equipments are dissembled. Clean all the parts using detergent and brush. Expose the parts to the steam. This is followed by rinsing with distilled water.

### (iii) Sterilisation of Equipments :

All the equipments, containers and closures are sterilised and then transferred to the compounding area.

### (iv) Compounding the Product :

During compounding all the components must be accurately measured and should be checked by second qualified person. Preferably liquids should also be prepared by weight so as to avoid the consideration of temperature of the component. The order of mixing the ingredients must be strictly followed.

### (v) Filtration of Solutions :

Parenteral solution must have clarity. Thus, the first step is to filter the solution using surface or depth filter. In this filtration operation, all particles greater than 2 μm are removed. This operation of clarification where all particles greater than 2 μm are removed is known as "Polishing". The polished solution is further subjected to filtration through membrane filter, where all particles and micro-organisms larger than 0.2 μm are removed making the solution sterile. This process is "cold sterilisation". This sterilised solution is stored in a collecting vessel where ion exchange occurs through bacteria retentive filter.

### (vi) Filling of Products :

The filling operation is carried out in an aseptic area. During this operation, the product is transferred from the bulk container to the final individual containers. In the filling area, air is filtered through HEPA filter and passes through laminar flow unit.

Filling of liquids is easier than the solids. Light duty machinery is suitable for low density liquids whereas heavy duty machinery is required for viscous, sticky and high density liquids. For filling the large volume of liquids, generally gravity filling or vacuum filling machines are used. Gravity filling is slower than vacuum filling. To deliver the small quantities, syringe type filler is used. In this, the stroke of the plunger of a syringe will deliver the required amount. For heavy and viscous liquids, piston valve is used.

Sterile solids may be filled by individual weighing. But it is a time consuming process. If the solid is granular i.e. have good flow properties, volume filling unit can be used.

### (vii) Sealing :

The containers once filled should be immediately sealed in the aseptic area. Ampoules are sealed by 'tip seal' or 'pull seal method'. In 'tip sealing method', tip of the ampoule is melted rapidly in a high temperature gas-oxygen flame. Rate of heating should be carefully considered.

Pull sealing method is used for sensitive material. In pull sealing, combustion products of the flame may not get access to the products. In this method, neck of the ampoule is heated below the tip. When the glass tip is sufficiently heated, grasp below the tip and softened glass is firmly pulled. During all this operation, ampoule is kept rotating.

Vials are sealed by closing the opening with rubber closure. The rubber closure can be inserted mannually using gloves. The closure must fit tightly. To carry out this operation rapidly machine can be used, but then closure surface is siliconised to reduce the roughness. Once rubber closures are fitted; aluminium caps are crimped so as to hold the closure in place. For this purpose, crimping machine is used.

**(viii) Sterilisation of Products :**

Product should preferably be sterilised in its final container. Immediately after filling and sealing, sterilisation should be undertaken. Generally, thermal methods are used for sterilisation of liquids. Autoclaving is carried out for various aqueous solutions. For dry solids and oily substances, dry heat sterilisation is carried out. Certain thermolabile products may require the components to be sterilised separately and processed under aseptic conditions. The effectiveness of the sterilising equipment must be regularly checked.

**QUALITY CONTROL**

The quality control has been carried out at three different stages : (i) Incoming stock, (ii) Processing and (iii) Finished product.

(i) Quality control of incoming stock involves regular assays of all the raw materials, and confirming them to the official monographs. The routine tests of the containers are carried out. The special checking involves (a) Pyrogen test for water for injection, (b) Glass test on the containers, and (c) Identity on rubber closures.

(ii) In the processing of a parenteral product, the quality is checked at various stages as conductivity of water in the preparation of water for injection; to check the volume of fill in the container. It also involves recording of temperature for thermal sterilisation. The labels of the product are checked.

(iii) The finished product is subjected to assay for active ingredient so as to confirm the availability of a given dose. Apart from this, the tests which are performed for parenterals are (a) Leaker test, (b) Clarity test, (c) Sterility test and (d) Pyrogen test.

**(a) Leaker test :** This test is necessary to check any crack or opening in the ampoules. This is required only for ampoules. It is explained in details in Chapter 17.

**(b) Clarity test :** Clarity test is basically to avoid the distribution and use of parenteral containing particulate matter. It is only recommended for solutions. The test procedure is discussed in Chapter 17.

**(c) Sterility test :** All lots of parenterals in their final container should be subjected to sterility test. The test is discussed in Chapter 17.

**(d) Pyrogen test :** Pyrogens are the metabolites of bacteria or dead micro-organisms; which increase the body temperature on injection. There are two methods of pyrogen testing.

**Biological Test :** It is based on the rabbits and development of fever in response to pyrogens. For this test, rabbits are selected because physiological response of rabbits to pyrogens is similar to that of the man.

The test procedure involves injection of the parenteral solution samples into the ear veins of three rabbits. The dose should not exceed 10 ml/kg over a 10 min. period. The rectal temperatures are taken with rectal thermocouples. Presence of pyrogen is indicated by rise in temperature within three hours.

But this test is only qualitative and do not give quantitative estimation. Similarly, this method has disadvantages like variability of response and influence of other factors on results. Some drugs can not be tested satisfactorily by this method due to their pharmacologic effect on the rabbits.

**Bacterial Endotoxin Test :** It is based on gelling of the reagent called Limulus amoebocyte lysate (LAL) in presence of bacterial endotoxins. Amoebocytes or the circulating blood cells of the horseshoe crab (*Limulus polyphemus*) contain a protein that clots in presence of pyrogens. Lyophilised powder of LAL in presence of pyrogens in solution causes gelation of solution within 30 min.

**Advantages :** It is simple, sensitive and reproducible.

**Limitation :** This test only detects gram negative organisms and not gram positive.

Pyrogen testing is more critical for large volume parenterals than small volume parenteral as more quantity of pyrogens will be injected. Similarly, the pyrogenic effect is more by I.V. route than I.M. route.

## PREPARATION OF INTRAVENOUS FLUIDS AND ADMIXTURES

Large volume parenterals intended to be administered intravenously are called 'intravenous fluids' or 'intravenous infusion' fluids. Intravenous fluids are available in packs from 150 ml to 1000 ml. Some containers of 250 ml capacity containing 50 ml or 100 ml are also available. These are used when dilution of drugs is to be carried out.

The intravenous fluids are used for the following purposes :

**(a) Basic nutrition :** In patients where the caloric intake is not satisfied by oral route. It mainly includes administration of proteins, carbohydrates and vitamins.

**(b) Electrolyte replenishment :** In conditions like burns, diarrhoea, vomiting etc. electrolyte disturbance occurs. In such cases, IV fluids are used.

(c) **To avoid dehydration.**

(d) **As a drug carrier.**

(e) **For total parenteral nutrition.**

**Intravenous Admixture :** When one or more sterile products are added to an I.V. fluid for administration, the resulting combination is known as 'intravenous admixture'.

Intravenous admixtures are sterile, free from particulate matter and pyrogens. Thus, preparation of intravenous admixtures require strict controls to be observed. Intravenous admixtures are generally extemporaneously prepared in pharmacies.

Preparation of intravenous admixture involves transfer of one or more small volume parenterals into an infusion container using a syringe or needle. Following steps are involved in the preparation.

(i) All components required for an admixture are selected, cleaned and placed in a sterile tray. Take admixture worksheet and labels. The components include LVP, SUP, additives, syringes, needles and membrane filter unit.

(ii) Precompounding inspection of large volume parenteral is carried out.

(iii) The trays are assembled in a suitable sized laminar air flow work bench.

(iv) All items in trays are wiped using 70% alcohol in laminar flow work bench.

(v) Compounding is carried out following aseptic techniques.

(vi) The completed admixture is checked, for appearance, integrity, label accuracy, final fluid level.

## TOTAL PARENTERAL NUTRITION (TPN)

It refers to the intravenous administration of calories, nitrogen and other nutrients in quantities sufficient to achieve tissue synthesis and anabolism. TPN is indicated in malignancy, pancreatitis, burns, sepsis, hepatic failure, renal failure, major alimentary tract surgery, in newborns, infantile dirrhoea, prematurity etc.

Dextrose is commonly used as a source of calories in TPN. Generally, 25% dextrose solution is administered via subclavian vein, where this hypertonic solution is immediately diluted by large volume of blood in vena cava.

Protein hydrolysate or amino acid injection will serve the nitrogen source. Amino acid injection contains all eight essential amino acids and non-essential amino acids in their L-form. Lipid emulsions may be used as calorie source and as a source of essential fatty acids.

Electrolytes which are commonly administered are sodium, potassium, magnesium, calcium, phosphate, and chloride. The general concentrations of these electrolytes required are given in Table 16.1.

**Table 16.1 : Concentration of Electrolytes**

| Electrolyte | Sodium | Potassium | Magnesium | Calcium | Phosphate | Chloride |
|---|---|---|---|---|---|---|
| Conc. required (M Eq) | 100 - 120 | 80 - 120 | 8 -16 | 5 - 10 | 40 - 60 | 100-120 |

Trace elements are zinc, copper, etc. Patients on long-term TPN therapy need vitamins and this also os to be supplied.

Once all these ingredients are mixed, there are chances of interactions and incompatibilities which may affect therapeutic efficacy of the preparation or increase its toxicity. Thus, the pharmacist involved in TPN should have a thorough knowledge of these aspects.

**Dialysis fluids :** In cases of renal failure, dialysis is an operation which mimic the filtration activity of the kidney. This dialytic therapy is divided into two types : (i) Dialysis done by the peritonial cavity i.e. peritonial dialysis; and (ii) Dialysis done by the blood stream i.e. haemodialysis.

In peritonial dialysis, fluid is administered into the peritonial cavity. The dialysis solutions available contain 1.5% and 4.5% dextrose, solutions which are made hypertonic so as to avoid transfer of water in intravascular compartment. The peritoneal cavity acts as a semipermeable membrane. The solution remains in the peritoneal cavity for 30 – 90 min. Daily peritoneal dialysis will require 30 – 50 lit. of dialysis solution. Tetracyclines, potassium chloride and heparin may be added to the peritoneal dialysis solution.

In haemodialysis, blood leaves the artery and passes through a dialysing unit. The electrolyte solution to bathe the dialysing membrane needs to be sterile; pyrogen free and free from particulate matter. After cycling through the dialyser, the blood enters the body vein.

## QUESTIONS

1. Define the term "parenterals". What are the various types of parenteral formulations ?
2. What are pyrogens ? Why they are required to be removed from parenteral products ? How they are removed ?
3. What are the various steps involved in preparation of parenterals ? Comment on each.
4. Write notes on :
   (a) Total parenteral nutrition
   (b) Pyrogen test
   (c) Adjuvants in parenteral processings
   (d) Dialysis fluids.

□□□

# 17 CHAPTER

# STERILITY TESTING

## INTRODUCTION

Sterility test is a technique used for checking the complete freedom from the viable contaminating micro-organisms. It is applied to substances, preparations or articles which are required to be sterile as per the Pharmacopoeia. In sterility test, we confirm the presence or absence of viable micro-organisms, in a specific sample (number of containers are taken from a batch of a product). The results from testing of this sample are used to predict the sterility of a complete batch. The sterility test procedures which are generally adopted have a major limitation that it does not give sufficient assurance of sterility of a terminally sterilised product i.e. products which are sterilised in their final sealed containers. The sterility testing involves the following steps:

1. Selection of sample size
2. Selection of quantity of product to be used
3. Method of testing
4. Interpretation of results.

**1. Selection of Sample Size :** From a given batch of product, sufficient number of containers should be selected as sample for testing. The sample size should be such that it assures the results of sterility testing.

**2. The minimum quantity of product** to be used for sterility testing depends mainly on the volume or weight in the container. The minimum samples to be used in each culture medium in the test for sterility are given in Table 17.1.

Table 17.1 : Quantity of product to be used for sterilliy testing

| Product | Volume in a Container | Sample Volume |
|---|---|---|
| Liquid | Less than 1 ml | All |
| | 1 - 4 ml | Half |
| | 4 - 20 ml | 2 ml |
| | 20 - 100 ml | 10% |

| Product | Weight in a Container | Sample Weight |
|---------|----------------------|---------------|
|         | Less than 50 mg      | All           |
| Solid   | 050 - 200 mg         | Half          |
|         | 200 mg or more       | 100 mg        |

**3. Sterility testing is carried out by two methods :**

(i) Direct inoculation method

(ii) Membrane filtration method.

Membrane filtration method is preferred for filterable aqueous preparations, alcoholic or oily preparations and for preparations miscible with or soluble in aqueous or oily solvents which do not have an antimicrobial effect in the conditions of the test.

**(i) Direct Inoculation Method :** In this method, the specified quantity of the preparation to be tested is transferred directly into the appropriate culture medium under aseptic conditions. Culture medium which is used for sterility testing provides ample nutrients, sufficient water and a suitable hydrogen ion concentration, and allows the vigorous growth of a small number of micro-organisms. The micro-organisms may be aerobics like saprophytes, pyogenic cocci, spore forming pathogenic organisms; or anaerobic or lower fungi like yeast and moulds.

The two media suggested for sterility test are

(a) Fluid Thioglycollate Medium, and

(b) Soyabean Casein Digest Medium.

(a) The fluid thioglycollate medium is mainly intended for the culture of anaerobic bacteria. In this medium, mercaptoacetic acid and glucose provide reducing conditions. Resarurin acts as an oxidation-reduction indicator and agar as a viscosifying agent reducing the inward diffusion of oxygen into the medium. Yeast extract acts as a growth factor. L-cystine is included to promote growth of certain *Clostridia*.

(b) Soyabean casein digest medium is intended for the growth of aerobic bacteria and fungi.

Inoculated fluid thioglycollate medium is incubated at 32°C, and the inoculated soyabean casein digest medium is incubated at 22°C for 7 to 14 days. Negative and positive controls are prepared, along with the samples. The product will pass the sterility test if none of the tubes with either media show turbidity at the end of the incubation period.

In cases where the parenteral product contains a bacteriostatic agent or the drug substance itself in the product possesses inherent bacteriostatic activity, suitable inactivating substance is added as given in Table 17.2.

**Table 17.2 : Inactivating substance to be added to parenterals**

| Antimicrobial Agent | Inactivating Method / Agent |
|---|---|
| (i) Alcohols | Dilution (1 to 50) |
| (ii) Penicillins | Penicillinase |
| (iii) Phenols, cresols | Dilution (1 to 50) or Polysorbate 80 (1%) |
| (iv) Sulfonamides | Para amino benzoic acid (PABA) (25 mg for each 5 g of sulfonamide) |
| (v) Cephalosporins | Cephalosporinase |
| (vi) Arsenic compounds | Thioglycollate |
| (vii) Quaternary Ammonium Compounds | Polysorbate 80 (3%) alongwith lecithin (0.3%) |
| (viii) Mercury compounds | Cystine + Polysorbate 80 |

**(ii) Membrane Filtration Method :** In this method, (a) the entire contents of the samples are filtered through a sterile membrane filter having a porosity of 0.45 μm. As 0.45 μm pore size is effective in retaining micro-organisms, it is recommended in the test. The filter discs used are about 50 mm in diameter.

(b) After filtration of sample through a sterile membrane, the membrane is washed with a sterile diluting fluid to remove traces of bacteriostatic agent.

(c) Then the membrane is aseptically removed and divided into two parts. One part is placed in 100 ml sterile fluid thioglycollate medium and the other is placed in 100 ml soyabean casein digest medium.

(d) Thioglycollate medium along with positive and negative control is incubated at 32°C for 7 days and soyabean casein digest medium with control at 22°C for 7 days.

(e) The product passes the sterility test if no turbidity appears at the end of the incubation period.

Filtration method has many advantages like wide applications; requires less medium and can be used for poorly soluble solids. But this method is expensive and requires a trained staff.

## PARTICULATE MATTER MONITORING

Parenteral products must be sterile, pyrogen free and free of any visible particulate matter. Particulate matter in parenteral solutions has been defined as *foreign insoluble material other than gas bubbles inadvertently present in a given product*. Every container whose contents show evidence of contamination with visible foreign material should be rejected. Particulate matter includes materials like cotton, glass, rubber, plastics, tissues, insect fragments, undissolved drugs, lint, hair, paint, plant fragments, metals, dust, paper fragments, wax or oil droplets, bacterial contamination and other unidentified materials.

### Significance of particulate matter monitoring :

Presence of particulate matter in intravenous solution may lead to phlebitis, fever and septicemia. It may cause occlusion of small blood vessels, capillary and arterial granulomas. Apart from this clinical significance, the presence of undissolved particles create suspicion about the quality of the product. Taking into consideration this significance, USP specifies that Large Volume parenterals should contain maximum 50 particles per ml $\geq 10$ µm and maximum 5 particles per ml $> 25$ µm. The small volume parenteral should not contain more than 10,000 particles per container having size 10 µm or greater and not more than 1,000 particles per container greater than 25 µm.

### Sources of particulate matter :

Particulate matter may arise from the product, containers, closures, manufacturing process and administration system. Particles may be product related when the solution is unstable or interacts with the container components. Type I glass used for containers contains barium oxide from which barium ions leach in the product. Barium ions may react with sulfate ions in the product to form barium sulfate crystals. Rubber closures contain various inorganic and organic materials which leach out. Product may get contaminated during removal from the container before administration.

### Detection of particulate matter :

Particle detection and measurement is carried out by the following methods or clarity tests.

(A) Non-destructive method : e.g. Visual inspection.

(B) Destructive method : e.g. Coulter counter filtration followed by microscopic examination.

Particles larger than 50 µm are detected by visual inspection against a black and white background with a light providing an intensity of illumination between 100 - 350 foot candles. This is mechanised to save labour time.

In a non-destructive light scattering method, a laser beam is focussed to a point within the sealed container. The contents of the container are agitated by shaking. These particles in motion enter the region exposed to the laser beam and the scattered light by particle is measured by a photomultiplier.

The destructive method of Coulter counter is used for detection of particles greater than 1 µm. It is based on the principle of electrolytic displacement thus the solution being tested must be an electrolyte. The change in the electrical resistance between the two electrodes is proportional to the volume of the particle. In another destructive method, the solution is filtered through the membrane filter and is then observed under the microscope.

**Identification of particulate matter :** The particles once detected are then identified by various procedures like microscopy, X-ray powder diffraction, mass microscopy, microchemical tests, polarised light microscopy and scanning electron microscopy. By identifying the particulate matter, it is easy to trace back its source and monitoring measures may be taken for improvement.

**Minimisation of particulate contamination :** May be obtained by the following 'Good Manufacturing Practices', during manufacture and 'Good Hospital Practices, during administration.

**Faulty Seals Packaging :**

The hermatically sealed ampoules for single dose parenteral products are subjected to small cracks. The cracks in the glass arise from thermal shocks due to rapid temperature changes or due to mechanical shocks, impact or abrasion. Thus, there should be some test such that

(i) It should detect leaks anywhere in the ampoule.

(ii) It must be non-destructive to both ampoule and its content for good ampoules.

(iii) It should give guarantee that all the leaking ampoules are detected.

(iv) The test procedure should take into account the nature of the product and its container.

**Leaker test :**

The leaker test is generally used to detect capillary pores, cracks or incomplete seals in the ampoules.

In this test the ampoules are completely immersed in a dye solution (1% methylene blue) in a vacuum chamber. The vacuum applied is not less than 27 inches of mercury. The vacuum is sharply released after 10 min. This procedure is repeated three times. If the seal is incomplete the dye will penetrate through openings in the ampoule and the contents of the ampoule will get coloured. In one modification, the ampoules in a dye bath are subjected to autoclaving for a short time and the ampoules with coloured contents are removed.

The leaker test should be carried out after every operation where there are chances of damage to the ampoules.

But leaker test shows presence of leaking ampoules but does not guarantee their absence.

## QUESTIONS

1. What is sterilization? State the importance of sterilization.
2. What is the test for sterility? How is it performed for sterilized liquid formulations?
3. What do you understand by particulate matter monitoring? How is it detected? Describe its significance.

# 18 CHAPTER

# OPHTHALMIC PRODUCTS

## (A) EYE DROPS

Eye drops are sterile aqueous or oily solutions or suspensions meant for instillation into the eyes. Ideal eye drops must possess the following properties :

(1) They should be completely *Sterile* at all times;

(2) They should be free from *Suspended particles*;

(3) They should contain preservative to keep the solution free from growth of micro-organism that may contaminate the drops during use;

(4) All eye drops must be *isotonic* with the lacrymal secretion;

(5) They should contain stable chemicals and solution must remain stable;

(6) They should have hydrogen ion concentration approaching the point of *Neutrality*;

(7) A preservative must not be present in eye drops meant for injured eye, as preservatives are a source of irritation.

**Containers :**

**Fig. 18.1 : Container for eye drops**

The eye drops are sent out in vertically fluted bottles fitted with a bakelite cap carrying a dropper. The bottles are either amber coloured or green in capacities of 4 ml to 60 ml. These bottles must confirm to alkalinity limit test. The bottles must not impart particles to the contents and the closures should not absorb the active constituents or the preservative added to the eye drops.

**Labelling :**

Name and concentration of the preservative (anti-microbial) compound used should be mentioned on the label. The words "*For external use only* " should be added to the label.

## PREPARATION OF EYE DROPS

**Preservatives:**

(a) Benzalkonium chloride in the concentration of 1 : 10,000 together with disodium ethylene diamine tetra acetic acid in the concentration 0.05 per cent may be used for preservation.

(b) Chlorobutanol 0.5 per cent is another agent of choice.

(c) Sodium metabisulphite in the concentration of 0.1 per cent is used as an antioxident.

Other useful eye drop preservatives are 1 : 25,000 solution of Phenylmercuric nitrate, and Methyl paraben and Propyl parabens.

Hydrogen ion concentration of tears lie between 7.2 to 7.4. The irritation of the eye rises with the rise in pH. Activity of some of the drugs, e.g. alkaloidal salt increases with rise in pH. In such cases a balance must be struck between higher activity and irritation. The adjustment is carried out by judicious use of buffer solutions. The commonly used buffers are solutions of phosphate buffers used in combination with normal saline.

The vehicle recommended for eye drops is normal saline or solution containing 2 per cent boric acid. Benzalkonium chloride is not suitable as a preservative for eye drops containing local anaesthetics.

The eye solutions are prepared as follows:

All apparatus used must be sterile and filling in the final container is carried out aseptically.

**Method 1 :** Sterilization of solution is carried out by filtration followed by aseptic transfer.

**Method 2 :** Sterilization is carried out in final container in an autoclave at 121°C for fifteen minutes.

**Method 3 :** Heating at 98°C to 100°C for thirty minutes after filtration and sealing in the final container. The eye drops must be freshly prepared.

**Base for Eye Ointment :**

Normally, yellow soft paraffin containing 10 per cent of wool fat is used. Before use, the base is melted and filtered to remove all particles of foreign matter and then sterilized.

The sterilization of the base is carried out in an oven. A little excess of base is taken. The collapsible tube which serves as a container is well washed and wrapped in parchment paper. The thermometer bulb should be inserted into a small air containing the excess of the base.

The base and the collapsible tubes are heated until the thermometer registers 150°C and then maintained there for one hour.

The ointment is then prepared by using a simple aseptic technique e.g., flaming scale pan and spatula and using tile whose surface is swabbed by acetone. When the ointment is completed, it is transferred to the jar in which the base is sterilized and it is warmed gently in order to make it pourable. The wrapping from the collapsible tube is removed. Its mouth is tightly closed and then it is placed cap downwards into containers containing cold water. Using a spatula, the ointment is poured into the collapsible tube. It is allowed to solidify and then the tube is closed. It is labelled.

### (B) EYE SOLUTIONS

Extemporaneous procedures.

1. **Solutions for application to traumatized eyes :**

   All drugs used in traumatized eye, by accident or surgery should be compounded with 2 per cent boric acid solution. All solutions intended for use during surgery should be filtered free of lint or other particulate matter and should be prepared without the addition of a preservative since all preservatives at bactericidal concentration are irritating to the inner structure of the eye. All such solutions should be dispensed in small containers (5 - 10 ml), glass bottles with screw caps for single patient only. The closed bottle plus a separate dropper, should be packed in a container that can be autoclaved.

2. **Solutions intended for application to the eyes with an impact corneal epithelium :**

   (1) Such solutions may be packed in multiple dose containers for general patient.

   (2) Stock bottles of sterile purified water, isotonic sodium-chloride solution, 2 per cent boric acid solution, and phosphate buffer at pH 6.8 to which preservatives are added should be available for the compounding of prescriptions to be used in the intact eye.

   (3) All intermediate containers, final containers and closures should be treated by boiling or sterilized with a suitable disinfectant.

   (4) The solutions should be made free of suspended particles by any equivalent which is cleaned and sterilized previously.

### (C) EYE LOTIONS

Eye lotions should be prepared with distilled water which is boiled for about 30 minutes, the measure, funnel and bottle should be well rinsed with a portion of the water before use. Eye lotions which contain only soluble substance should be sent out clear and bright. To achieve this, the lotion before, adjustment to volume should be filtered through filter paper and sufficient boiled water allowed to pass through the filter paper to produce the required volume.

**Isotonicity of Ophthalmic Solutions :**

   (1) An isotonic ophthalmic solution causes less discomfort than one that is paratonic;

   (2) Sterility and clarity is essential.

Ophthalmic solutions are required to be sterilized when prepared and great care must be exercised subsequently to prevent contamination in use.

The common methods of sterilization are :

   (i) Autoclaving

   (ii) Bacterial filtration.

## Preservation :

Preservatives are not to be used when solutions are intended for instillation or injected into the chamber of the eye. Such solutions are for a single use or single dose containers. Such solutions are autoclaved before use. Preservatives are used for other ophthalmic solutions. The commonly used preservatives are methyl paraben 0.05 percent, propyl paraben 0.02 per cent, and phenyl mercuric nitrate 1 : 25,000 etc.

## Exercise 1 :

$R_x$

| | |
|---|---|
| Atropine sulphate | 0.5 g |
| Distilled water | 8 ml |
| Normal saline solution | ad 50 ml |

**Label :** The Eye Drops.

### Method :

Dissolve atropine sulphate in water. Make up the volume with normal saline. Filter. Transfer to the final container and autoclave at 121°C for fifteen minutes and seal.

## Exercise 2 :

$R_x$

| | |
|---|---|
| Sulphacetamide sodium | 1.5 g |
| Distilled water | ad 30 ml |

**Label :** The Eye Drops.

### Method :

Dissolve sulphacetamide in distilled water. Filter. Autoclave at 121°C for fifteen minutes in final container and dispense.

## Exercise 3 :

$R_x$

| | |
|---|---|
| Zinc sulphate | 600 mg |
| Distilled water | 10 ml |
| Boric acid solution 2% | at 60 ml |

**Label :** The Eye Drops.

### Method :

Dissolve zinc sulphate in 10 ml of water. Add sufficient quantity of 2 per cent boric acid solution to produce 60 ml. Filter. Place in the final container and autoclave at 121°C for fifteen minutes and dispense.

## (D) EYE OINTMENTS

Unless otherwise mentioned, 5 gm in small sterilized collapsible tubes, should be dispensed.

Indian pharmacopoeia suggests the following formula for eye ointment base.

R$_x$

| Liquid paraffin | 10 g |
| Wool fat | 10 g |
| White soft paraffin | 80 g |

Melt all the ingredients, add liquid paraffin and filter the mixture through coarse filter paper placed in the heated funnel. Then heat the mixture at 150°C for one hour. Allow it to cool.

### Exercise 4 :

R$_x$

| Hydrocortisone acetate | 625 mg |
| Liquid paraffin | 2.5 g |
| Wool fat | 2.5 g |
| White soft paraffin | 20.0 g |

**Prepare :** An Eye Ointment.

**Label :** Use as directed by the physician.

### Method :

Melt the wool fat and white soft paraffin and add liquid paraffin. Sterilize at 150°C for one hour.

Powder the hydrocortisone acetate very finely and triturate with the melted base in a sterile mortar. Add sufficient base to produce the required weight and continue trituration until the base attains room temperature.

### Exercise 5 :

R$_x$

| Benzyl penicillin | 10,000 units |
| Liquid paraffin | 1 g |
| Wool fat | 1 g |
| Yellow soft paraffin | 8 g |

**Prepare :** The Eye Ointment.

**Label :** Use as directed by the physician.

### Method :

Melt wool fat and yellow soft paraffin and then add liquid paraffin. Filter through a coarse filter paper. Sterilize at 160°C for 1 hour in a hot air oven. Cool and then add penicillin with trituration.

## QUESTIONS

1. Define each of the following : Eye drops, Eye lotions and Eye solution. Describe the method of preparation of eye solution and eye ointment.
2. Why are ophthalmic preparations sterilized ? Describe the ideal requirements of eye drops.
3. What are preservatives ? Name five preservatives used in ophthalmic products.
4. Describe the containers and labelling conditions for eye drop and eye ointments.

# BIBLIOGRAPHY

1. **Aulton Michael E.** Editor, Pharmaceutics - The Science of Dosage Form Design, First ELBS Edition 1990. Longman Group (FE) Ltd. U.K.

2. **Rawlins E. A.** Editor, Bentley's Textbook of Pharmaceutics. First ELBS Edition 1979. Reprint 1984. Bailliere Tindall, Eastbourne, East Sussex, U.K.

3. **Alfonso R. Gennaro**, Editor Remington's Pharmaceutical Sciences, 18$^{th}$ Edition, 1990, Mack Publishing Company, Easton, Pennsylvania, 18042 U.S.A.

4. **Herbert A. Lieberman**, Leon Lachman, Editors, Pharmaceutical Dosage Forms - Tablets Volume I, 1980, Marcel Dekker, Inc., 270, Madison Avenue, New York 10016.

5. **S. J. Carter**, Editor "Cooper and Gunn's Tutorial Pharmacy", Sixth Edition. CBS Publishers and Distributors, Shahdra, Delhi 110032, by arrangement with Pitman London.

6. **Dittert L.W.**, "Sprowl's American Pharmacy"; J.B. Lippincott Co. 1974. Philadelphia.

7. **Ansel H.C.**, "Introduction to Pharmaceutical Dosage Forms" 1969, Lea and Febiger, Philadelphia.

8. **Martin E. W.**, "Dispensing of Medication", Mack Publishing Co. 1971, Pennsylvania.

9. **Lawrence C. A.**, Block SS, "Disinfection, Sterilisation and Preservation" 1968, Lea Febiger, Philadelphia.

10. **Mithal B. M.**, "Text Book of Pharmaceutical Formulation" 1983, Vallabh Prakashan, Delhi.

11. **Gunn-C and Carter S. J.**, "Dispensing for Pharmaceutical Students", Pitman London.

12. **E. G. Thomesseni**, "Modern Cosmetics" by Universal Publishing Corporation.

13. **Balsam M. S. and E. Sagarin**, "Cosmetics Science and Technology" vol. 1, 2, 3, John Wiley and Sons N. Y.

14. **Breuer M. M.**, "Cosmetic Science" Vol. 1, 2, Academic Press. London.

15. **Wilkinson J. B. and Moor R. J.**, "Harry's Cosmeticology" Longman Scientific and Technical, England, 7$^{th}$ edition.

16. Pharmacopoeia of India Supplement 1975, Ministry of Health, Government of India, Delhi.

17. "Pharmacopoeia of India" Volume I and II, Third Edition 1985, Government of India, Ministry of Health and Family Welfare, Delhi.

18. Pharmacopoeia of India. Third Edition Addendum (I) 1989, Ministry of Health and Family Welfare Government of India, Delhi.

19. Pharmacopoeia of India. Third Edition Addendum (II) 1991, Ministry of Health and Family Welfare Government of India, Delhi.

20. The Standards of Weights and Measures Act, 1976.

21. The Standards of Weights and Measures (Packaged commodities) Rules 1977.

22. The Standards of Weights and Measures (Enforcement) Act, 1985.

# INDEX

| | | | |
|---|---|---|---|
| Acacia emulsions | 11.12, 11.14 | Degree of flocculation | 10.9 |
| Adjuvants | 16.4 | Dentifrics | 15.2 |
| Aerosol | 8.5 | abrasives | 15.3 |
| Alligation method | 1.16 | detergents | 15.3 |
| Antioxidants | 7.5, 16.4 | formulation | 15.3 |
| Antiperspirants | 15.12 | humectants | 15.4 |
| Apothecaries system | 1.12 | requirements | 15.2 |
| Avoirdupois system | 1.12 | therapeutic | 15.4 |
| Bentonite | 10.3 | Deodorant | 15.13 |
| Bleaches | 15.8 | formulation | 15.13 |
| Sunscreen | 15.9 | ingredients | 15.13 |
| Body odour | 15.12 | mechanism | 15.13 |
| Bottle method | 11.10 | Depilatories | 15.19 |
| Brilliantines | 15.18 | agents | 15.19 |
| Bulk powders | 4.4 | ideal | 15.19 |
| Cachets | 4.1 | Diabetic syrup | 5.3 |
| Chemical incompatibility | 2.3 | Diffusible solids | 10.2 |
| benzoates | 2.7 | Displacement value | 14.4 |
| of emulsifiers | 2.9 | determination | 14.5 |
| of metals | 2.4 | Dialysis fluids | 16.12 |
| of soluble barbiturates | 2.8 | Dose | |
| of soluble iodides | 2.6 | paediatric | 3.2 |
| Clarity test | 16.9 | table | 3.3 |
| Cleansing creams | 15.5 | veterinary | 3.10 |
| Colorants | 5.4 | Douches | 8.4 |
| Cold cream | 15.7 | containers | 8.4 |
| Cosmetics | | labelling | 8.5 |
| classification | 15.1 | Dry gum method | 11.9 |
| definition | 15.1 | Dusting powders | 4.10 |
| facial | 15.1 | Ear drops | 8.1 |
| Cracking | 11.3 | containers | 8.1 |
| Creaming | 11.3 | labelling | 8.1 |

| | | | |
|---|---|---|---|
| Elixirs | 6.1 | label | 18.1 |
| containers | 6.1 | preparation | 18.2 |
| definition | 6.1 | preservatives | 18.2 |
| labelling | 6.1 | Eye solution | 18.3 |
| storage | 6.1 | Facial cosmetics | 15.5 |
| Electrolysis | 15.19 | Faulty seal packaging | 18.3 |
| Elixirs | 6.1 | Flavours | 5.4 |
| containers | 6.2 | Fusion method | 12.5 |
| Emolliments | 15.5 | Gallon | 1.13 |
| Emulsifying agent | 11.1, 11.5 | Gargles | 7.2 |
| Emulsifying wax | 12.6 | containers | 7.2 |
| Emulsion | | labelling | 7.2 |
| additives | 11.4 | Granules | 4.1 |
| containers | 11.2 | Hair dressings | 15.17 |
| definition | 11.1 | men's | 15.18 |
| detection | 11.2 | women's | 15.17 |
| evaluation | 11.4 | Hair removers | 15.18 |
| formulation | 11.12 | Hospital prescription | 1.10 |
| label | 11.2 | Incompatibility | 2.1 |
| machines | 11.11 | Indiffusible solids | 10.2 |
| paediatric | 11.19 | Infusion fluids | 16.2 |
| stability | 11.3 | Insufflations | 4.11 |
| theories | 11.5 | Intravenous fluids and | 16.10 |
| types | 11.1 | admixtures | |
| with egg yolk | 11.8 | Imperial system | 1.12 |
| Epilation | 15.18 | In-patient prescription | 1.10 |
| Eutectic mixtures | 4.3 | Irish moss emulsion | 11.16 |
| Explosive mixtures | 4.3 | Jellies | |
| Eye drops | 18.1 | containers | 13.1 |
| Eye liner | 15.12 | gelling agents | 13.1 |
| Eye lotions | 9.9 | label | 13.1 |
| Eye shadow | 15.12 | preservatives | 13.2 |
| containers | 18.1 | LAL test | 16.10 |

| | | | |
|---|---|---|---|
| Leaker test | 16.9 | definition | 5.1 |
| Liniments | 9.1 | disadvantages | 5.1 |
|    action | 9.2 | label | 5.2 |
|    containers | 9.1 | paediatric | 5.14 |
|    definition | 9.1 | preparation | 5.5 |
|    difference from lotion | 9.6 | vehicles for | 5.3 |
|    labelling | 9.1 | Moisturisers | 15.1, 15.6 |
|    storage | 9.1 | Nasal drops | 8.3 |
| Lipstick | 15.10 |    containers | 8.3 |
| Lotions | 9.5 | Ointments | 12.1 |
|    action | 9.7 |    absorption | 12.1 |
|    classification | 9.6 |    additives | 12.5 |
|    containers | 9.6 |    hydrocarbon | 12.1 |
|    definition | 9.5 |    ideal | 12.2 |
|    difference from liniment | 9.6 |    water miscible | 12.2 |
|    labeling | 9.6 |    water soluble | 12.2 |
|    storage | 9.6 | Ointment bases | 12.1 |
| Mascara | 15.12 |    containers | 12.1 |
| Massage creams | 15.8 |    label | 12.1 |
| Metric system | 1.14 |    preparation | 12.5 |
| Moulded tablets | 4.1 |    storage | 12.1 |
| Mouth wash | 7.1 | Oleoresin emulsion | 11.17 |
|    containers | 7.1 | Out-patient prescription | 1.11 |
|    definition | 7.1 | Paraffin ointment | 12.6 |
|    labelling | 7.1 | Parenteral | 16.1 |
| Methyl cellulose | 10.3 |    adjuvants | 16.4 |
| Methyl cellulose emulsion | 11.17 |    formulation | 16.2 |
| Mixtures | |    large volume | 16.2 |
|    advantages | 5.1 |    manufacture | 16.5 |
|    classification | 5.5 |    non-aqueous vehicles | 16.4 |
|    containers for | 5.1 |    processing | 16.6 |
| | |    quality control | 16.9 |

| | | | |
|---|---|---|---|
| requirements | 16.1 | in-patient | 1.10 |
| small volume | 16.2 | out-patient | 1.11 |
| vehicles | 16.3 | parts | 1.1 |
| Particulate matter | | veterinary | 1.10 |
| monitoring | 17.3 | Preservatives | |
| Pastes | 12.12 | containers | 13.4 |
| classification | 12.12 | kaolin | 13.5 |
| Percentage calculations | 1.19 | mustard | 13.5 |
| Pessaries | 14.6 | storage | 13.6 |
| Physical incompatibility | 2.1 | Pyrogen test | |
| Posology | 3.1 | Rouge | 15.11 |
| Poultice | 13.3 | Sealing faulty | 16.8 |
| Powders | | Sedimentation volume | 10.7 |
| advantages | 4.1 | Shampoo | 15.14 |
| bulk | 4.4 | acid-balanced | 15.17 |
| containing small doses | 4.6 | additives | 15.16 |
| disadvantages | 4.1 | baby | 15.17 |
| dusting | 4.11 | classification | 15.17 |
| effervescent | 4.9 | conditioning | 15.16 |
| efflorescent | 4.3 | formulation | 15.16 |
| external | 4.3 | ingredients | 15.15 |
| hygroscopic | 4.2 | medicated | 15.15 |
| mixing of | 4.2 | properties | 15.14 |
| wrapping of | 4.4 | Silverson emulsifier | 11.11 |
| Prescription | 1.1 | Simple ointment | 12.5 |
| checking | 1.5 | Snuffs | 4.4 |
| community | 1.9 | Sodium C.M.C. | 10.3 |
| compounding | 1.5 | Specific gravity Calculations | 1.19 |
| for TPN | 1.11 | Sprays | 8.5 |
| handling | 1.5 | Stabilizers | 5.4 |
| hospital | 1.11 | Sterile solids | 16.2 |
| imperial system | 1.12 | Sterile suspensions | 16.2 |

| | | | |
|---|---|---|---|
| Sterility test | 16.9 | Syrup | 6.2 |
|    direct inoculation method | 17.2 |    containers | 6.2 |
|    membrane filtration method | 17.3 |    medicated | 6.2 |
|    sample size | 16.9 |    storage | 6.2 |
| Stoke's law | 11.3 |    uses | 6.3 |
| Suppositories | 14.1 | Tablet triturates | 4.1 |
|    advantages | 14.1 | Therapeutic incompatibility | 2.2 |
|    disadvantages | 14.2 | Thickening agents | 10.2 |
|    ideal | 14.1 | Throat paints | 7.3 |
|    moulds | 14.3 |    C.P.T. | 10.1 |
|    preparation | 14.3 |    containers | 7.2 |
|    types | 14.1 |    drops | 5.4 |
| Suppository Base | 14.3 |    labelling | 7.2 |
|    cocoa butter | 14.3 |    linctuses | 5.4 |
|    glycerogelatin | 14.3 |    storage | 7.2 |
|    ideal | 14.3 | Trituration method | 12.5 |
| Suspension | 10.1 | Types of incomp. | 2.1 |
|    container | 10.1 | Vanishing cream | 15.1, 15.6 |
|    deflocculated | 10.9 | Veterinary | |
|    flocculated | 10.9 |    prescription | 1.10 |
|    ideal | 10.1 | Water for injection | 16.3 |
|    label | 10.1 | Wet gum method | 11.9 |
|    preparation | 10.1 | Wetting agents | 10.4, 11.9 |

❏❏❏

www.ingramcontent.com/pod-product-compliance
Lightning Source LLC
Chambersburg PA
CBHW062133160426
43191CB00013B/2295